IMAGES
of America

FRANKLIN COUNTY

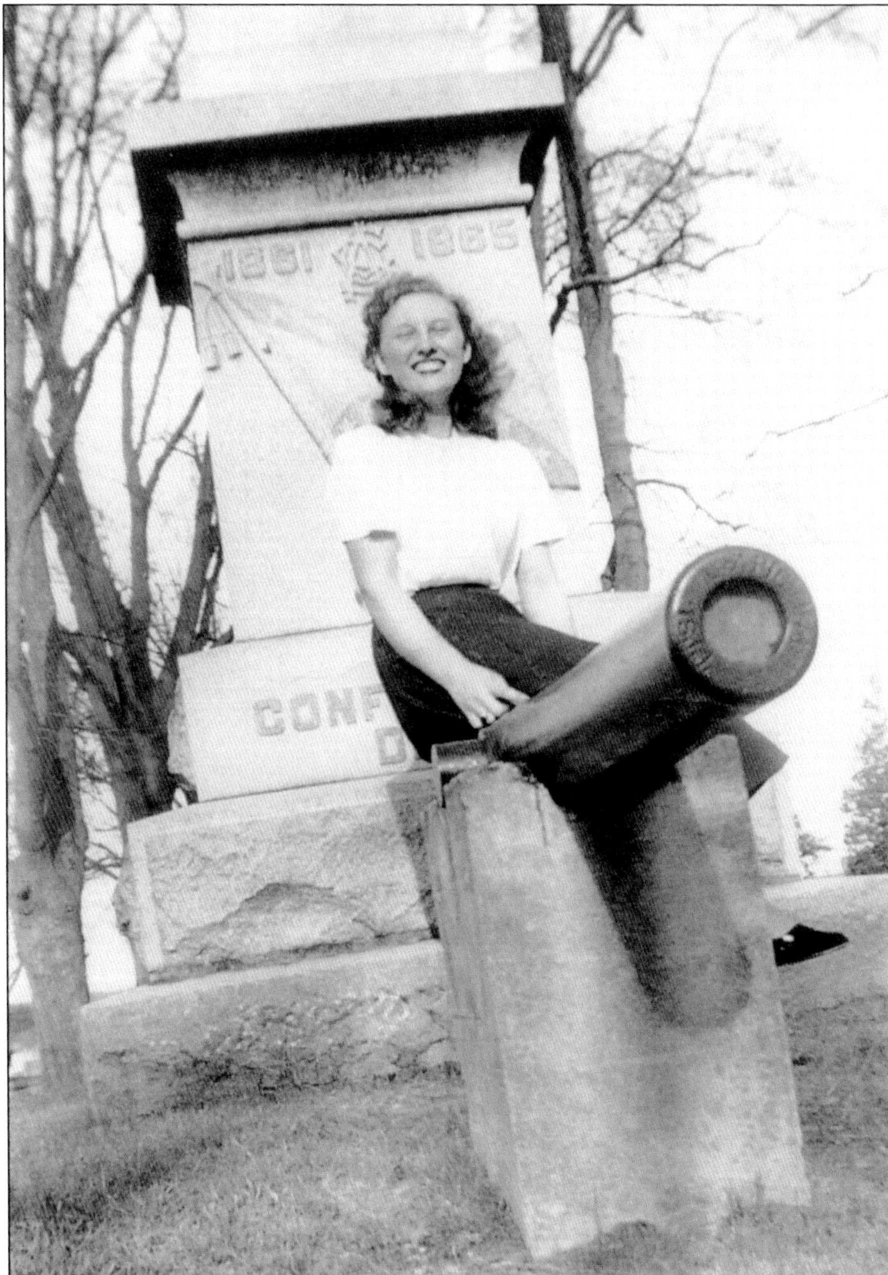

Inspiration for this book came from the guidance of Eloise Garris Taylor, who taught me very early in life to respect my elders, embrace my past, and strive to preserve the history of all that came before me. She would have loved every minute of this journey. (Courtesy of the Eloise Garris Taylor collection.)

On the Cover: Officials and citizens pose for a photograph at the April 16, 1937, dedication of the newly renovated Franklin County Courthouse. See page 31 for more information. (Courtesy of Carolyn Patterson.)

IMAGES
of America

FRANKLIN COUNTY

Diane Taylor Torrent

ARCADIA
PUBLISHING

ISBN 978-1-4671-2216-0

Published by Arcadia Publishing
Charleston, South Carolina

Printed in the United States of America

Library of Congress Control Number: 2014930475

For all general information, please contact Arcadia Publishing:
Telephone 843-853-2070
Fax 843-853-0044
E-mail sales@arcadiapublishing.com
For customer service and orders:
Toll-Free 1-888-313-2665

Visit us on the Internet at www.arcadiapublishing.com

To Dr. Neeraj Agrawal, whose wisdom and patience saved my life, and to my husband, Stephen Charles Torrent, whose love makes my life worth living

Contents

Acknowledgments

This book would not have been possible without the many historians and photographers whose passion it was to record, collect, and preserve the history of Franklin County. Family photographers caught their loved ones in a moment in time, historians strove to capture memorable events, and everyday citizens snapped a mundane street scene that today gives us a glimpse into their lives.

I would especially like to thank those few who contributed their time, photographs, and, especially, their wisdom and knowledge in collecting many of the images. Freddie Edwards, whose influence spans from teacher to mentor, graciously contributed the postcard images from his personal collection and offered insight into the life of Louisburg's past. Sammie Beasley, who has spent years striving to collect and identify the images that define Franklin County, offered advice, photographs, and his extensive knowledge of Franklin County history. John Seibel, who worked alongside Beasley to bring many of Louisburg's street scenes to life, provided photographs and assistance with locating others who shared our interest.

My gratitude to the staff of the Franklin County Courthouse for assisting me in perusing its halls, nooks, and crannies for photographs it housed. It produced many long-forgotten, unseen treasures and brought to light the enormity of the records contained within its historic walls. Information gleaned from reels of microfilm housed at the Franklin County Library provided the headlines of Franklin County. The events found on those reels aided in correctly identifying, dating, and telling the story of many images.

A special thank-you to the gracious members of the Heritage Society of Franklin County for their guidance in producing a local history book. Their experience in gathering, compiling, and writing a historical volume was of great assistance.

Most of all, I would like to thank the many citizens who searched through their own family albums, attics, and basements to lend their memories to make this book possible. I am grateful to each one who took the time to tell the story of their ancestors and provide the photographs that defined who they were.

Introduction

On January 20, 1779, the North Carolina General Assembly met in Halifax and approved an act to divide Bute County into Warren and Franklin Counties. John Norwood, Matthew Thomas, and Joseph Norris were named to locate and purchase a central location for a county seat. Book one, page one of *Franklin County Deeds* describes the 100 acres of land chosen along the Tar River. The land was purchased from Patewills and Jacobina Milner for $1,000 current money, and commissioners Osborn Jeffreys, William Green, William Hill, William Brickell, and John Hunt were appointed to lay off the land in lots, which were awarded through a lottery. Though records reflect the presence of settlers in this area of the Piedmont long before this act, this day in 1779 marks the birth of Franklin County.

The county seat of Louisburg sprung from the original 100 acres. At the dawn of the 1800s, the town was a thriving trade route. Stores, mills, and at least 20 houses were in place by 1810, and the stagecoach was making three stops weekly. The Franklin Male Academy was under the direction of Matthew Dickinson by 1805. It was soon followed by the Louisburg Female Academy. The 1835 discovery of gold on John Portis's land brought growth to the Wood community, with a rush of settlers and prospectors. Franklinton grew around the Raleigh-Gaston Railroad and incorporated into a town in 1842.

By 1850, the Franklin County Courthouse was completed, and the census recorded Franklin County citizens engaged in the everyday business of merchants, hotel keepers, wheelwrights, carpenters, stonecutters, blacksmiths, tailors, barbers, coach makers, physicians, teachers, and gunsmiths. The 1860 census gave the population at around 14,000, over half of which were slaves.

The Civil War took its toll on Franklin County families, as 1,400 men went to war and 1,000 returned. The county was spared the physical devastation of the war, but Louisburg College's grounds were subjected to an occupation by Union soldiers from May through July 1865.

The South's reconstruction had begun, and the 1870s saw industrial growth along Sandy Creek, as Col. Jordan Jones began operating a gristmill at Laurel. Louisburg's Edwin Wiley Fuller published his novel *Sea Gift* in 1871, and production of newspapers, suspended during the war, resumed when J.A. Thomas purchased what would become the *Franklin Times* in 1875. That same year, on March 17, the post office and railroad stop at Pacific were incorporated into the town of Youngsville.

The county celebrated its centennial in 1879, attracting the largest assembly of citizens to date to the Franklin Academy's grove. A parade, speeches, bands, and a picnic all culminated in a grand ball. In Franklinton, Dr. Moses Hopkins founded Albion Academy during the centennial year, marking an educational milestone as the first colored school in the county.

The county's population had risen to over 20,000 by 1880, and tobacco markets in Louisburg and Youngsville were prospering. Louisburg's market expanded when the 10-mile track of railroad to Franklinton was completed, making travel for business and pleasure easily accessible. The Franklinton railroad also contributed to the success of the Sterling Cotton Mill, built by Samuel C. Vann in 1895, providing employment and mill housing.

The new century brought modern conveniences, with telephone services connecting Louisburg, Centerville, Franklinton, and Youngsville. Water and sewer lines were in by 1905, and in 1906, Dr. R.F. Yarborough drove the first automobile into the county. A new town was added when the railroad stop at Bunn was incorporated in 1913.

In 1914, the United Daughters of the Confederacy dedicated a monument to Franklin County's fallen Civil War soldiers. The keynote speaker was county native Thomas W. Bickett, who became governor of North Carolina in 1917. Governor Bickett's administration saw the state through the dark years of World War I, when Franklin County lost 36 of its sons to the cause.

The 1920s saw an increase in education under the supervision of Edward L. Best, with the addition of schools in Cedar Rock and Franklinton. Electricity was introduced to rural communities, and roadway-paving projects were under way. Postwar prosperity brought consumer goods back to the populace, and the economy once again began to thrive. The mid-1920s saw Billy T. Person become the first of many airplane owners in the county. The county's first pilot, Louisburg's William Winston, taught Charles Lindbergh as an Army instructor in 1925.

Thousands attended the July 4, 1929, sesquicentennial ceremonies to proudly celebrate the past 150 years. The stock market crash was just around the corner, but optimism was high as the Roaring Twenties wound down. However, by the 1930 census, Franklin County's nearly 30,000 residents were in the grip of the Depression. As businesses closed and banks failed, a new form of entertainment offered an affordable distraction when talking pictures came to Louisburg in 1929 and Franklinton in 1930. Also increasing morale was the repeal of Prohibition in 1933, which resulted in the legalization of the sale of spirits in Louisburg and Franklinton in 1936. Renovation of the courthouse began in 1936, providing much needed employment, and the rededication in 1937 was attended by hundreds.

The war years of the 1940s saw Franklin County lose Bunn's Malcolm Leigh in the attack on Pearl Harbor, as well as another 51 locals before the surrender of Japan. The remainder of the 1940s saw the county slowly recover, as rationing decreased and employment increased. In 1946, it was announced that roadwork was to begin on a bypass to downtown Louisburg, and Bickett Boulevard was born. Franklin Memorial Hospital opened its doors in 1951, and by the end of the 1950s, the county had its own radio station, WYRN. In 1955, a new drive-in theater opened outside of town, and growth along the new bypass included the Murphy House restaurant, Dick's Drive-In, and full-service gas stations. The 1960s and 1970s showed an increase in activity, as more and more downtown businesses moved to the more spacious bypass. In 1977, Franklin County saw the golden arches of the McDonald's chain rise on Bickett Boulevard, which would become just one of many fast food restaurants, chain stores, and mega-marts marking their growth into today's market.

So sums up the 235-year history of a county born in the throes of the American Revolution. However, the history of a county is not limited to the names that were recorded or the events remembered. As W.F. Yarborough stated in his speech at the county's 150-year celebration, "The true history of Franklin County has not and never can be written . . . it is locked in the archives of the hearts of the multitude that are in the graves that are unknown and unremembered." Through the efforts of the county's original historians, Edward Hill Davis and Daniel T. Smithwick; the more recent works of Thilbert H. Pearce and Lib Cheatham; and those who continue their work today, Sammy Beasley, Joe Elmore, Maury York, Freddie Edwards, and so many others, along with the Heritage Society of Franklin County, those archives are being unlocked and shared.

The real history of Franklin County exists in the faces of its people, in the landmarks left by its forefathers, and in the promise to its future generations that their legacy will be preserved.

One

Founding a County around the Courthouse Square

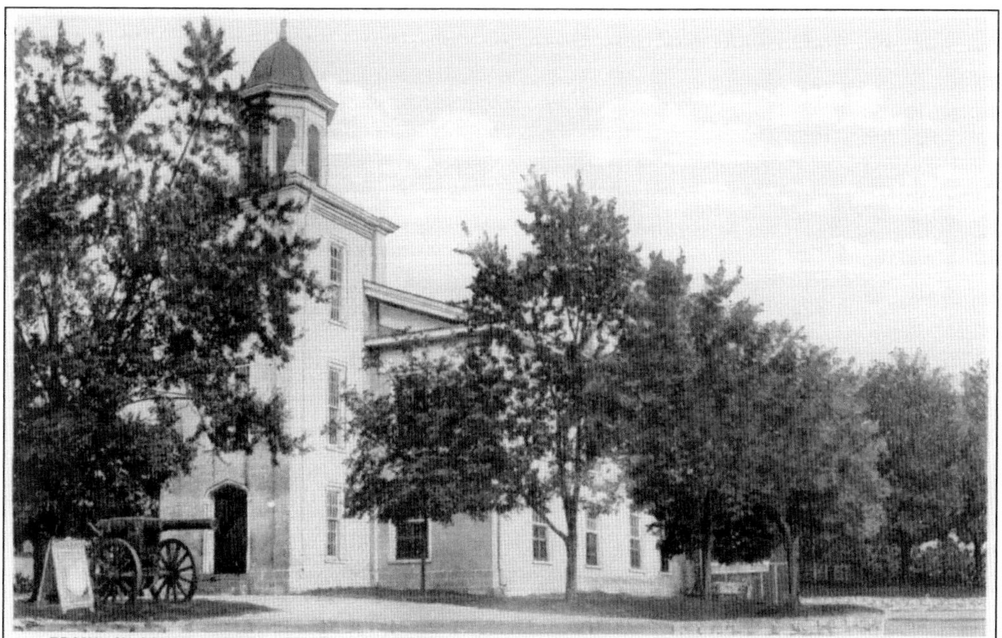

The act establishing Franklin County required that the commissioners, John Norwood, Matthew Thomas, and Joseph Norris, locate the new courthouse in a central location convenient to water. Built along the Tar River, the twice-renovated courthouse still sits on the land chosen in 1849. The bell tower, seen here in this 1900-era postcard, was not completed until after the Civil War. (Courtesy of Freddie Edwards.)

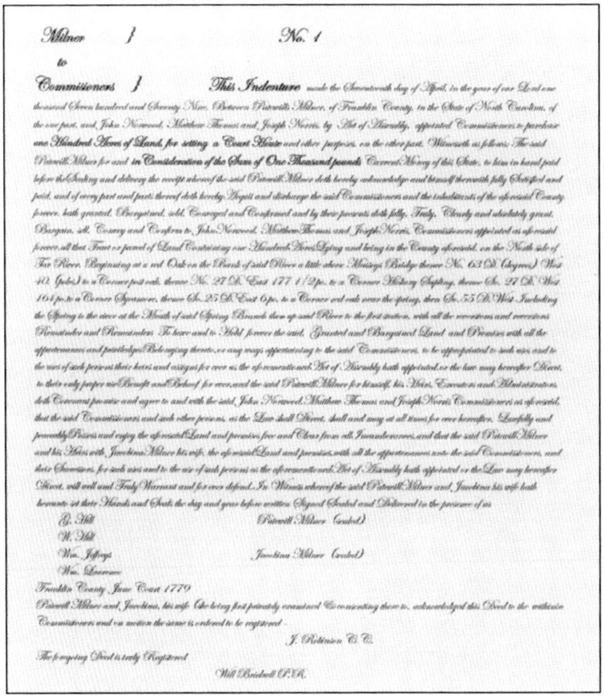

Milner }
to
Commissioners }

No. 1

This Indenture made the Seventeenth day of April, in the year of our Lord one thousand Seven hundred and Seventy Nine, Between Patewills Milner, of Franklin County, in the State of North Carolina, of the one part, and John Norwood, Matthew Thomas and Joseph Norris by Act of Assembly, appointed Commissioners to purchase **one Hundred Acres of Land, for setting a Court House** and other purposes, on the other part. Witnesseth as follows: The said Patewill Milner for and **in Consideration of the Sum of One Thousand pounds** Current Money of this State, to him in hand paid before the Sealing and delivery the receipt whereof the said Patewill Milner doth hereby acknowledge and himself therewith fully Satisfied and paid, and of every part and parts thereof doth hereby Acquit and discharge the said Commissioners and the inhabitants of the aforesaid County forever, hath granted, Bargained, sold, Conveyed and Confirmed and by their presents doth fully, Truly, Clearly and absolutely grant, Bargain, sell, Convey and Confirm to John Norwood, Matthew Thomas and Joseph Norris, Commissioners appointed as aforesaid forever, all that Tract or parcel of Land Containing one Hundred Acres Lying and being in the County aforesaid, on the North side of Tar River, Beginning at a red Oak on the Bank of said River a little above Massey's Bridge thence No. 63 D. (degrees) West 40. (poles) to a Corner post oak, thence No. 27 D. East 177 1/2 po. to a Corner Hickory Sapling, thence So. 27 D. West 164 po. to a Corner Sycamore, thence So. 25 D. East 6 po. to a Corner red oak near the spring, then So. 55 D. West Including the Spring to the river at the Mouth of said Spring Branch then up said River to the first station, with all the reversions and reversions Remainder and Remainders To have and to Hold forever the said, Granted and Bargained Land and Premises with all the appurtenances and priviledges Belonging thereto, or any ways appertaining to the said Commissioners, to be appropriated to such uses and to the uses of such persons their heirs and assigns for ever as the aforementioned Act of Assembly hath appointed, or the law may hereafter Direct, to their only proper use Benefit and Behoof for ever, and the said Patewill Milner for himself, his Heirs, Executors and Administrators, doth Covenant promise and agree to and with the said, John Norwood, Matthew Thomas and Joseph Norris Commissioners as aforesaid, that the said Commissioners and such other persons, as the Law shall Direct, shall and may at all times for ever hereafter, Lawfully and peaceably Possess and enjoy the aforesaid Land and premises free and Clear from all Incumbrances, and that the said Patewill Milner and his Heirs with Jacobina Milner his wife, the aforesaid Land and premises, with all the appurtenances unto the said Commissioners, and their Successors, for such uses and to the use of such persons as the aforementioned Act of Assembly hath appointed or the Law may hereafter Direct, will well and Truly Warrant and for ever defend. In Witness whereof the said Patewill Milner and, Jacobina his wife hath hereunto set their Hands and Seals the day and year before written Signed Sealed and Delivered in the presence of us

G. Hill — Patewill Milner (sealed)
W. Hill
Wm. Jeffreys — Jacobina Milner (sealed)
Wm. Lawrence

Franklin County June Court 1779
Patewill Milner and, Jacobina, his wife (She being first privately examined & consenting there to, acknowledged this Deed to the withinin Commissioners and on motion the same is ordered to be registered.

J. Robinson C. C.

The foregoing Deed is truly Registered

Will Bricknell P.R.

This copy of the indenture for the land purchased to construct the Franklin County Courthouse hangs on the courthouse wall, alongside photographs of the building throughout its history. Patewills (1734–1788) and Jacobina Milner (1745–1827) were extensive landowners when they sold the 100 acres for $1,000 current money in June 1779. The deed is recorded in the *Franklin County Deeds* book one, page one. (Author's collection.)

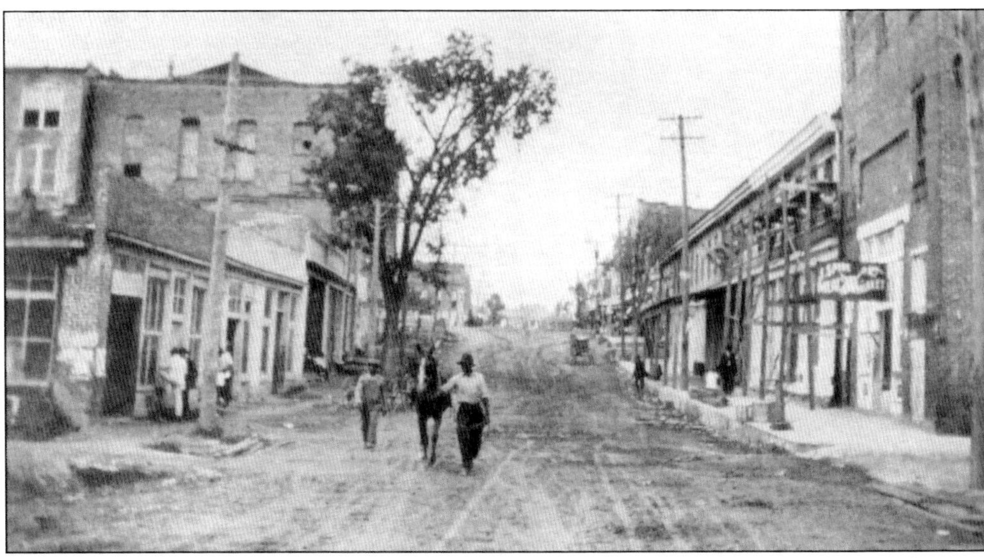

On October 27, 1779, the North Carolina General Assembly passed a law establishing the town of Louisburg. With the courthouse in place, 100 half-acre lots were assigned on a grid, forming the layout of the surrounding town. Commissioners conducted a lottery at a cost of $40 per lot, and settlers began building homes and businesses on the banks of the Tar River. By the time this photograph was taken around 1910, the thriving town of merchants, warehouses, and educators was 131 years old. With a railroad and telephone, electric, and sewer systems, Louisburg's residents were enjoying all the conveniences of modern living. In this view of a yet-to-be-paved Nash Street, one can see a few landmarks that still stand today. At the far end of the street is the Egerton-Pruitt House, built in 1905 for merchant Frank N. Egerton (1853–1924). (Courtesy of Sammy Beasley.)

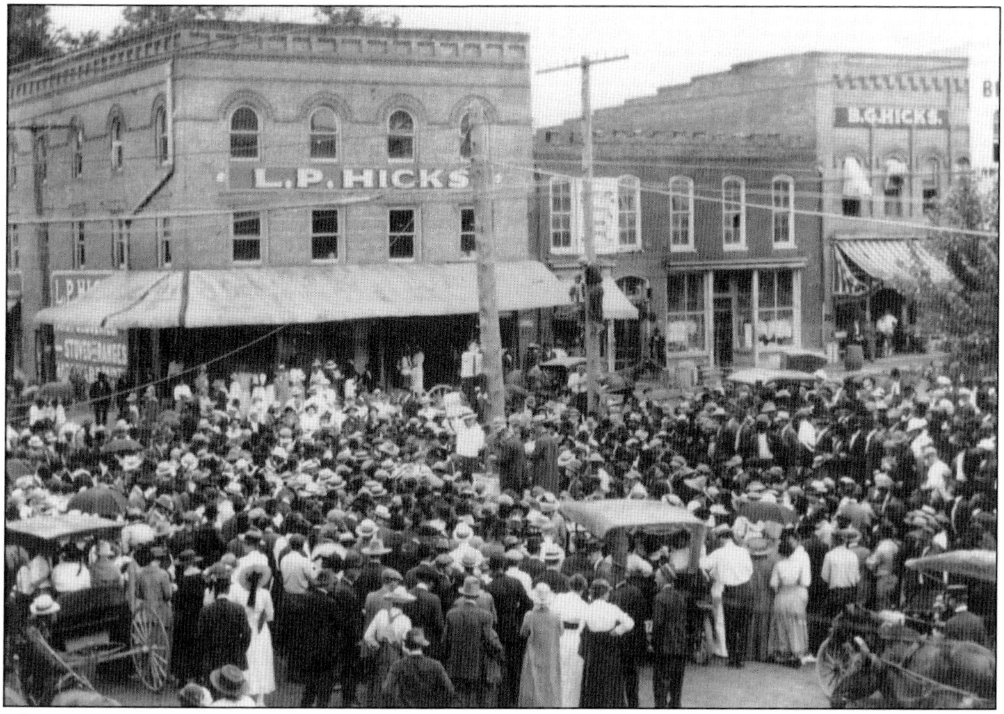

The L.P. Hicks store sat at the intersection of Nash and Main Streets, historically known as Hick's Corner. The three-story building was constructed in 1899 at a cost of $4,000 and still stands today. Here, a crowd gathers in the courthouse square as onlookers climb poles to get a better view. (Courtesy of Louisburg Town Hall.)

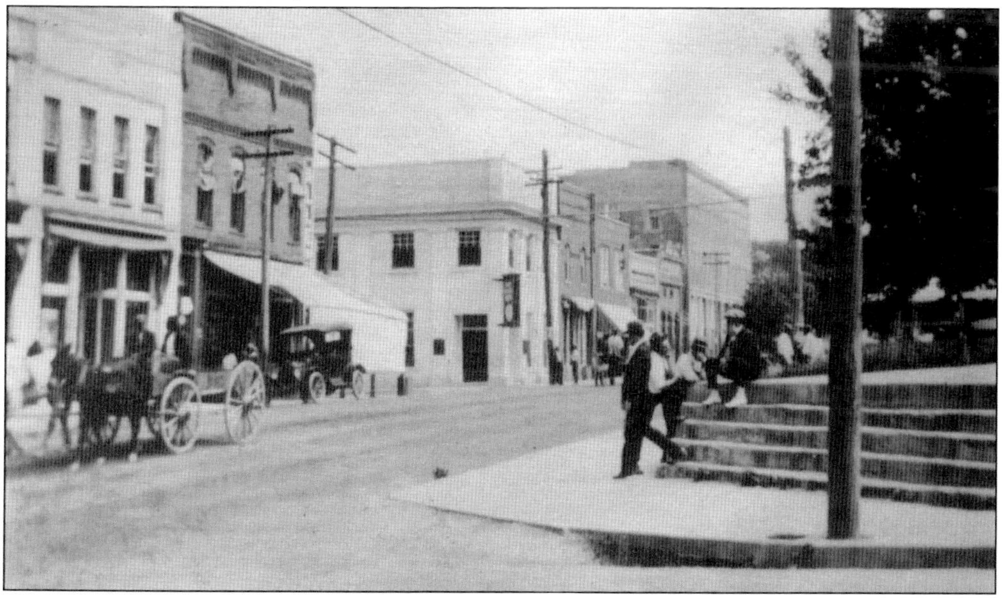

In the years prior to the 1936 renovation of the courthouse, the steps surrounding the square offered a gathering place for Louisburg's visitors. Looking north from the corner of Main and Court Streets, the unpaved roads and sidewalks teemed with activity in this early-1900s photograph. (Courtesy of Sammy Beasley.)

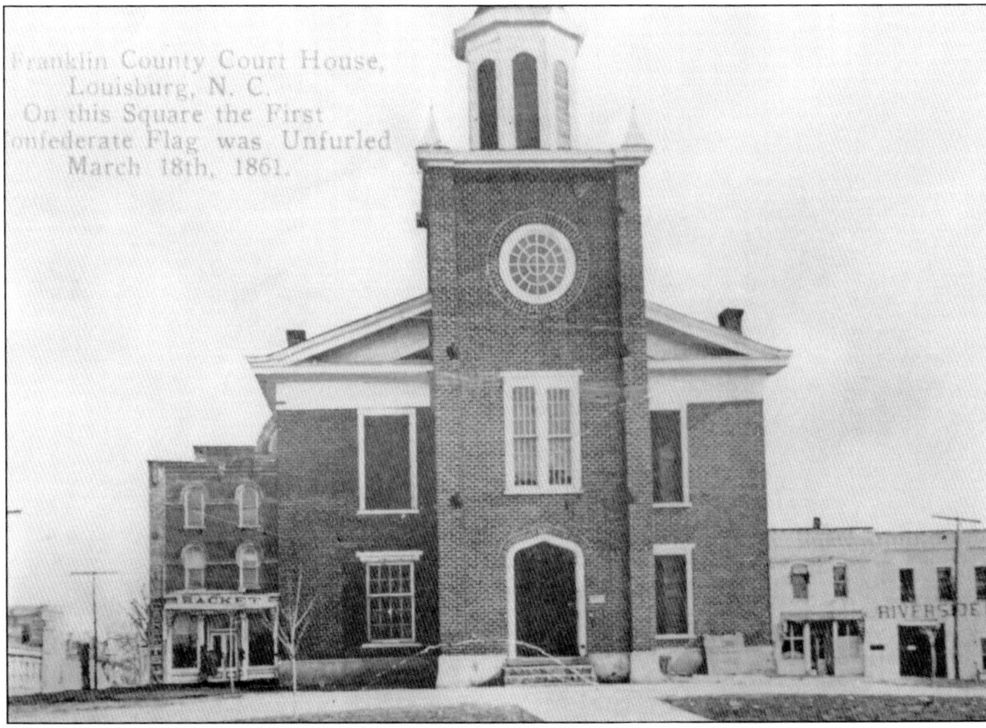

The original design of the courthouse included a bell tower, an A-frame roof, and a central hallway. The footprint was much smaller in this 1890s photograph, allowing a view of the Opera House and the Racket Store to the left and the Riverside Warehouse to the right. (Courtesy of Franklin County Courthouse.)

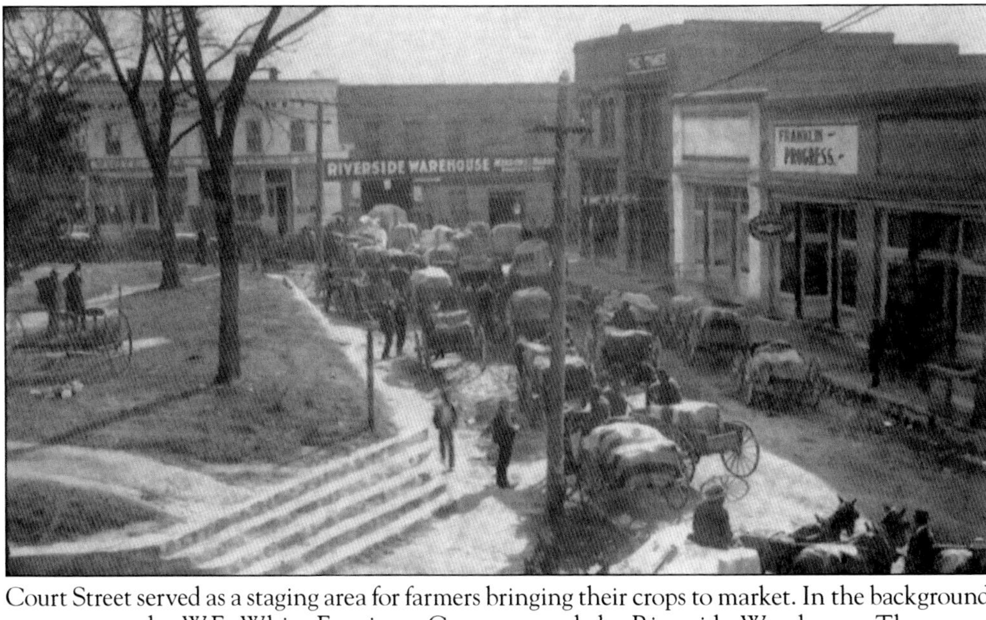

Court Street served as a staging area for farmers bringing their crops to market. In the background, one can see the W.E. White Furniture Company and the Riverside Warehouse. The row of buildings to the right housing the *Franklin Times* and *Franklin Progress* offices still stands today. (Courtesy of Sammy Beasley.)

The *Franklin Times* was located on Court Street in Louisburg from 1909 until 1956, when it moved to its present location on Bickett Boulevard. Once known as the *Franklin Courier*, its first issue was printed on February 11, 1870, but its origins can be traced back even further to the *Louisburg Union*, published in 1846. These reporters took a break from typesetting to pose for the camera. (Courtesy of Sammy Beasley.)

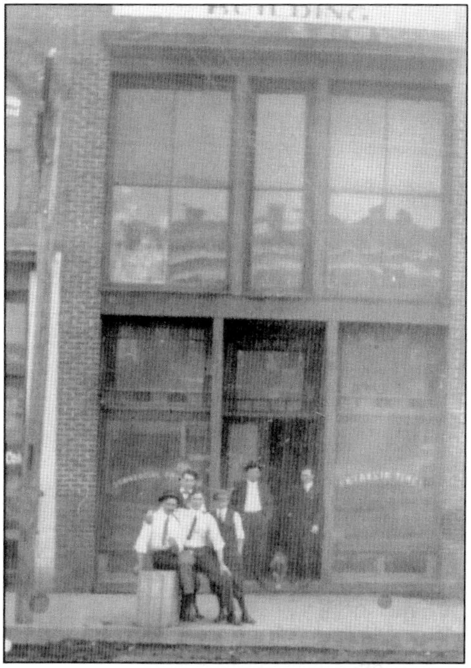

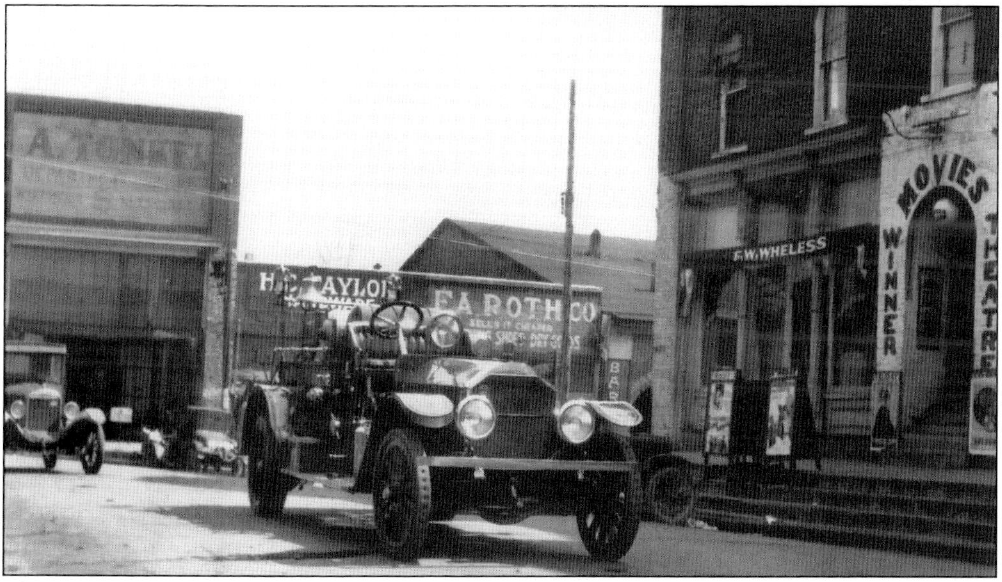

The Louisburg Opera House was located behind the courthouse on the corner of Market and East Nash Streets. On the second floor, the Opera House provided entertainment ranging from vaudeville to the latest movies of the day. Downstairs storefronts included clothing sales, a 5 and 10¢ store, candy shops, and law offices. In June 1945, a lightning strike destroyed the building and damaged the third floor of the adjacent structure, which housed the Masonic Lodge. Plans to rebuild failed, and the space serves as a parking lot today. The 1921 American LaFrance Type 75 fire engine in the photograph still belongs to the Louisburg Fire Department. After its retirement in 1952, the engine was sold to a farmer who used it to irrigate his fields. It was then sold to collectors and fire truck enthusiasts. In 2012, "Maude," as the engine was affectionately named, returned to the Louisburg Fire Department. (Courtesy of Louisburg Town Hall.)

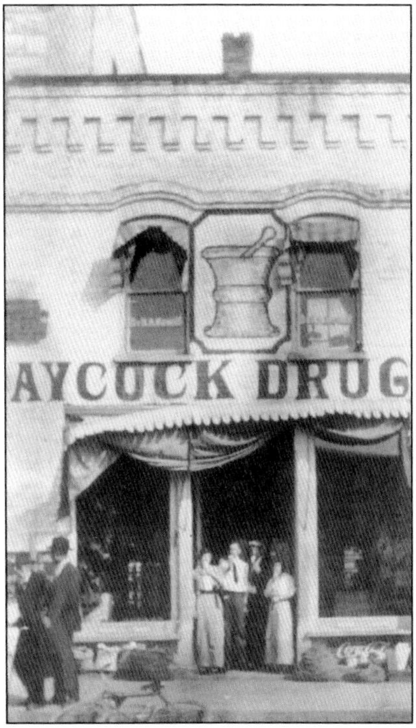

In its prime location behind the courthouse on Market Street, Aycock Drug Company served as a doctor's office, apothecary, and soda shop. Advertisements in the *Franklin Times* announced sales of everything from household items and fine stationery to ladies' hats and toys from Santa Claus. Patrons are seen here enjoying an ice cream treat. (Courtesy of Sammy Beasley.)

Though uncommon in Franklin County's usually mild climate, snow periodically blankets the streets of Louisburg. The Franklin County Courthouse is seen here in the late 1920s. Found among the old records in the courthouse basement, this photograph can be dated by the movie marquee announcing the viewing on Friday and Saturday of the new Rin Tin Tin film, *The Night Cry*, a silent black-and-white film that debuted in 1926. Renovations to the courthouse in 1936 changed the facade of the bell tower, placing this photograph somewhere between 1926 and 1936. The small handwritten sign tacked to the pole warns of a $5 fine if cars are left on the street past 1:00 a.m. In the background, the edge of the *Franklin Times* office on Court Street can be seen just behind the courthouse. (Courtesy of Franklin County Courthouse.)

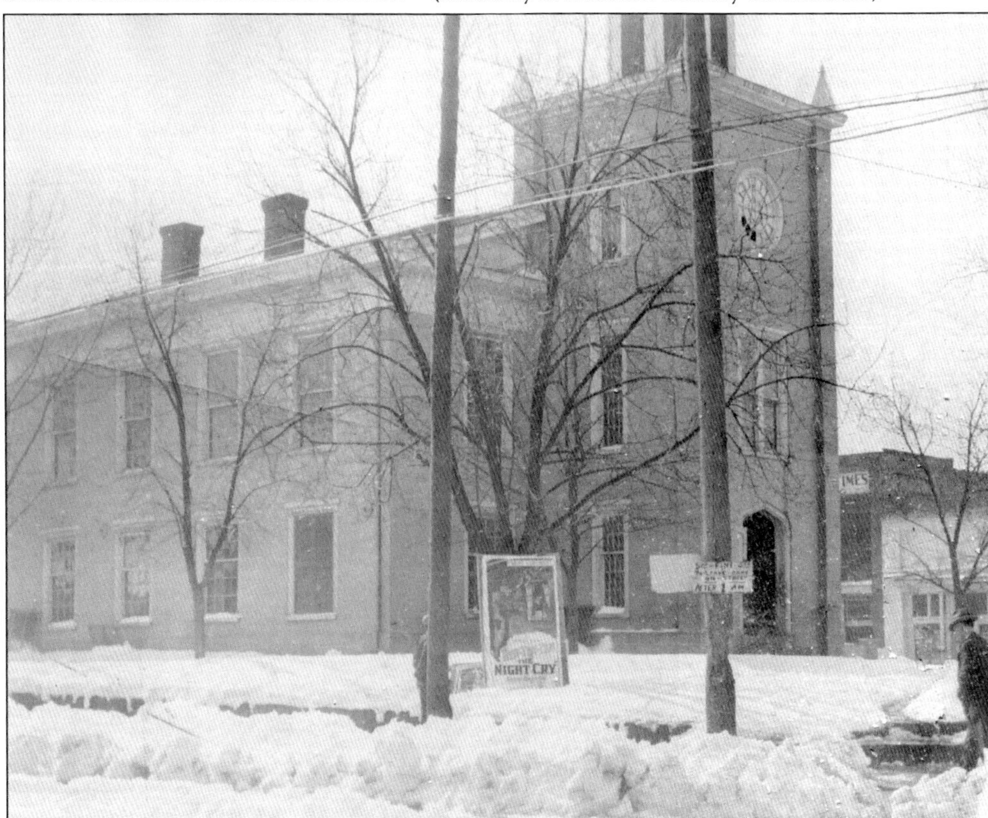

With Main Street at his back, this unidentified young man sits in the snow along Court Street near the courthouse. In the background are the W.E. White Furniture Company and the Hardware Company, with a sign that is still visible on the building today. This may have been an unexpected or unseasonable storm, as the gentleman does not appear to be dressed for the event. (Courtesy of Sammy Beasley.)

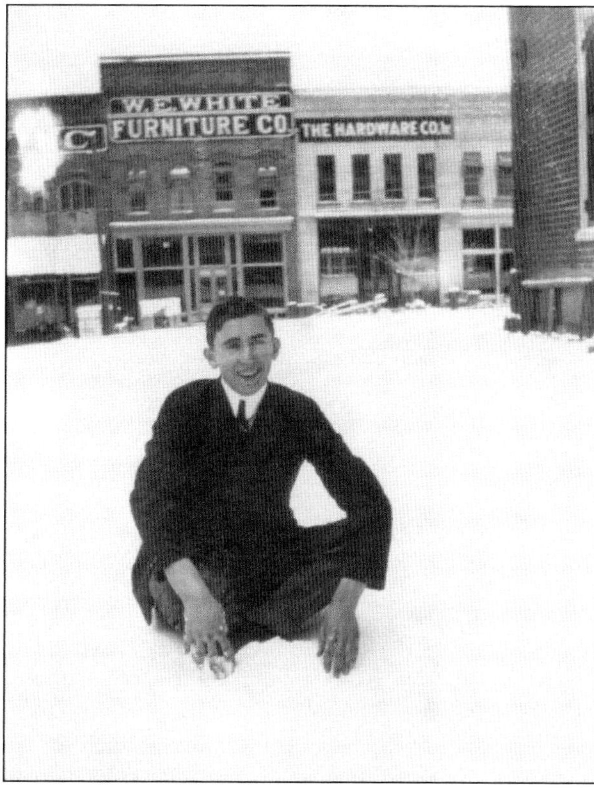

Looking towards the Tar River on Main Street, the dirt road and bridge are barely passable in this snow-covered state. The Union Warehouse can be seen to the right, and the Toy Land at the C.C. Hudson Store to the left was no doubt a popular destination in this winter wonderland. (Courtesy of Louisburg Town Hall.)

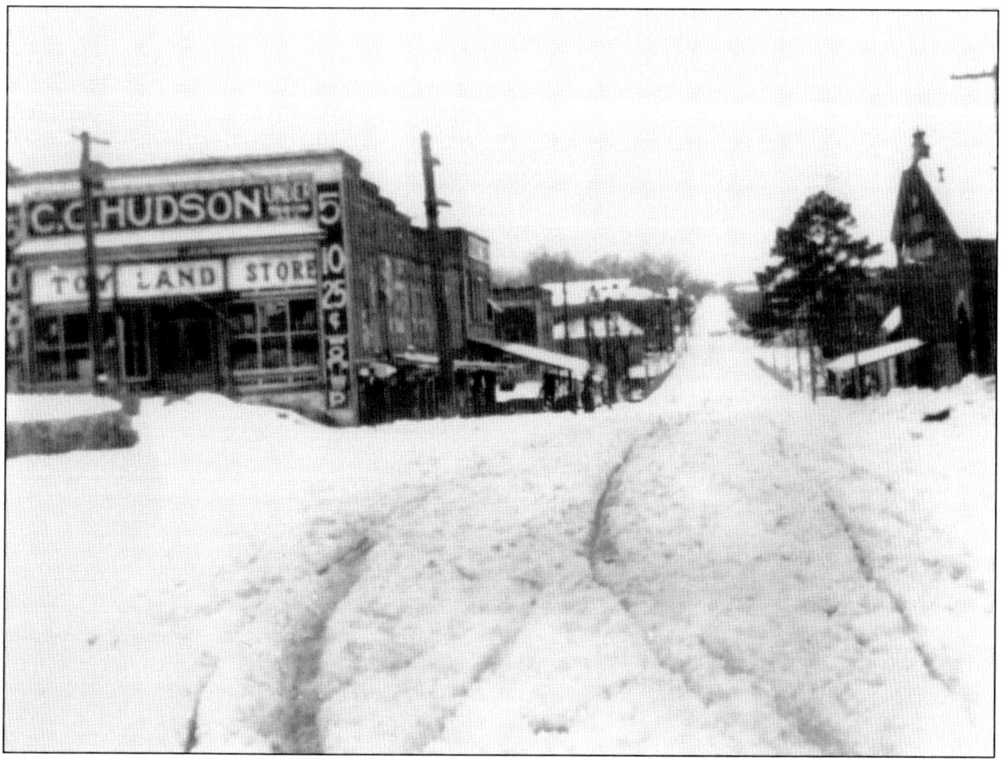

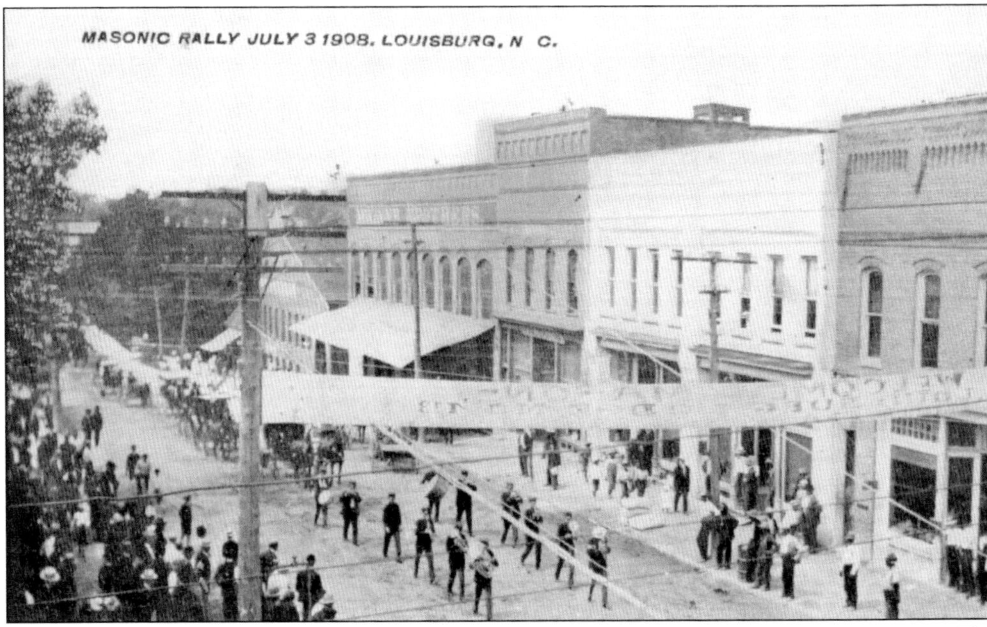

In this 1908 postcard, a Masonic rally parades north past the courthouse on Main Street. The Masons have a long history in Franklin County, with orders dating to the beginnings of the county, when the Blandford-Bute Lodge formed in 1766. The Franklinton Masonic Lodge No. 123 was organized in 1849. (Courtesy of Freddie Edwards.)

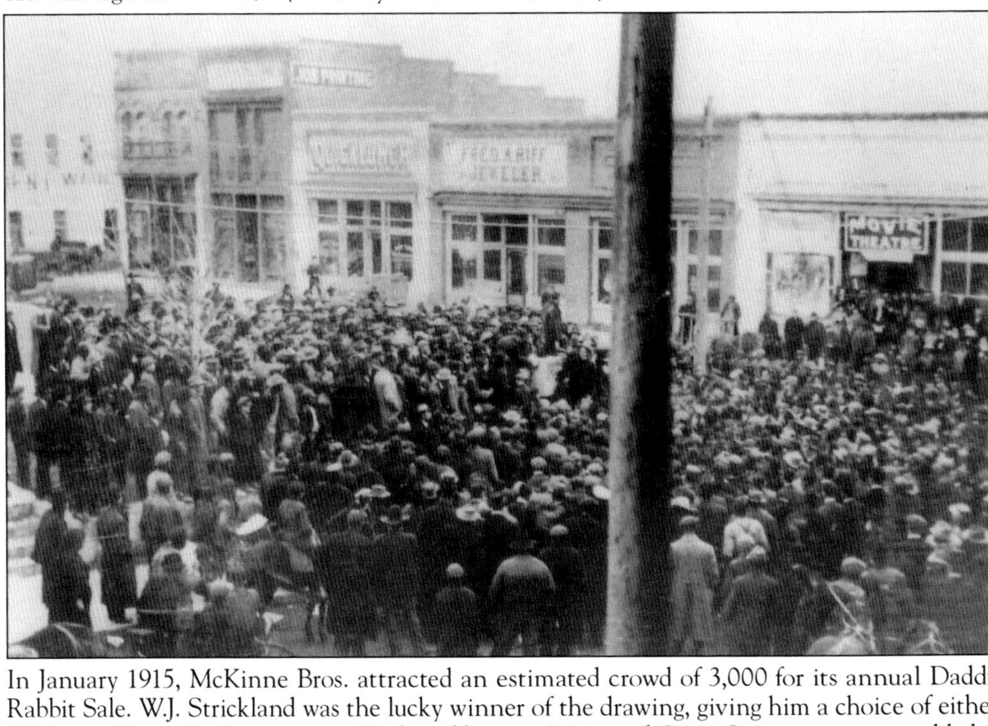

In January 1915, McKinne Bros. attracted an estimated crowd of 3,000 for its annual Daddy Rabbit Sale. W.J. Strickland was the lucky winner of the drawing, giving him a choice of either $500 in gold or a Ford touring car. Gathered here on Main and Court Streets, patrons could also visit the Quick Lunch, Fred A. Riff Jewelers, or the newly opened movie theater on the corner. (Courtesy of Sammy Beasley.)

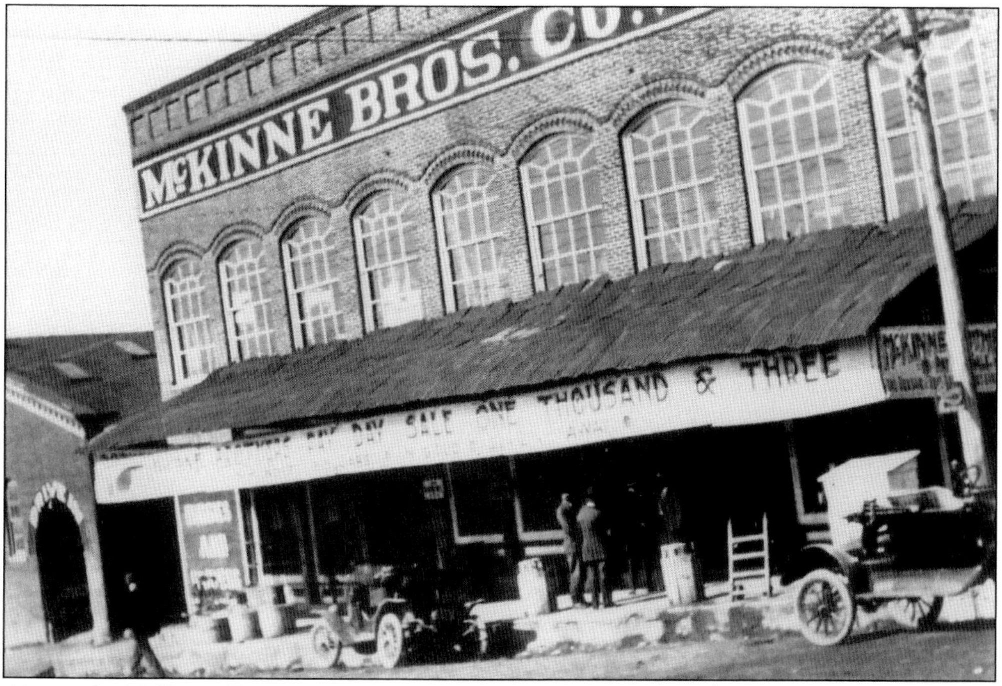

Above, the McKinne Bros. sign announces a "Pay Day Sale," where $200 in gold would be given away. Located on Main Street in front of the courthouse, the McKinne Bros. carried farm supplies, horses, buggies, and sundries, as well as serving as cotton brokers. Seen below, brothers Frank B. McKinne (1872–1946), David F. McKinne (1878–1965), and Malcolm McKinne (1884–1964) came from a family of merchants in Johnston County to open their successful farm supply business in Louisburg. Descendants of the McKinnes continued to operate the store until the 1990s when the building was replaced with the Judge Hamilton H. Hobgood Courthouse Annex. (Above, courtesy of Sammy Beasley; below, courtesy of Ray Strawbridge.)

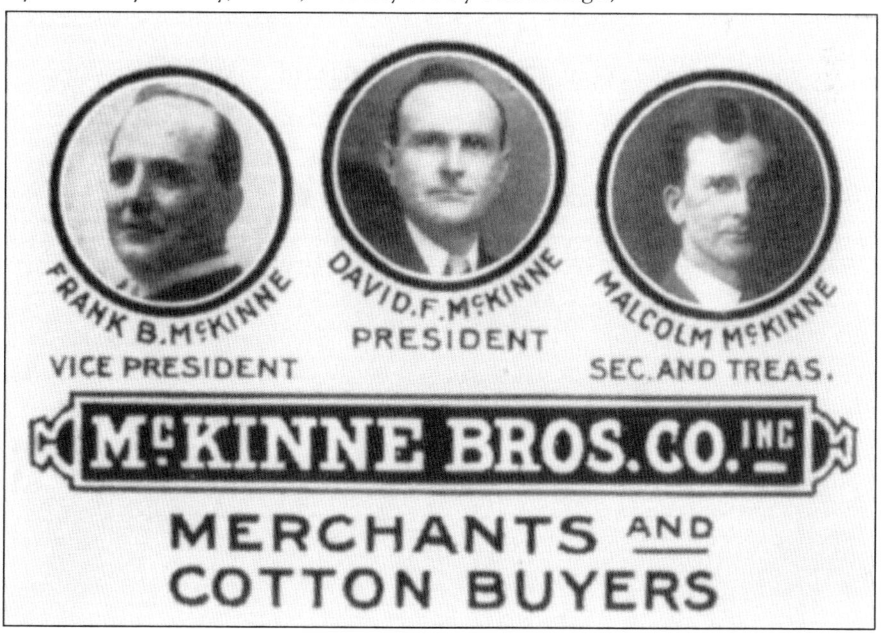

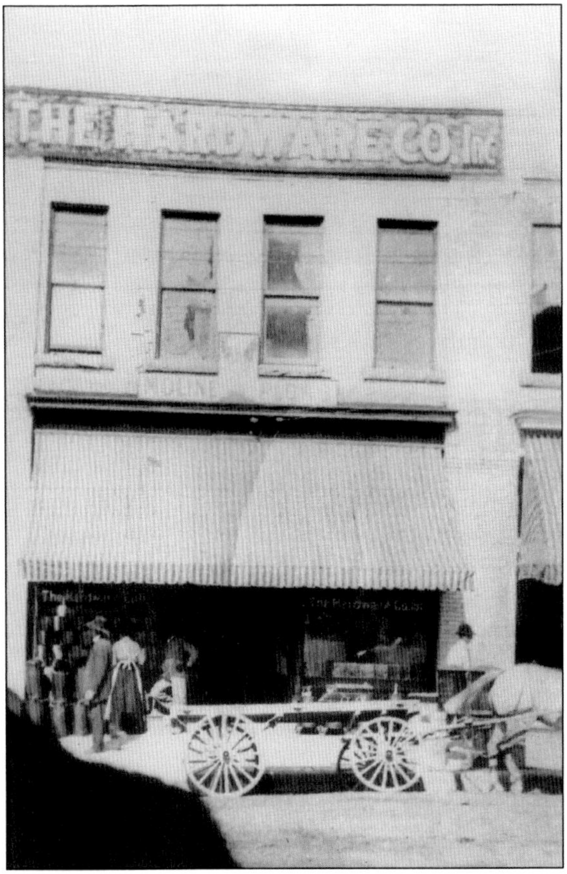

The sign above The Hardware Company, Inc., awning announces the sale of Moline plows, made by a horse-drawn plow company formed in the 1870s. It was located along Main Street next to the White Furniture Company and the McKinne Bros. farm supply, an area of downtown Louisburg that bustled with shoppers. (Courtesy of Sammy Beasley.)

The Hardware Company, Inc., building still stands today on North Main Street facing the courthouse, and a faint hint of the original sign can still be seen on the white brick building. Though empty today, it was the home of Rowe's Men's Shop for many years. (Author's collection.)

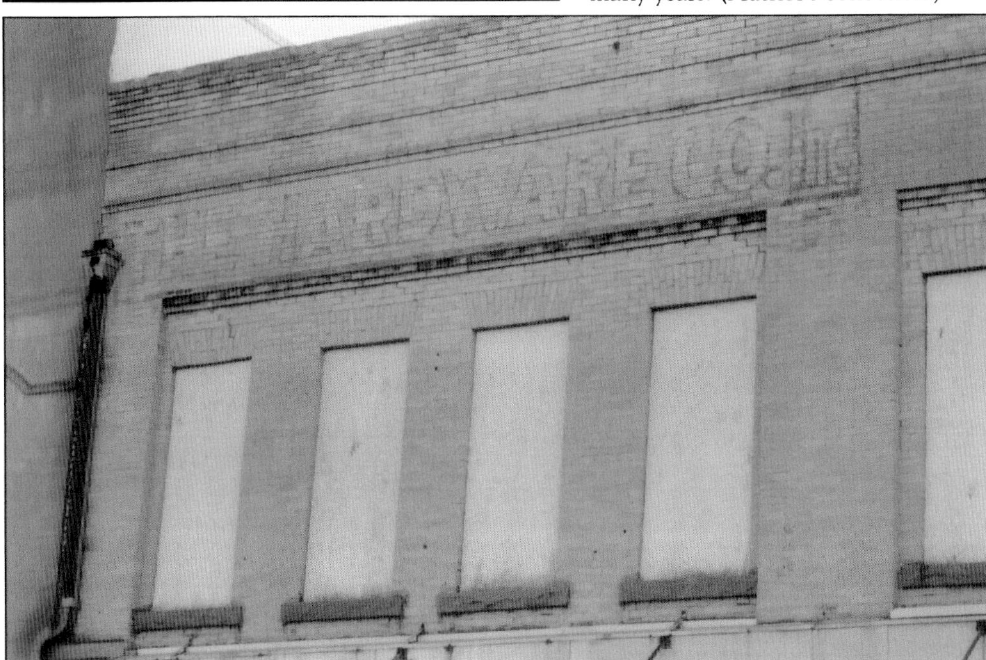

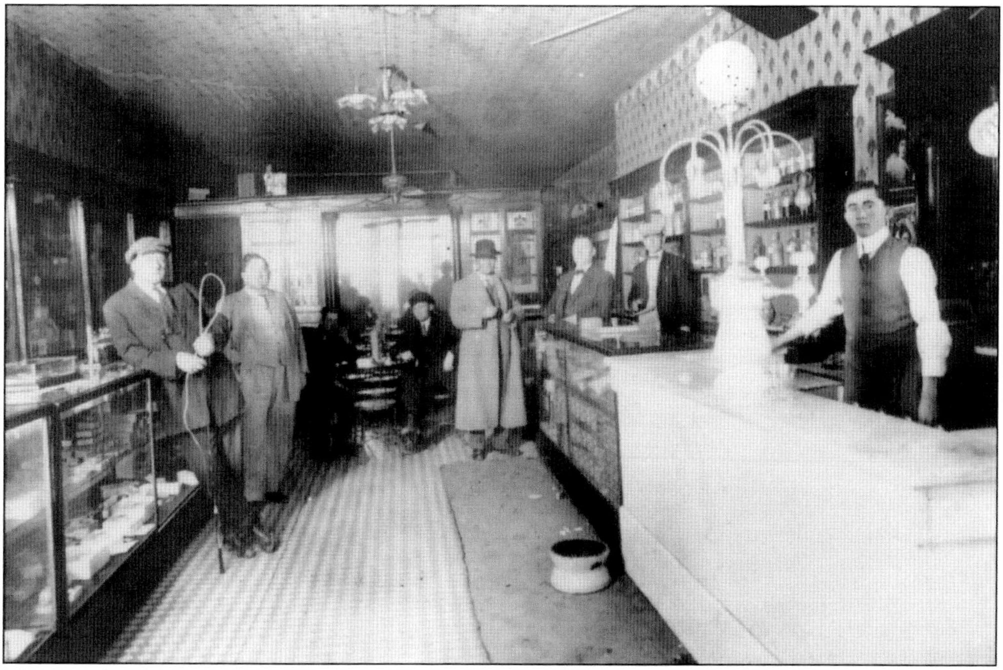

The Beasley-Alston Drug Company opened in 1915 on the corner of Court and Market Streets, next to the *Franklin Times* office, and was partly owned by William Fuquay Beasley (1869–1930). Beasley ran many diverse businesses, including a cotton gin, a sawmill, livery stables, a meat market, and a hogshead plant, which made barrels for storing tobacco. Benjamin Williamson and Beasley are seen here on the left with other unidentified patrons. (Courtesy of Sammy Beasley.)

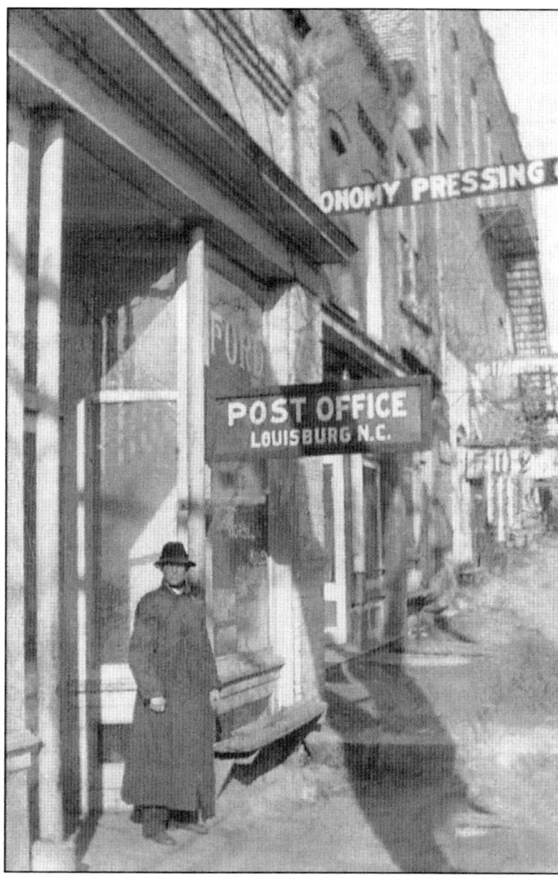

V.C. Williams stands by a storefront post office on East Nash Street in the days when mail was handled by shopkeepers. In the early 1900s, rural post offices were located in Alert, Bunn, Cedar Rock, Centerville, Cheaves, Dickens, Franklinton, Ingleside, Justice, Katesville, Laurel, Letha, Louisburg, Mapleville, Mitchener, Moulton, Oswego, Pilot, Pocomoke, Privett, Pughs, Ransom's Bridge, Riley, Royal, Stallings, Sutton, Views, Wood, and Youngsville. (Courtesy of Ted Gupton.)

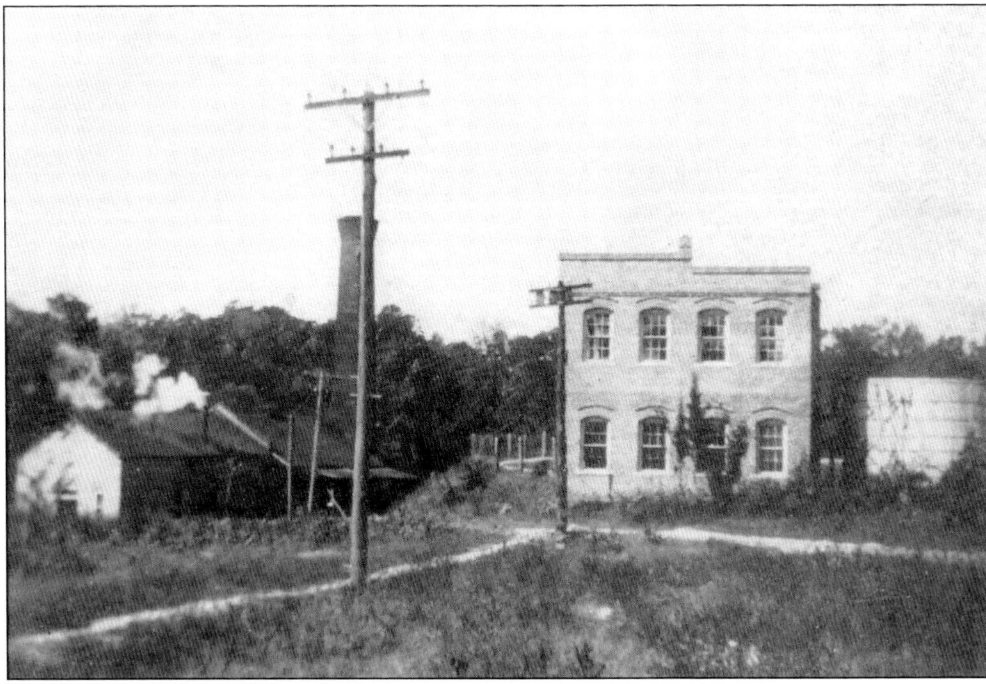

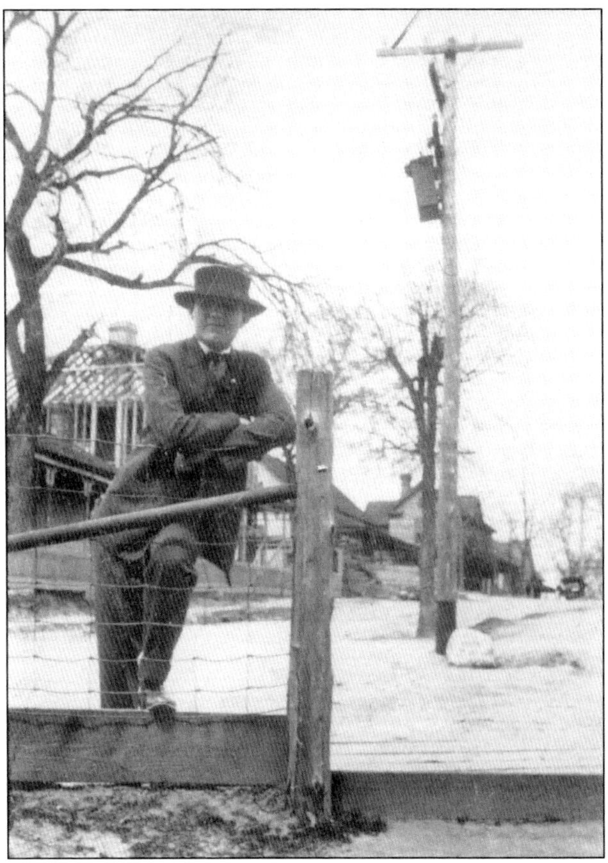

Modern conveniences arrived in Franklin County in 1905 when George E. Tenny of Spartanburg, South Carolina, was contracted to build a water and sewer system. On September 8, 1905, civil engineer John W. Hayes was awarded the contract to purchase materials and oversee construction of the town's electric plant. In this early scene, poles can be seen running from buildings alongside water-holding tanks. (Courtesy of Sammy Beasley.)

Telephone service was provided by the Henderson Telephone Company and arrived in Louisburg prior to 1905. In the early years, the operator, Susan Temperance Alston (1880–1970), worked six days a week, taking only Sundays off. This street scene shows an unidentified man and street in Louisburg with poles, a transformer, and lines overhead. (Courtesy of Sammy Beasley.)

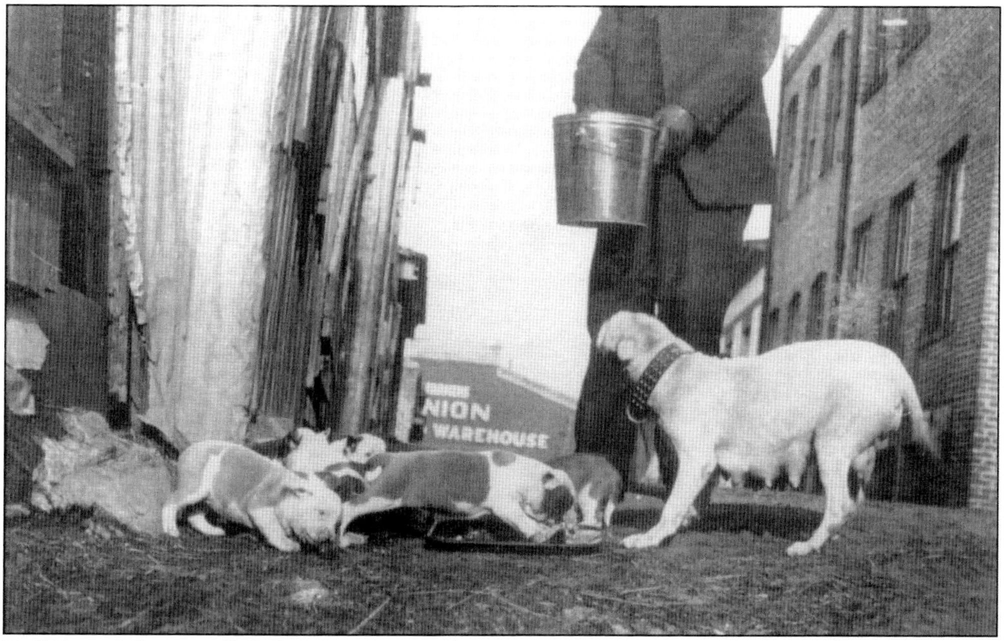

Bull Run Alley paralleled Court Street where Johnston Street connects North Main Street to Bickett Boulevard. In March 1955, Louisburg's city council ordered the alleyway cleaned, disinfected, and closed and for those loitering in the alleyway to be arrested. The back street had been a popular café and restaurant respite at day's end, but it had evolved into a hideaway of bars and outdoor restrooms. (Courtesy of Sammy Beasley.)

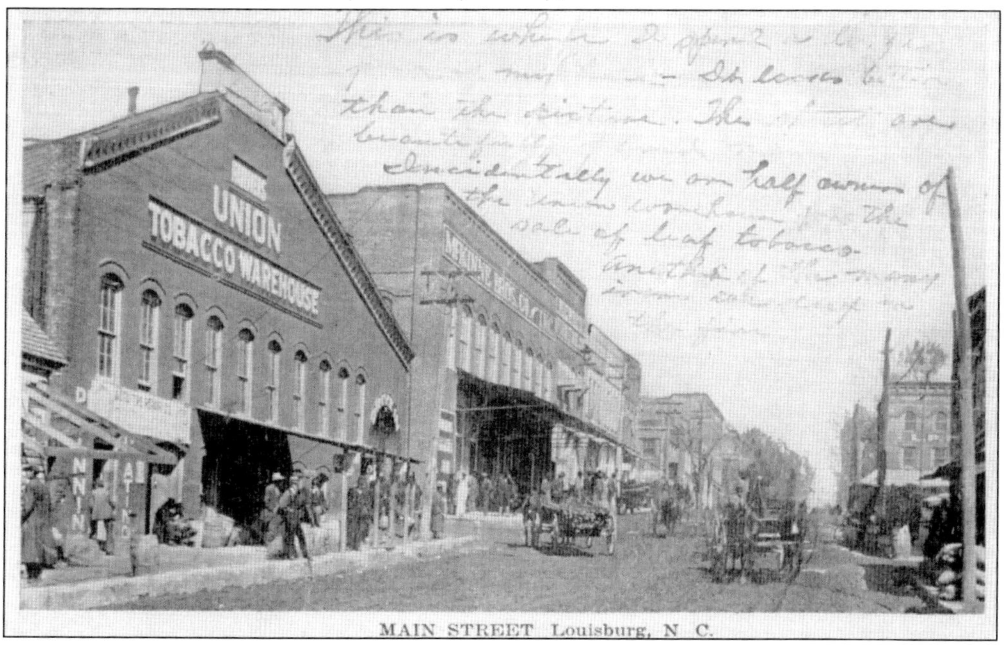

This early postcard shows the bustling activity as patrons gather in front of the Union Warehouse and McKinne Bros. The Union Tobacco Warehouse once stood on North Main Street at the end of Bull Run Alley, next to where the new Judge Hamilton Hobgood Courthouse Annex stands today. (Courtesy of Freddie Edwards.)

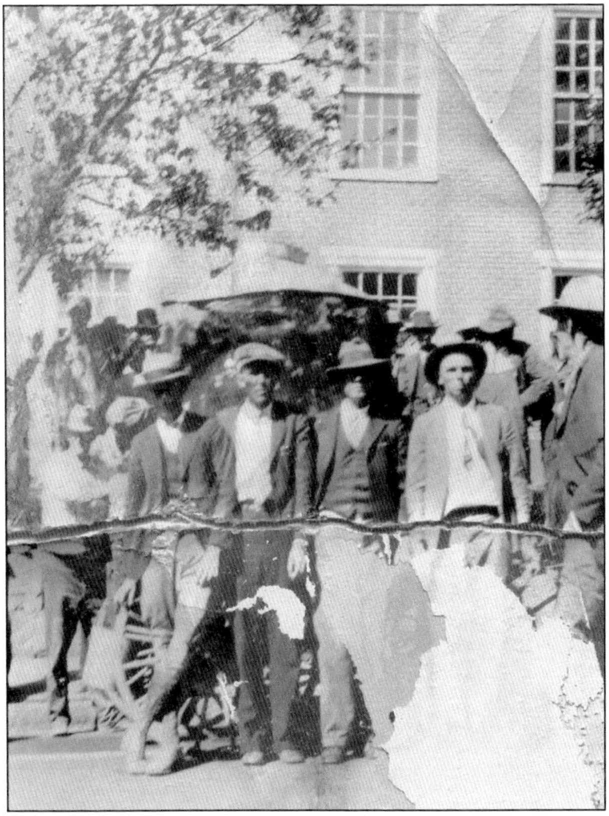

The two photographs on this page were found among the lost records in the courthouse basement in 2013. Here, a group of men gather at a street cart around the courthouse square. Perhaps it shows a midday lunch break, as some of the men are in work clothes and a few are in business attire. (Courtesy of Franklin County Courthouse.)

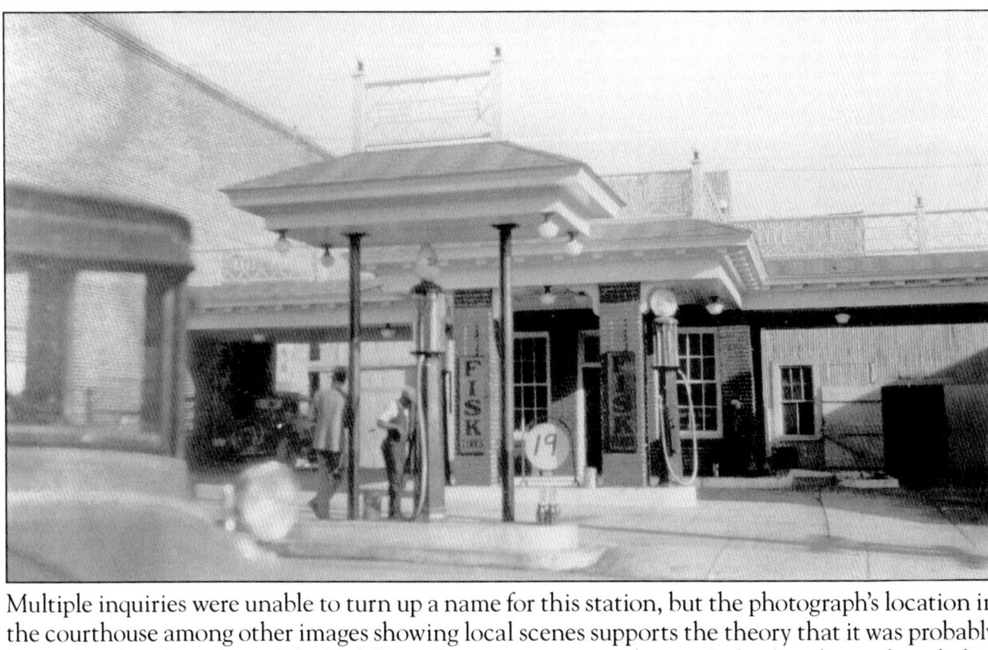

Multiple inquiries were unable to turn up a name for this station, but the photograph's location in the courthouse among other images showing local scenes supports the theory that it was probably located within Louisburg. The Fisk Tire Company, seen in the sign's displayed, was founded in 1898 and remained in business until the 1940s, when it was acquired by the US Rubber Company (now Uniroyal). (Courtesy of Franklin County Courthouse.)

By October 1905, the 125-foot-tall steel standpipe at right held 125,000 gallons of water and the sewer systems were in operation. Louisburg's citizens finally had running water, with the sewers discharging into the Tar River. The pipe stood behind the old Mills School for 75 years until an updated system replaced the obsolete storage pipe. The Wade Moore Construction Company took on the responsibility of removing the 275,000 pounds of steel to make way for a parking lot on the campus of Louisburg College. In the photograph below, a local sixth-grade class of students poses for a photograph at the base of the massive standpipe in the 1920s. (Both, courtesy of Sammy Beasley.)

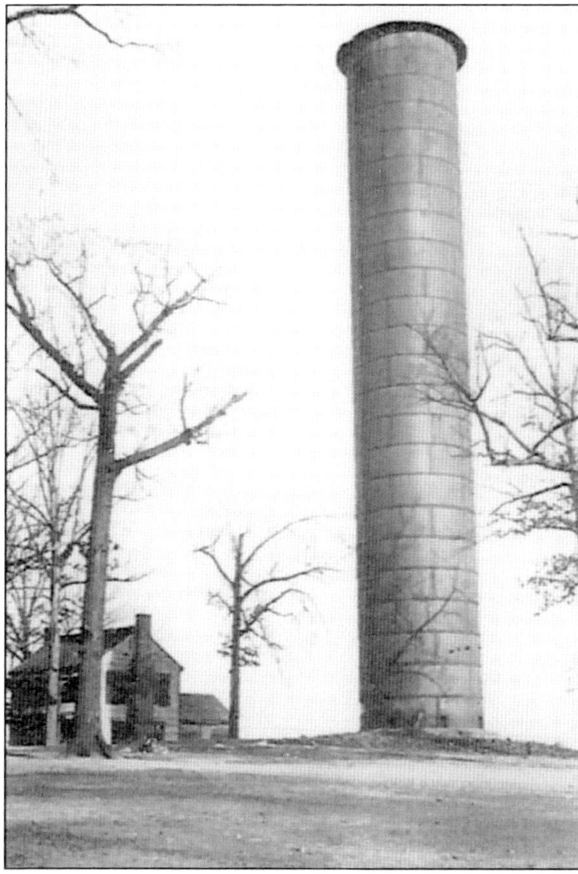

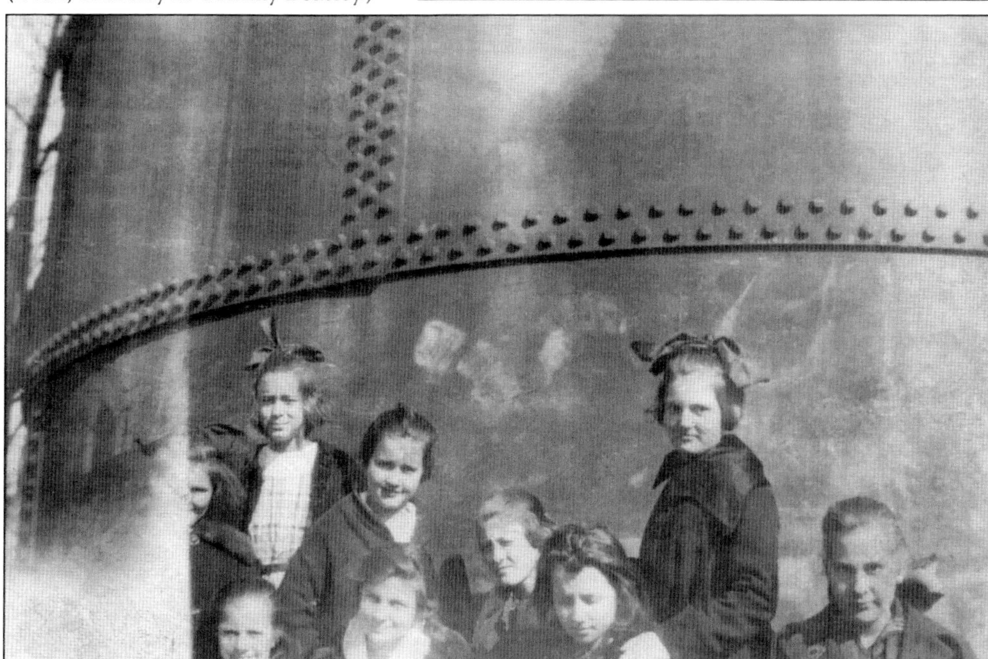

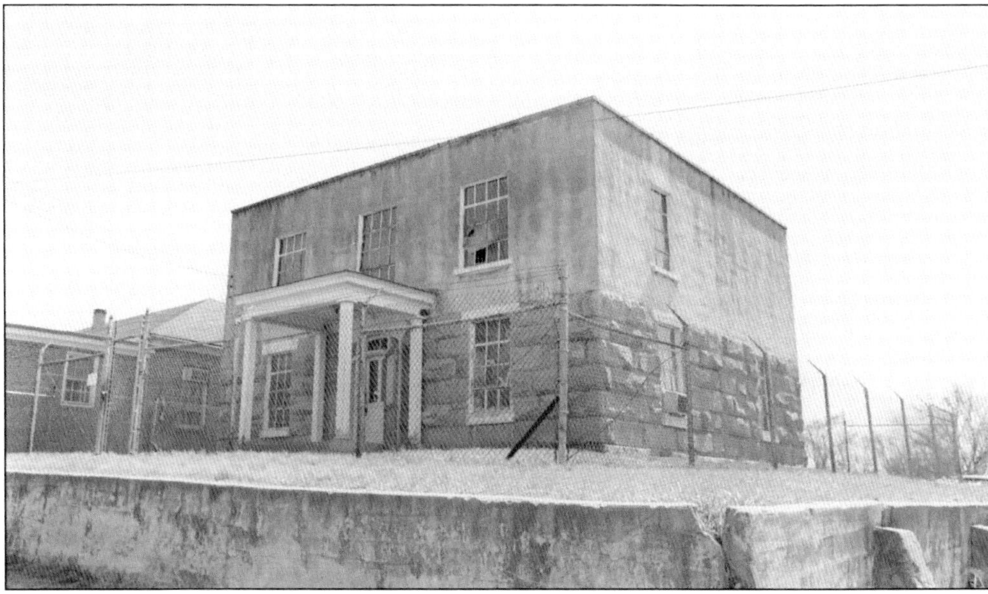

Built in 1874, the jail on East Nash Street was originally constructed of granite with an A-frame roof, and it was surrounded by a wooden fence. When a new facility opened on Market Street in 1975, hopes were that the historic building would one day house a museum, but it stands empty today, with the wooden fence replaced with a chain-link fence. (Courtesy of Sammy Beasley.)

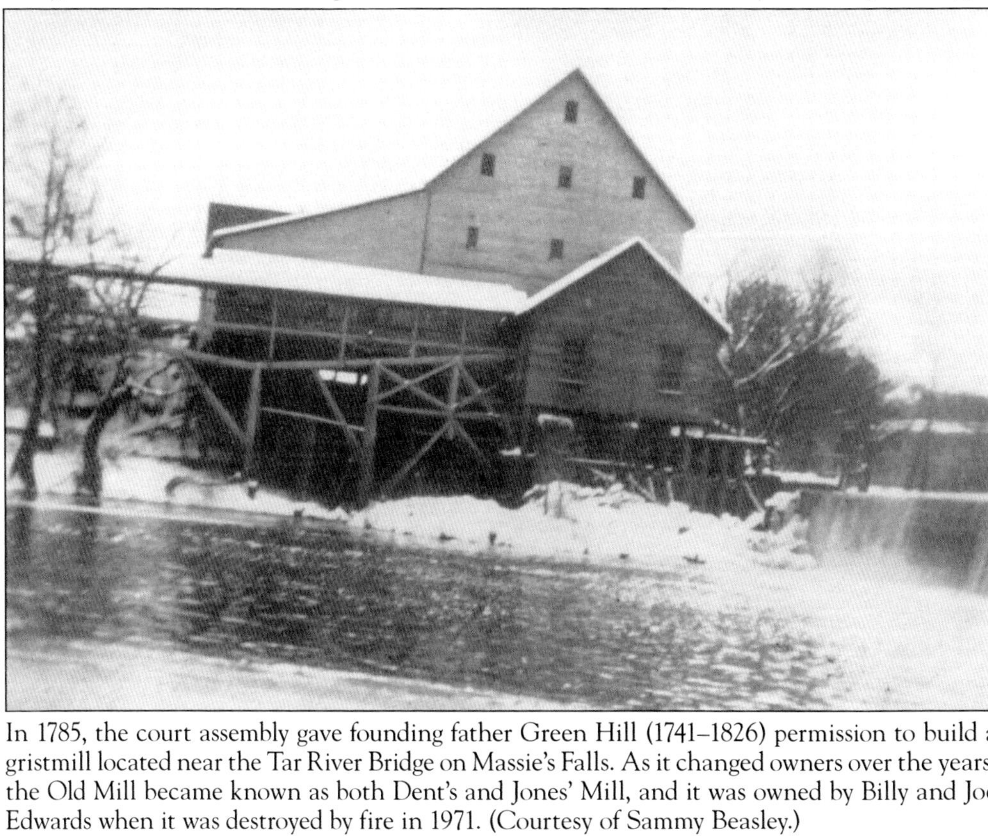

In 1785, the court assembly gave founding father Green Hill (1741–1826) permission to build a gristmill located near the Tar River Bridge on Massie's Falls. As it changed owners over the years, the Old Mill became known as both Dent's and Jones' Mill, and it was owned by Billy and Joe Edwards when it was destroyed by fire in 1971. (Courtesy of Sammy Beasley.)

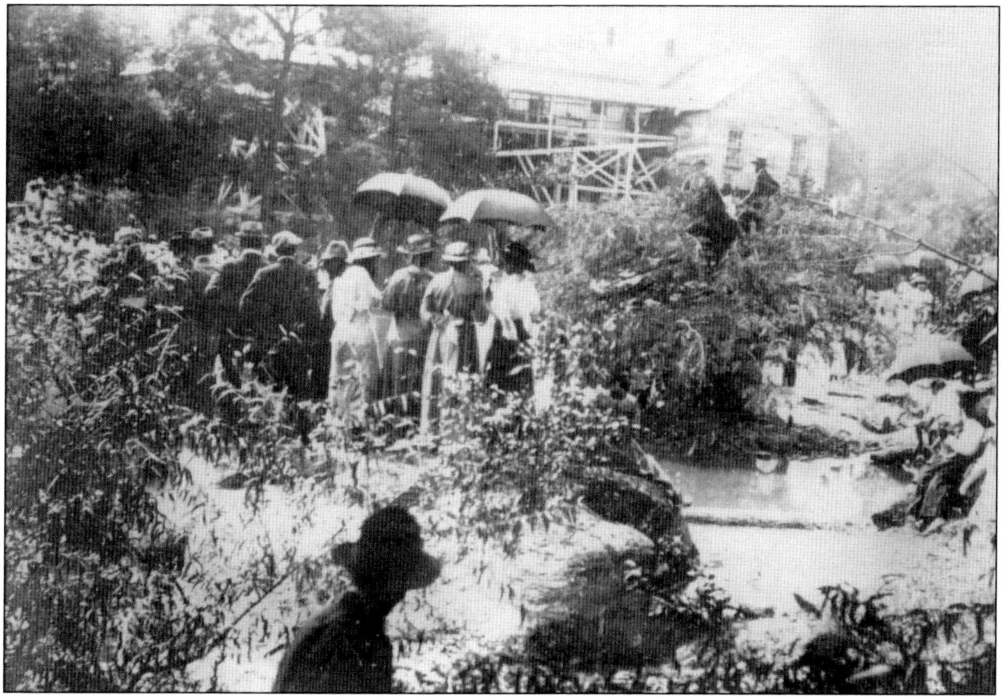

Seen from the south side of the Tar River, the Old Mill at Massie's Falls provides the backdrop for this gathering on the river. The once-busy waterway was used not only to power the gristmill, but also for recreation, baptisms, and cooling on a hot day. Though the cause for this social event is obscured by the spectators and brush, their clothing suggests a baptism. (Courtesy of Sammy Beasley.)

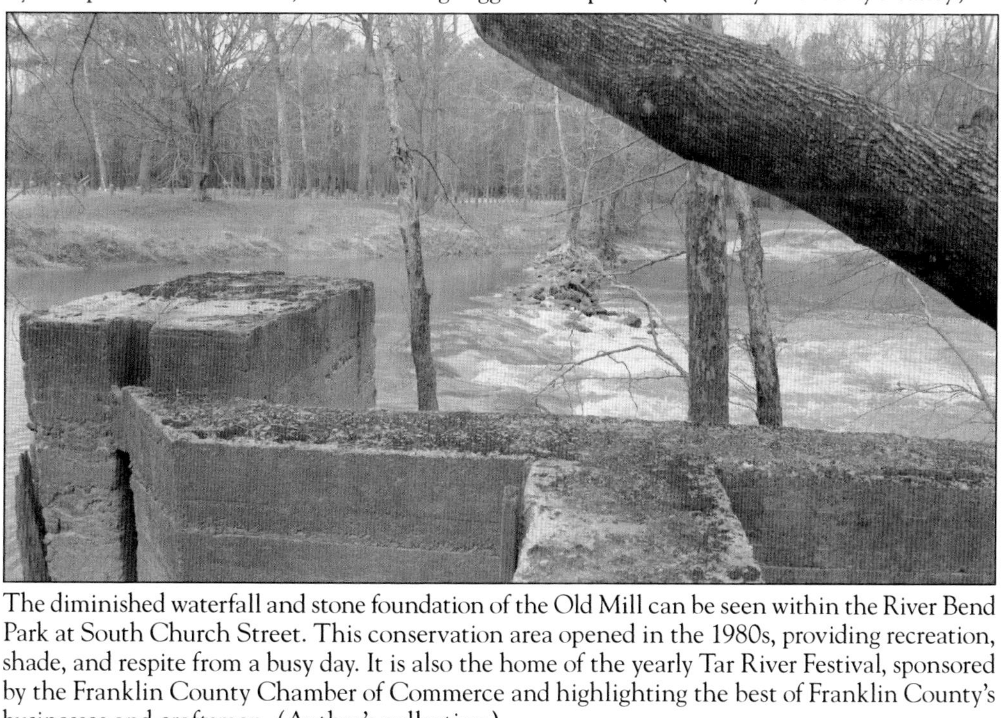

The diminished waterfall and stone foundation of the Old Mill can be seen within the River Bend Park at South Church Street. This conservation area opened in the 1980s, providing recreation, shade, and respite from a busy day. It is also the home of the yearly Tar River Festival, sponsored by the Franklin County Chamber of Commerce and highlighting the best of Franklin County's businesses and craftsmen. (Author's collection.)

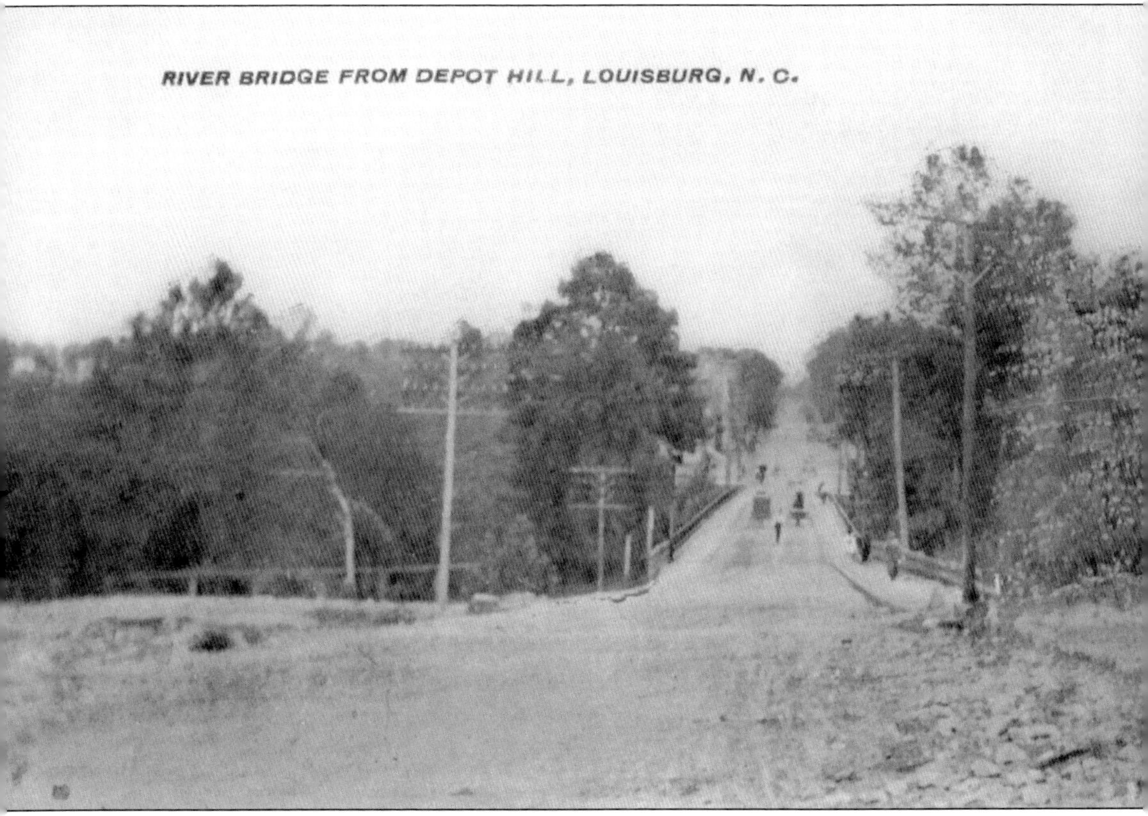

Depot Hill was the home of the Seaboard Air Line Railway freight depot, on South Main Street at the Tar River Bridge. This 1910 postcard gives a view of the bridge from Depot Hill showing the state of the dirt roads. Residents often found it difficult to navigate ruts created by wagons, weather, and the new motorcars. (Courtesy of Freddie Edwards.)

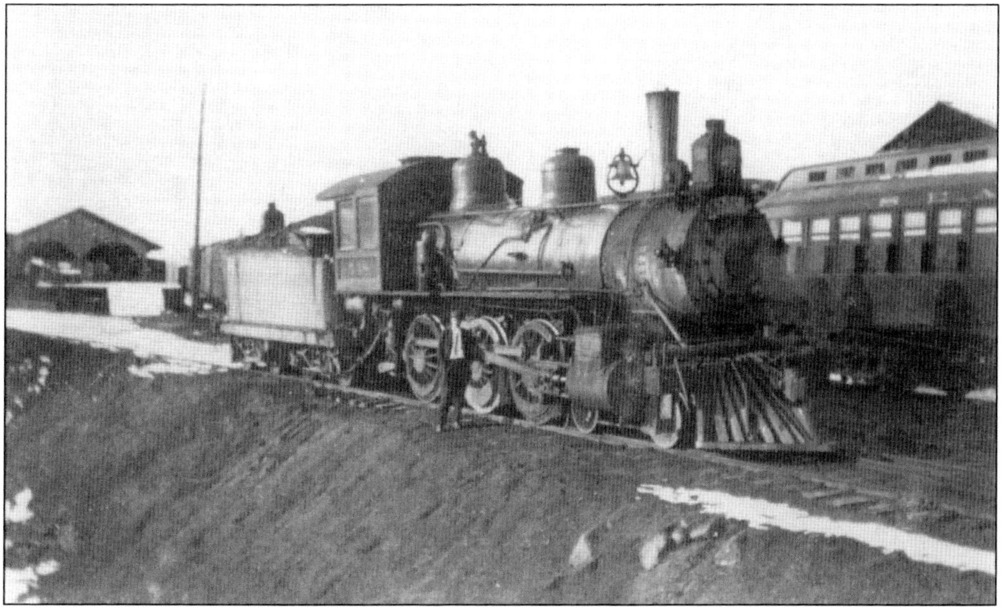

Construction of a 10-mile rail between Louisburg and the Raleigh & Gaston junction in Franklinton was completed in 1885, and it eventually became the Seaboard Air Line. The station was conveniently located on Depot Hill along the Tar River, near the town's cotton and tobacco warehouses. Two 35-minute round-trips per day between Louisburg and Franklinton allowed citizens to easily conduct business and return home the same day. (Courtesy of Sammy Beasley.)

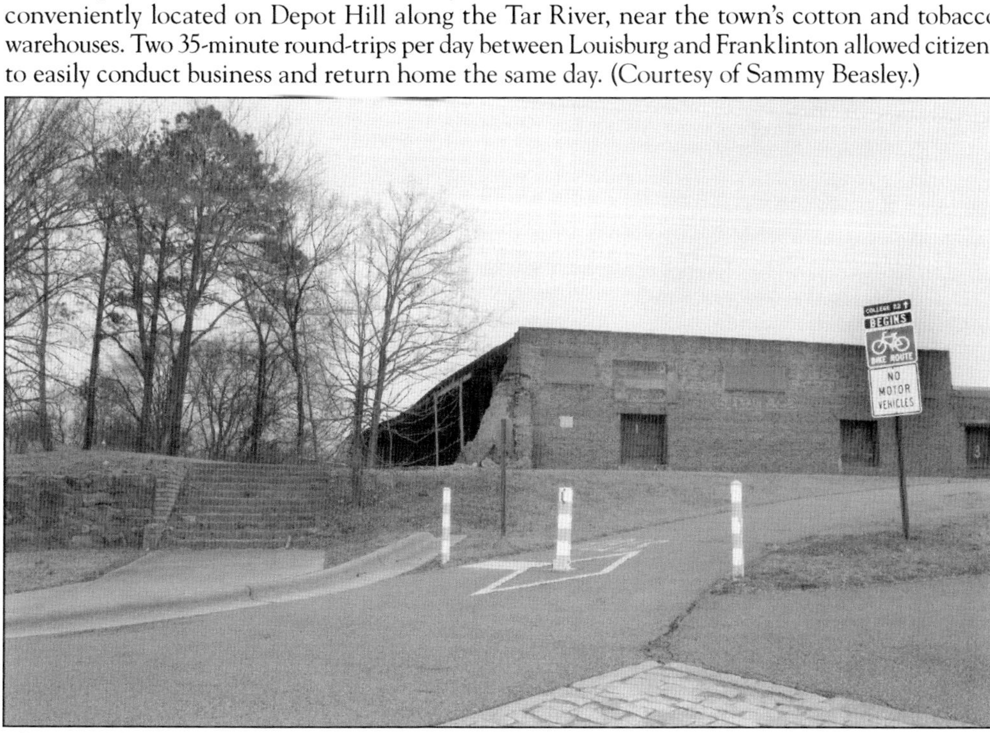

The crumbling train station on Depot Hill marks the beginning of the 2.2-mile Louisburg Bike Trail, which follows the former Seaboard Air Line rail corridor from the depot to Vance Granville Community College on Highway 56 West. The bike trail was built with a grant from the State of North Carolina and a long-term lease of the corridor from the North Carolina Department of Transportation's Rail Division. (Author's collection.)

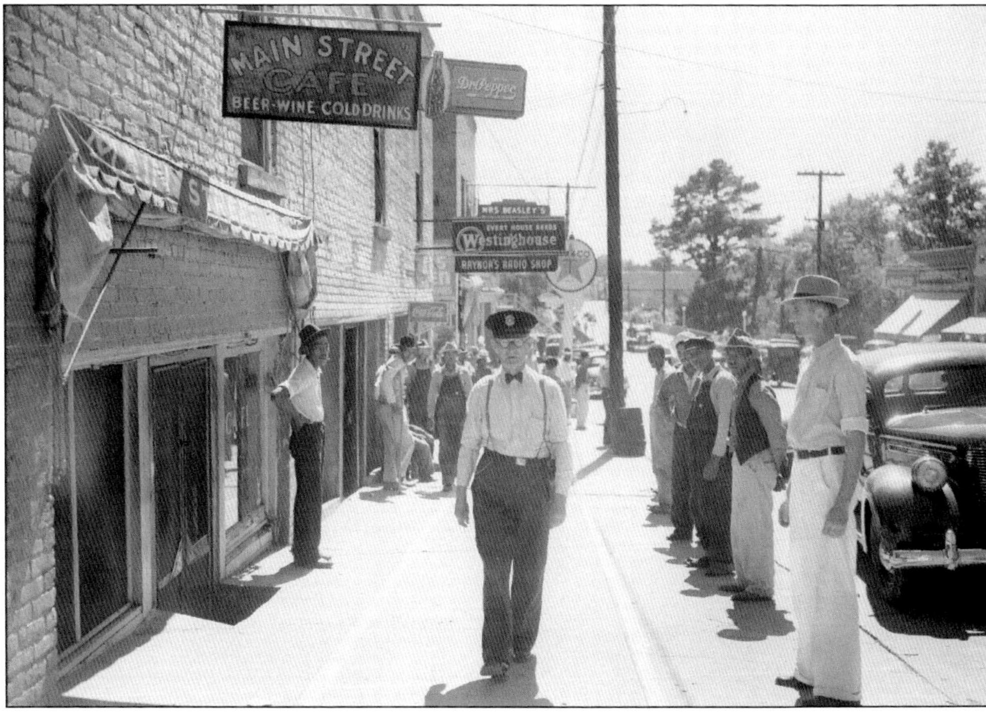

Growth in the 1930s created congestion in Louisburg, on the roadways and the sidewalks. Downtown businesses catered to so many pedestrians that the sidewalks became difficult to navigate. Forward-thinking townspeople drew sidewalk lines, allowing for walking in the middle lane and standing on the outside lanes. There is no word on the penalty for standing in the walking lane or walking where one should be standing. In the 1939 photograph above, an officer is seen walking from South Main Street towards the courthouse. In the background to the left are the Main Street Café, Raynor's Radio Shop, Beasley's Café, and the Texaco station. Across the street is the Louisburg Supply Company. Below is the same area of Main Street looking north. In the background is Hicks Store, and Boddie's Drug Store is to the left. (Both, courtesy of the State Archives of North Carolina.)

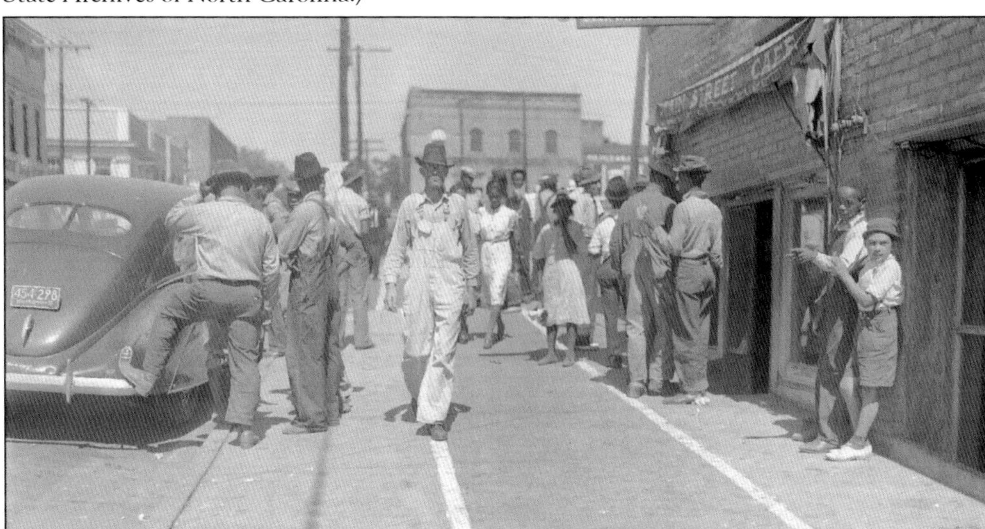

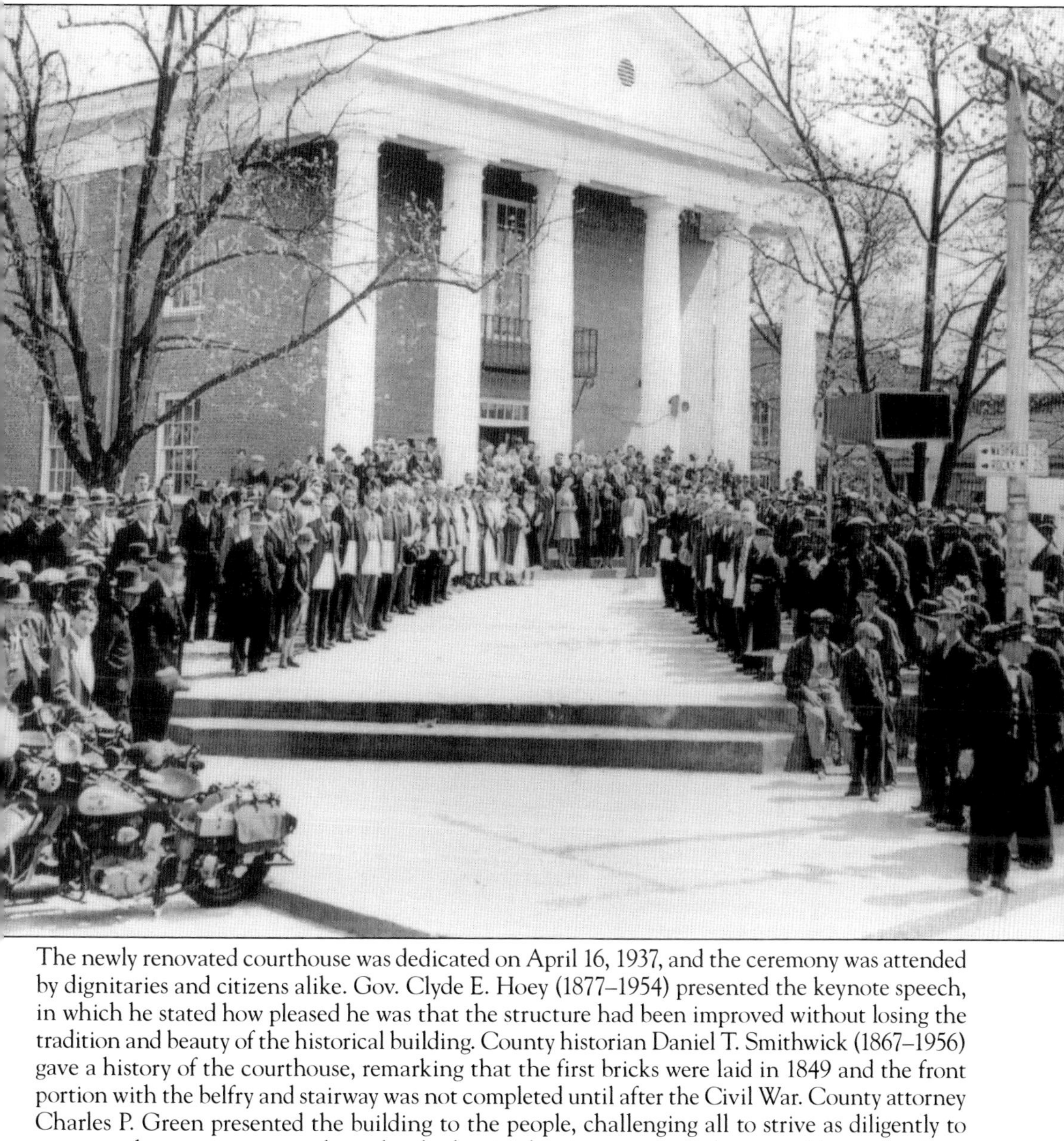

The newly renovated courthouse was dedicated on April 16, 1937, and the ceremony was attended by dignitaries and citizens alike. Gov. Clyde E. Hoey (1877–1954) presented the keynote speech, in which he stated how pleased he was that the structure had been improved without losing the tradition and beauty of the historical building. County historian Daniel T. Smithwick (1867–1956) gave a history of the courthouse, remarking that the first bricks were laid in 1849 and the front portion with the belfry and stairway was not completed until after the Civil War. County attorney Charles P. Green presented the building to the people, challenging all to strive as diligently to preserve the structure as each worker had strived to improve it. A bronze tablet at the front entrance commemorates the day and all those involved. Also in attendance were Masons, Eastern Star members, and schoolchildren, who were given the day off from their studies to attend the historic event. Citizens admired fresh flowers in every room as they were given the grand tour of the newly refreshed offices. (Courtesy of Carolyn Patterson.)

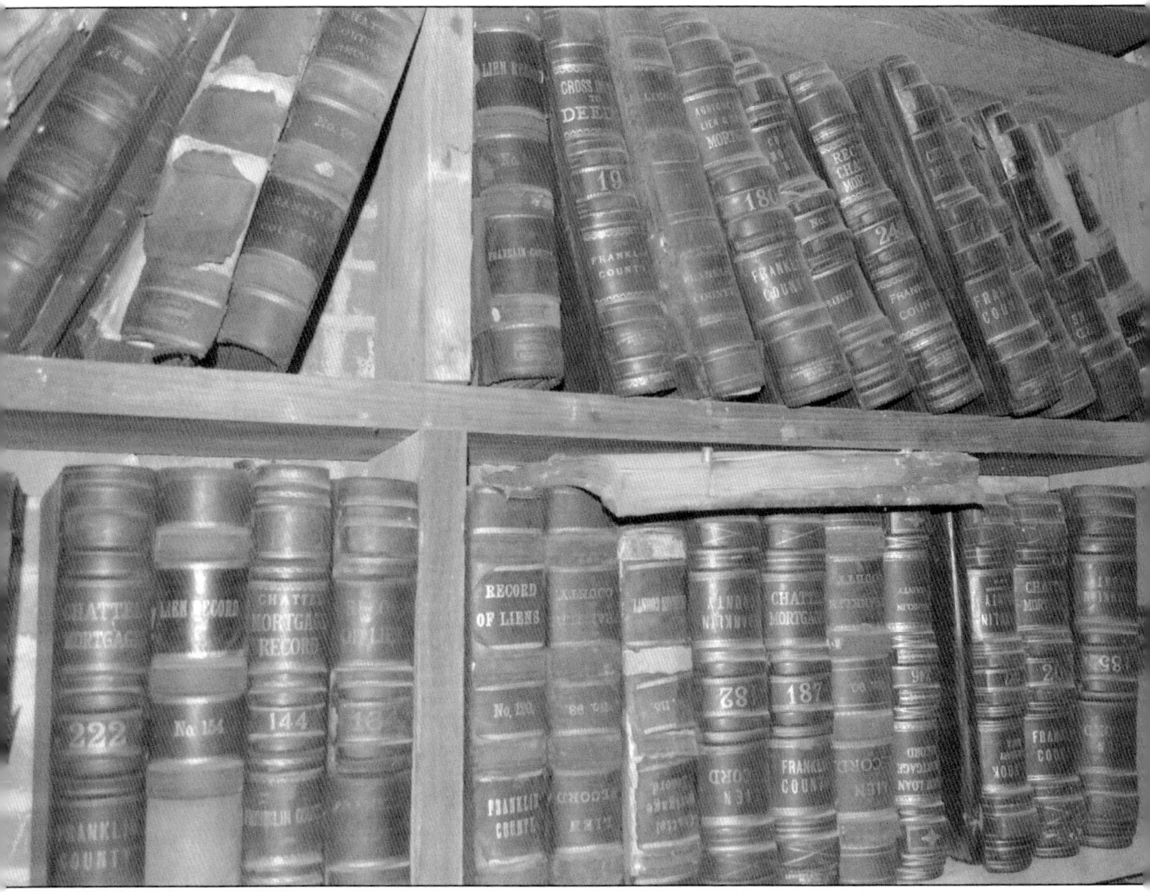

Franklin County gained worldwide attention in December 2013 when historical records dating from the early 1800s were discovered and then subsequently destroyed. Prior to 1965, the long-forgotten books, ledgers, boxes, documents, letters, and loose papers had been stored in the damp courthouse basement, most likely due to space constraints in the upper rooms. Despite the efforts of local historians and concerned citizens to save the records and worldwide attention thanks to social media, the county management, along with officials from the North Carolina State Archives, believed the records to be dangerous due to the presence of mold and moved to burn the entire contents of the basement on December 6, 2013. (Author's collection.)

Two

Starting a Family, Building a Home

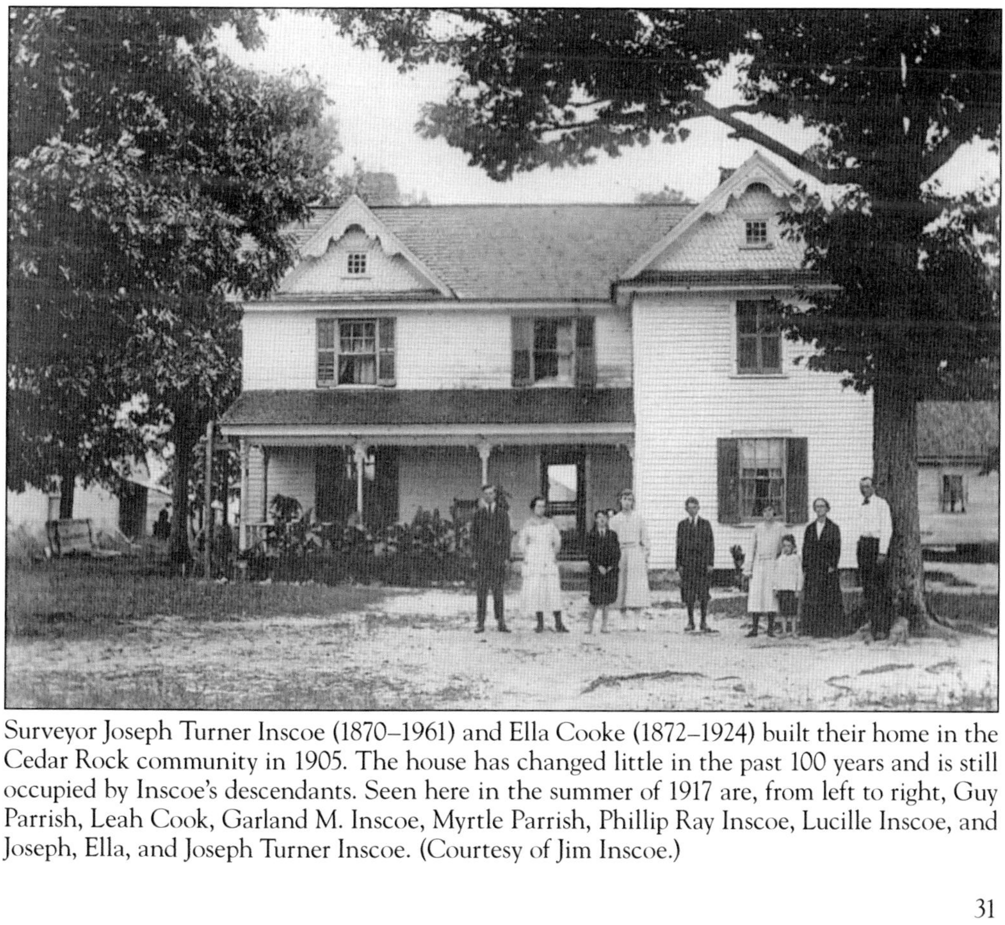

Surveyor Joseph Turner Inscoe (1870–1961) and Ella Cooke (1872–1924) built their home in the Cedar Rock community in 1905. The house has changed little in the past 100 years and is still occupied by Inscoe's descendants. Seen here in the summer of 1917 are, from left to right, Guy Parrish, Leah Cook, Garland M. Inscoe, Myrtle Parrish, Phillip Ray Inscoe, Lucille Inscoe, and Joseph, Ella, and Joseph Turner Inscoe. (Courtesy of Jim Inscoe.)

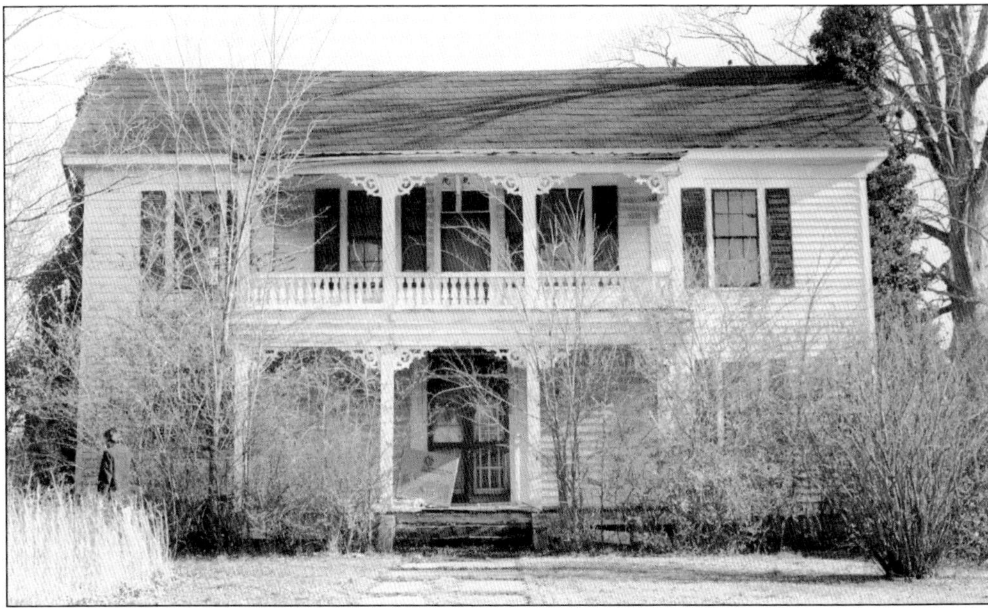

Patewills and Jacobina Milner sold 100 acres of land to county commissioners to establish the town of Louisburg. The home they shared with their 11 children stood at 205 Cedar Street until at least 1990, when it was listed in Vickie E. Mason's *The Historic District of Louisburg, North Carolina.* (Courtesy of the State Archives of North Carolina.)

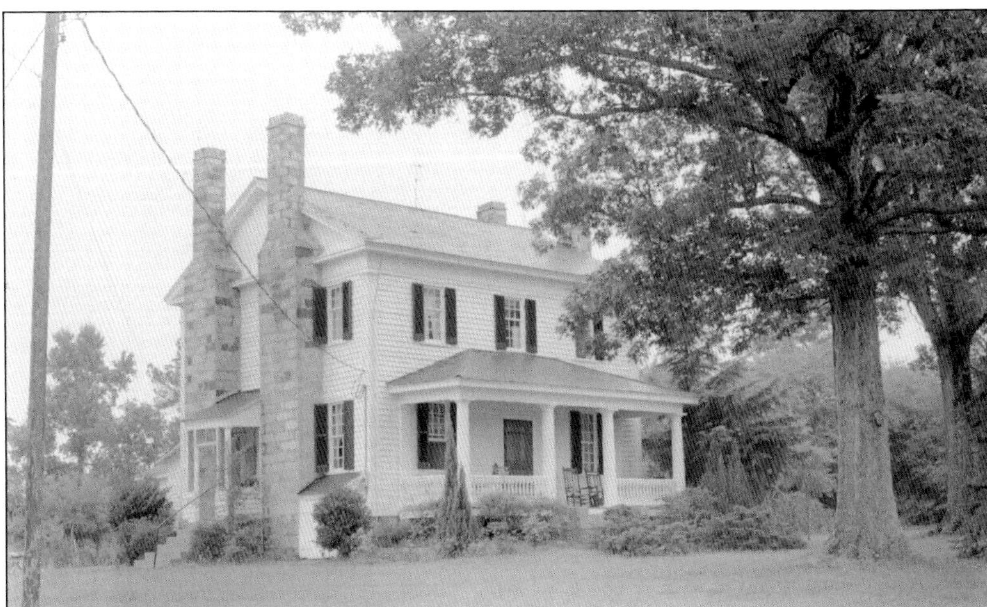

The Dean Farm, located on Highway 56 East was added to the National Register of Historic Places in 1975 due to its architectural significance. Built between 1825 and 1849, the house has remained in the Dean family and continues to be the sight of family reunions and friendly gatherings. (Courtesy of the State Archives of North Carolina.)

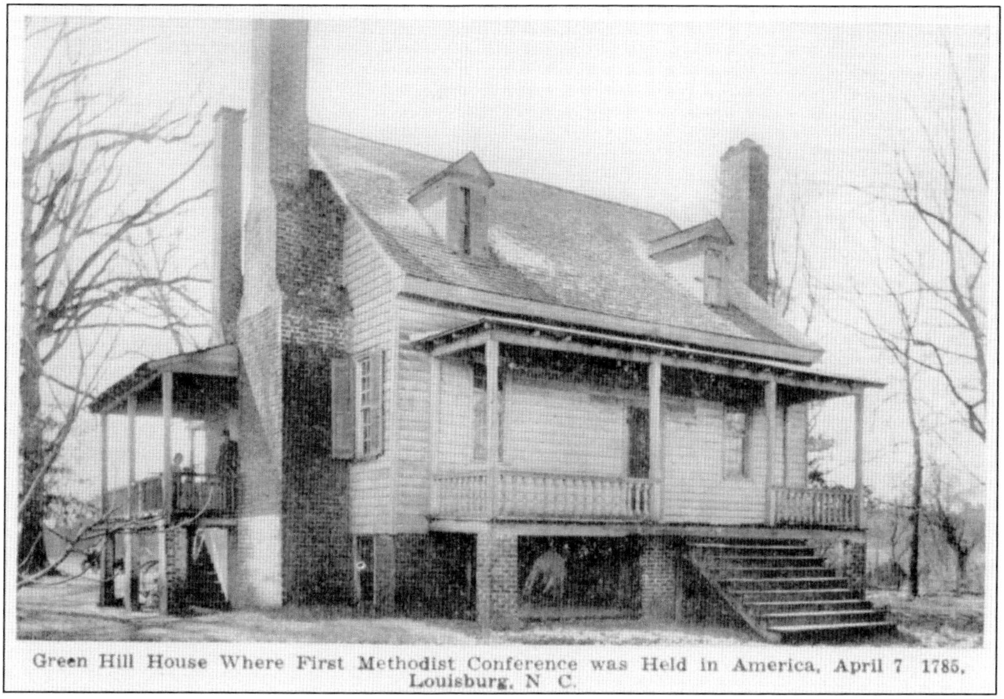

In April 1785, the first Methodist conference held in North Carolina was convened at the home of Green Hill (1741–1826), just south of Louisburg. Hill served as one of Franklin County's first representatives to the North Carolina General Assembly and was a prominent landowner and Methodist preacher. The home, built in the 1760s, is now owned by descendants of the Hill family and maintains much of its original charm. (Courtesy of Freddie Edwards.)

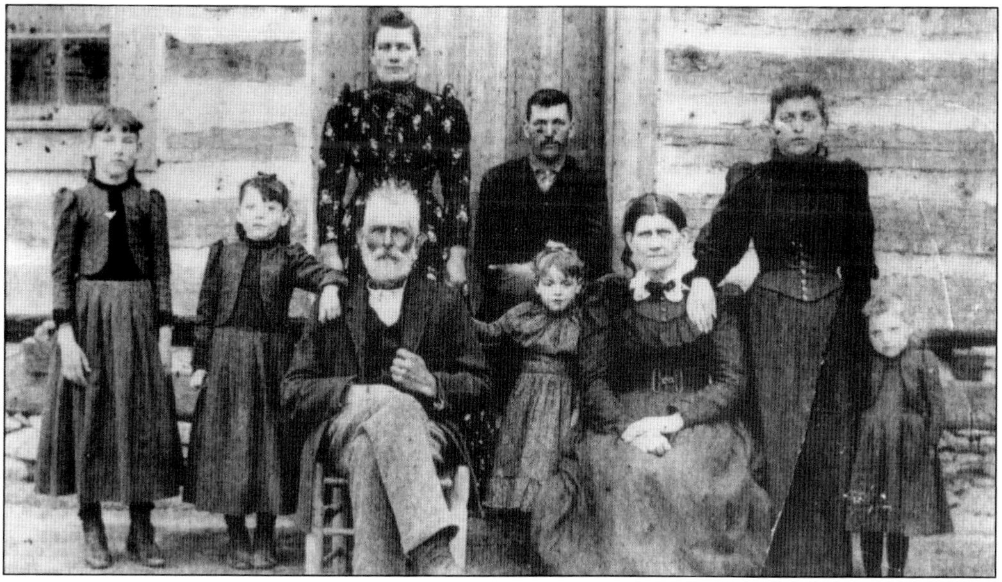

Confederate veteran Norman Nicholas "Nick" Strickland (1841–1907) and his wife, Charlotte Tharrington (1848–1940), pose with their family in front of their log-hewn home in Franklinton Township in the late 1890s. Their son Norman Pressley Strickland (1874–1950), who served in the state militia, is seated in the doorway. (Courtesy of Carrie Daniels.)

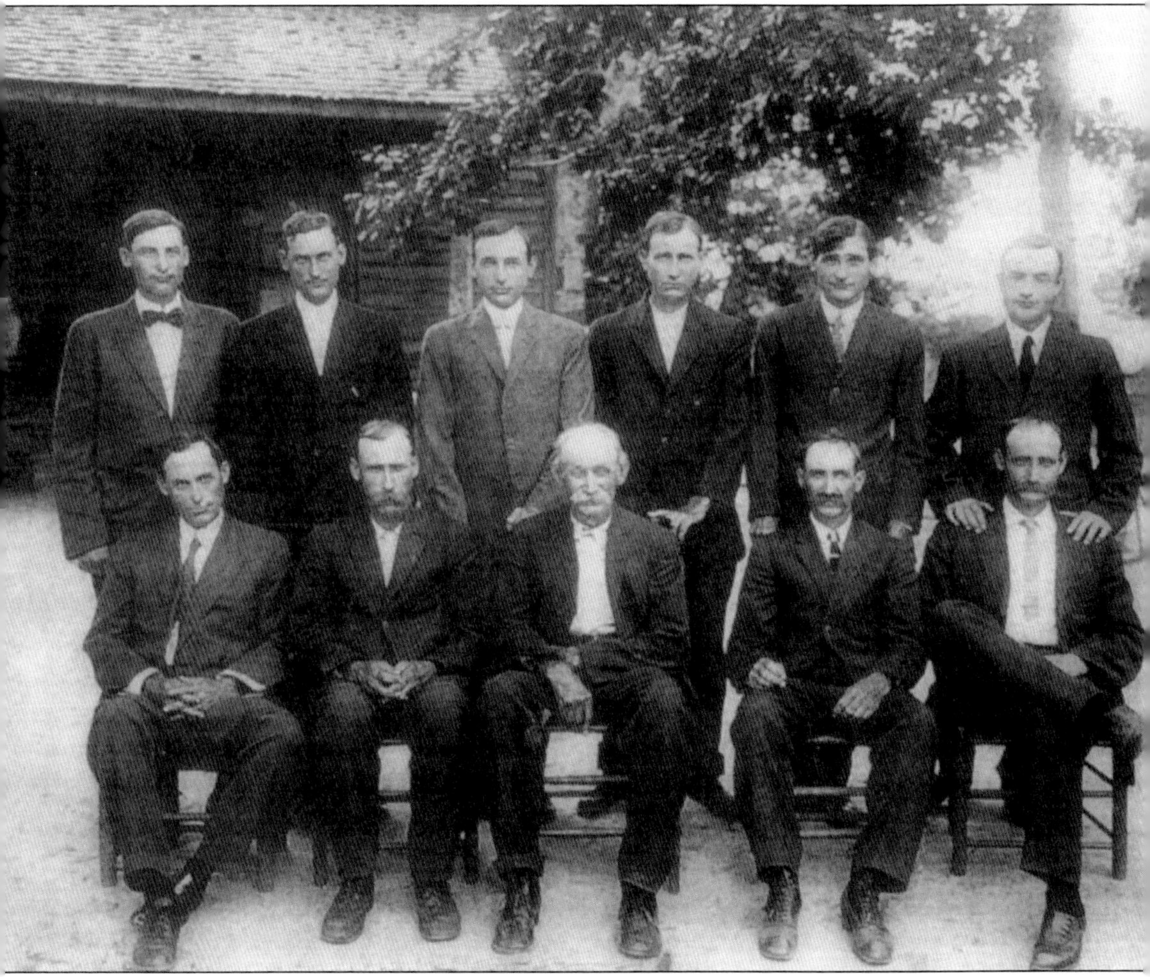

Wesley Radford (1843–1920) married Cleopatra "Patie" Evans (1850-1892) on February 24, 1870. Together, they were responsible for populating much of the Gold Mine community. They had 10 sons and 4 daughters before Cleopatra passed away at the age of 42. With so many young children to look after, Wesley quickly remarried Havanna Inscoe (1860–1930). Seen here from left to right are (seated) John Wesley (1879–1950), James Hilliard (1872–1955), Wesley, William Archibald (1871–1960), and Nat Colloc Radford (1880–?); (standing) Phillip Augustus (1891–1920), Rufus Robert (1889–1960), Doctor Emmett (1887–1950), Henry Coleman (1885–1952), Osborn R. (1888–1946), and Lucius J. Radford (1885–1918). The photograph was likely taken just prior to October 12, 1918, since Lucius J. passed away on that date. Not pictured are the daughters, Tealy Arelia (1874–1955), Lucy T. (1876–?), Mary Freeman (Burnette, 1878–1955), and Cary E. (1885–?). (Courtesy of Shirley Varker Gragg.)

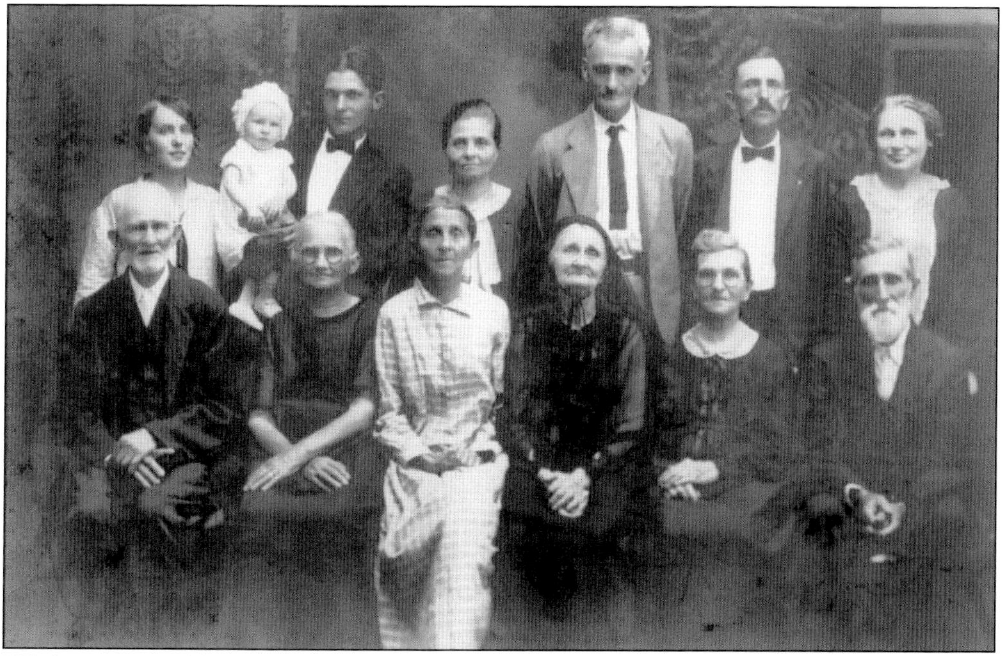

While some Franklin County natives were not captured in any photographs, lucky little Lucy Adcock of Epsom was photographed here with five generations of her ancestors. She is in the second row being held by her parents, Aldred and Lonie Adcock. With them are, from left to right, (first row) great-grandparents Mr. and Mrs. Joseph Adcock, Mrs. J.D. Hoyle, great-great-grandmother Mrs. John Hamm, and great-grandparents Mr. and Mrs. Louis Ayscue; (second row) grandparents George and Katie Adcock, and Mr. and Mrs. Peter Ayscue. (Courtesy of Cindy Hunt Carroll.)

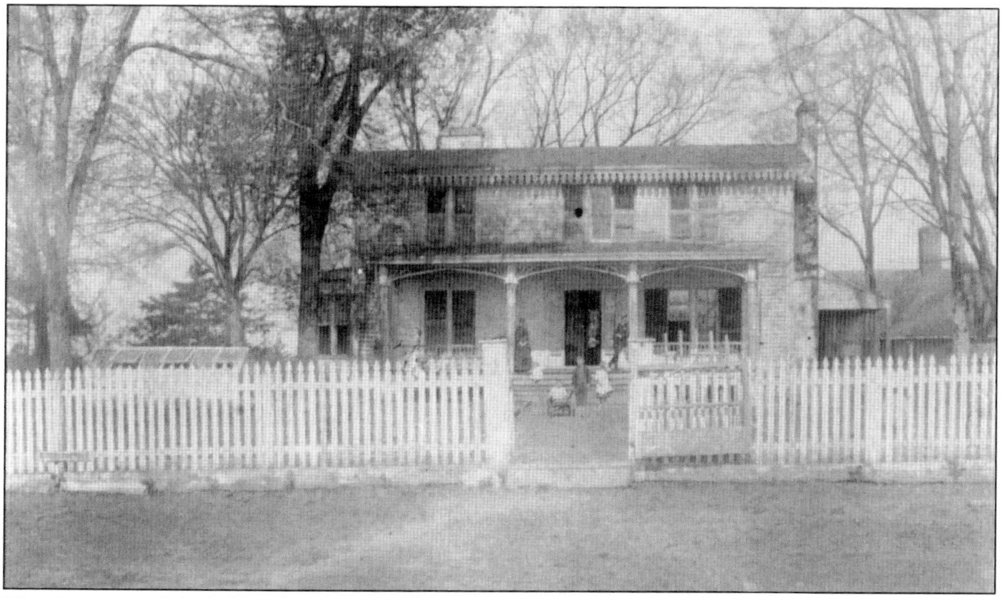

This home was labeled by the State Archives of North Carolina as "Buffalo Hill in the Louisburg vicinity on the north side of SR 1223, just west of 1224 circa 1888." This would be in the Mitchener's Pond area on Phelps and May Roads. A search of the area found a beautifully restored home. (Courtesy of the State Archives of North Carolina.)

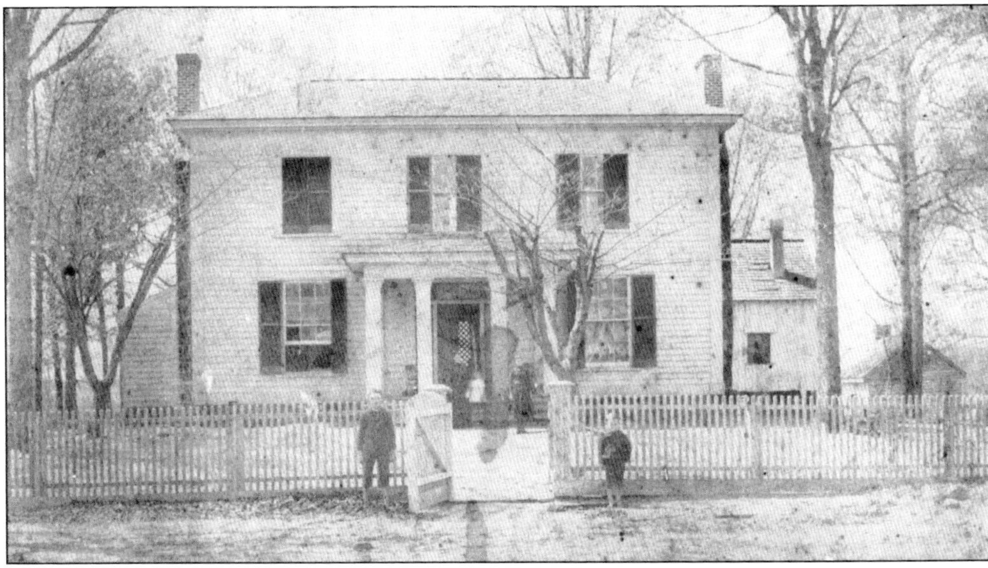

The Terrell House, on the south side of Highway 56, a half mile west of Route 401 in Louisburg, is seen here just 10 years after its construction. Built in 1880, the home still stands in a grove of trees just outside of town. (Courtesy of the State Archives of North Carolina.)

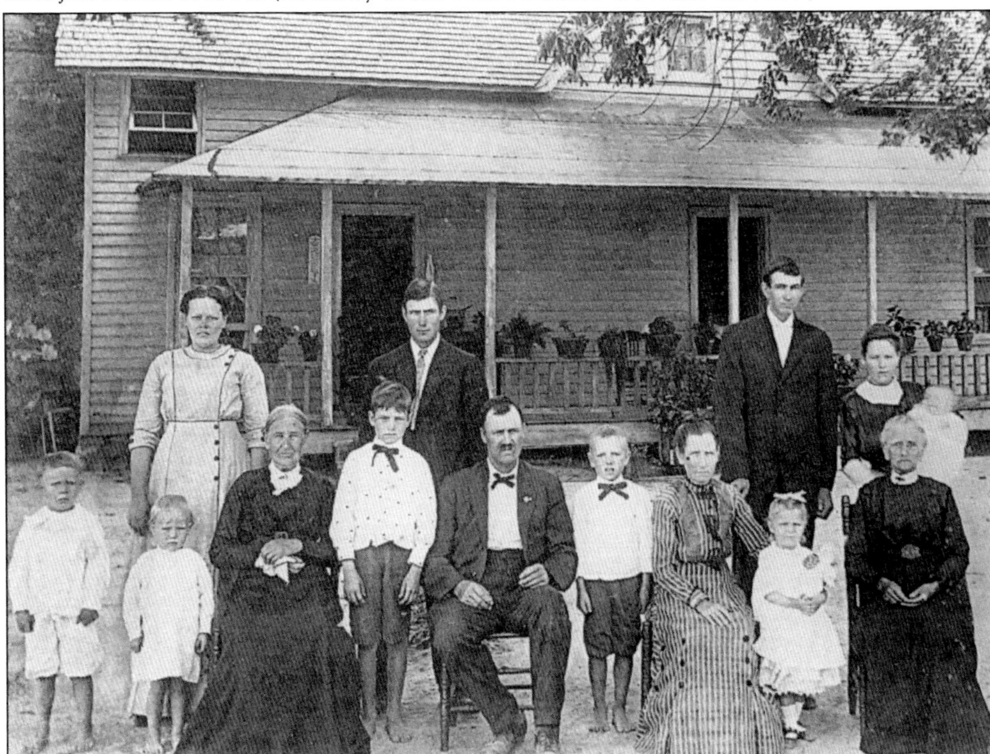

The family of Emmett Macon Newman (1867–1941) lived in the Epsom area and attended Liberty Christian Church. Emmett and his wife, Martha Lou Moore (1866–1918), had six children: James D., Mamie C., Lucy Belle, Henry B., Bennett Murdock, and Mary Olive. The family members in this photograph were not identified. (Courtesy of Jim Newman.)

Three

Making a Living, Running a Business

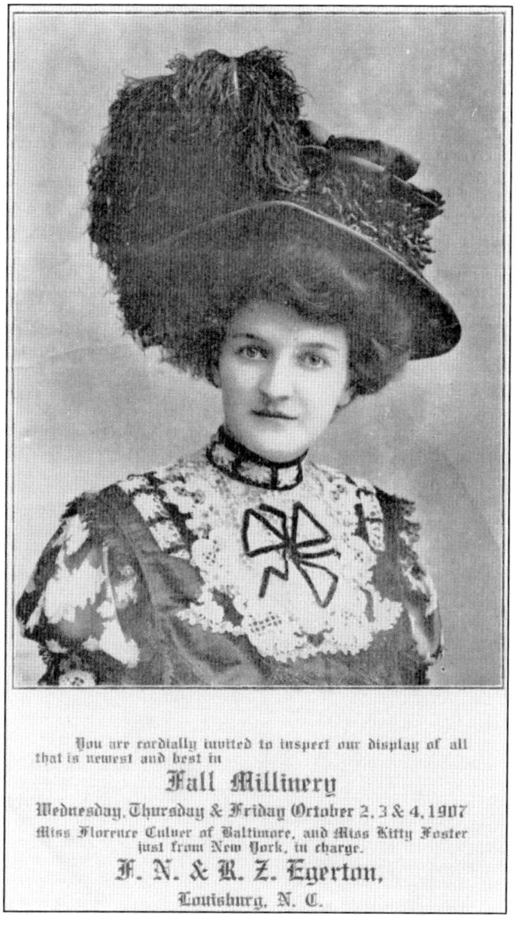

Millinery is the designing and manufacturing of hats. In the late 1800 and early 1900s, fashionable outfits were incomplete without this crowning accessory. Run by Frank Nicholas Egerton (1853–1924) and Robert Zolicoffer Egerton (1863–1915), F.N. & R.Z. Egerton's store in Louisburg provided the ladies of Franklin County with the latest in headwear from 1877 until it closed in 1910. (Courtesy of Freddie Edwards.)

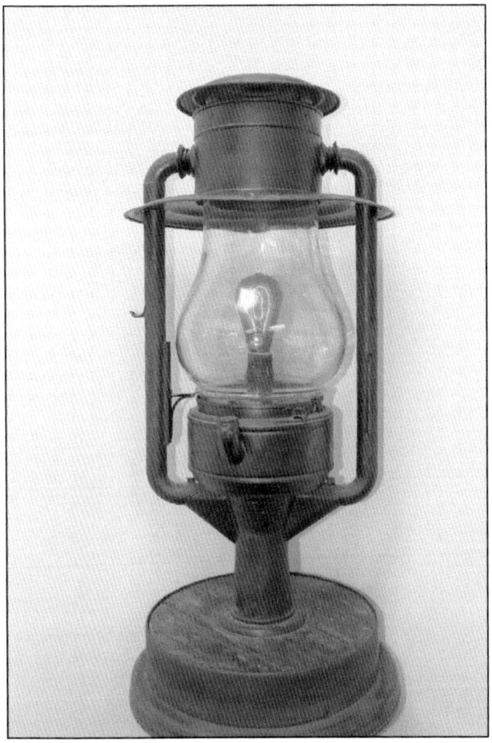

The position of lamplighter for Louisburg was held by one man, John Sullivan (1833–1888), who was responsible for lighting and extinguishing the kerosene streetlights. So faithful was he that, following his death, town commissioners and businessmen paid to lay him to rest at Oakwood Cemetery. This lamp was salvaged by Lucy Allen's father, converted to an electric light, and donated to the Louisburg Town Hall. (Author's collection.)

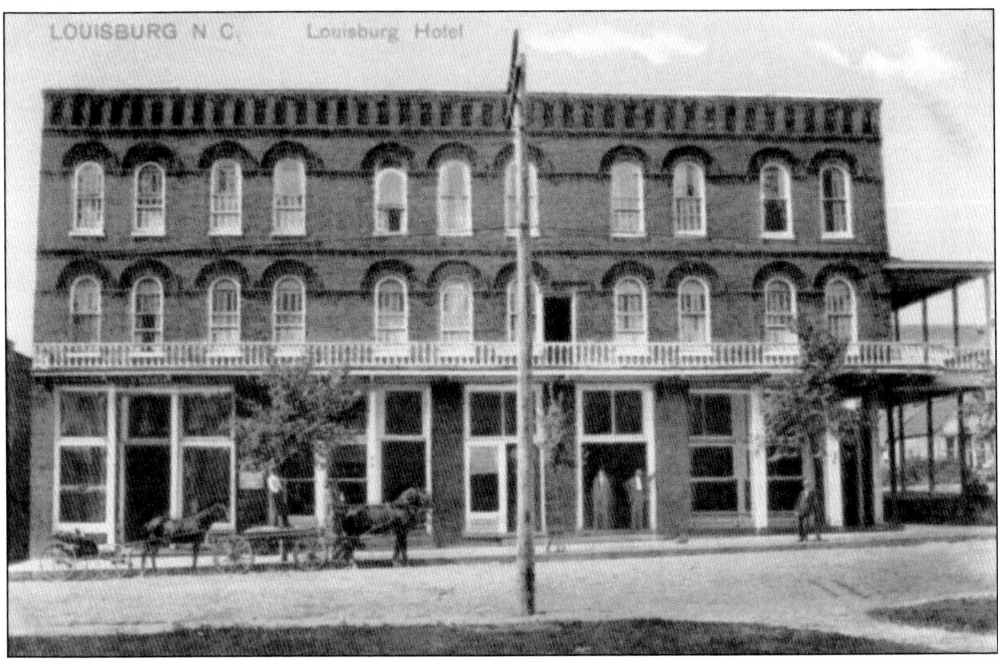

Louisburg's location on the stage route between Raleigh, Norfolk, and Richmond made it a perfect stopover for weary travelers. The Louisburg Hotel was one of many in town and was heralded as one of the best stops on the route. This postcard shows the hotel on Main Street, close to where the post office stands today. An October 12, 1914, kitchen fire destroyed the hotel. (Courtesy of Freddie Edwards.)

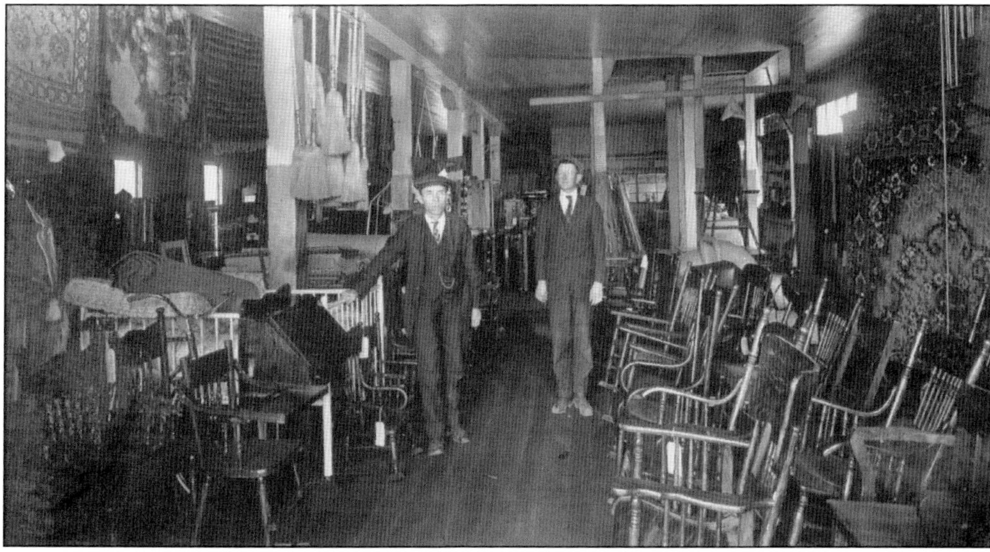

This photograph is believed to be of the Brown Furniture Company, established in 1915 by J.L. Brown. It was located on Main Street in Youngsville in the same building that also housed the Youngsville Bottling Works, founded by Will C. Young in 1911. The Bottling Works produced orange, strawberry, ginger, and cola drinks using their own well, located in the back right corner of the store. (Courtesy of Youngsville Town Hall.)

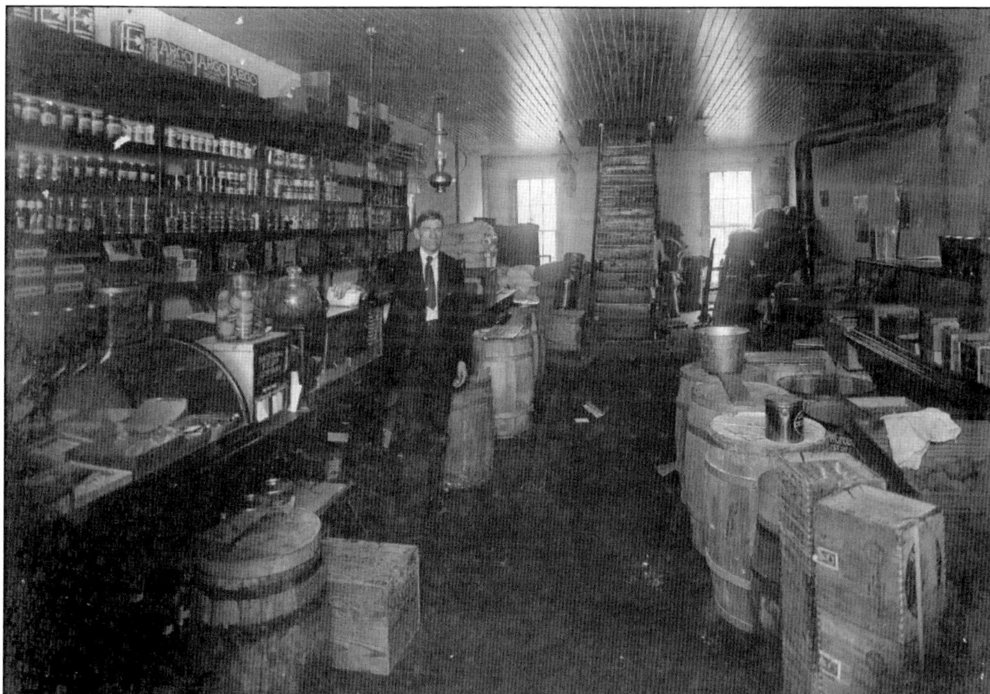

Little is known about the photograph above, showing a typical store along Youngsville's Main Street in the early 1900s. Barrels of flour, rice, and other household staples mixed with canned goods and tobacco products to offer one-stop shopping. This may have been the Union Store Company, which operated in Youngsville in 1906. (Courtesy of Youngsville Town Hall.)

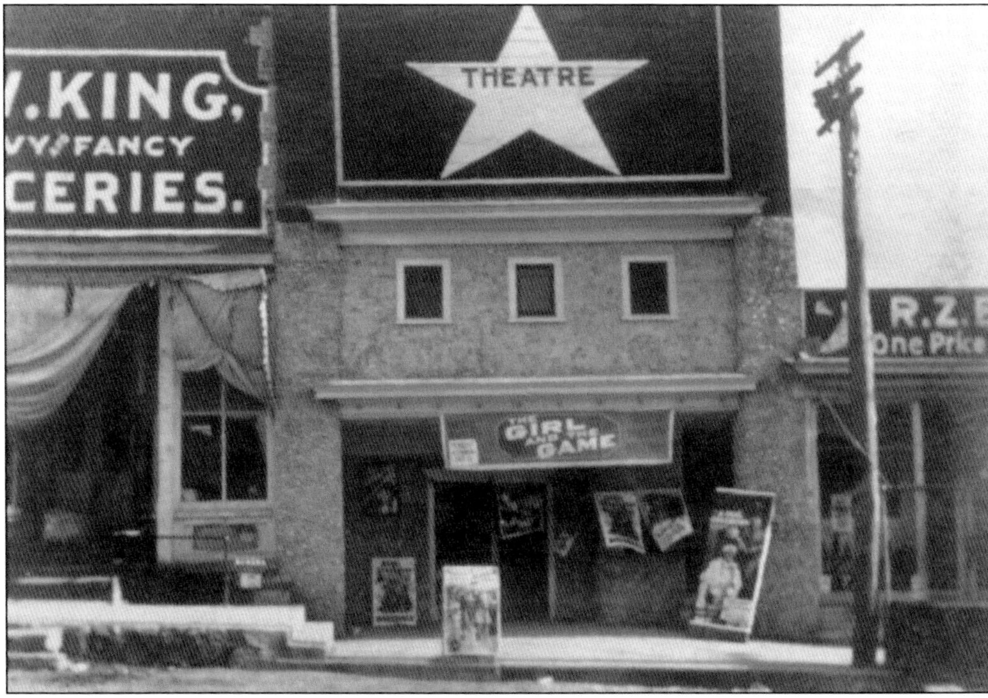

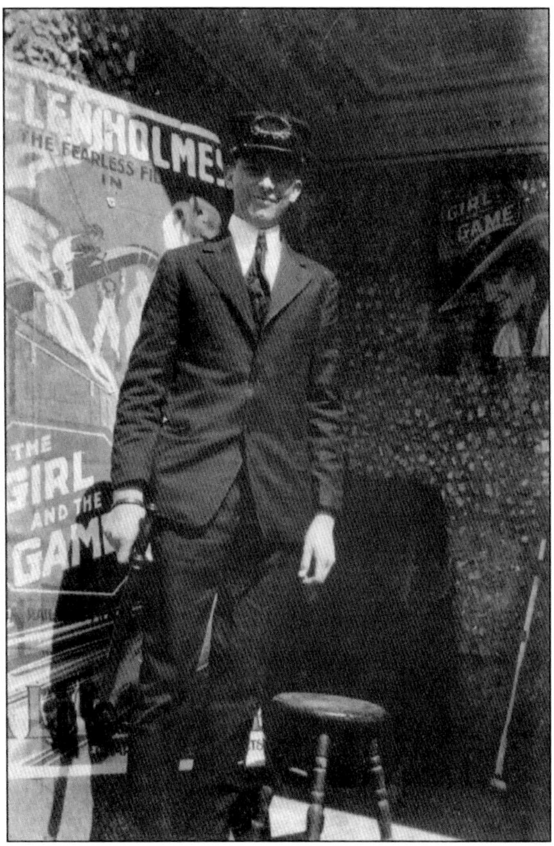

The marquee at the Star Theatre announces the showing of the 1916 black-and-white silent film, *The Girl and the Game*, starring Helen Holmes (1893–1950). The Star Theatre was located on Nash Street at the intersection of Nash and Market Streets. Weekly advertisements in local newspapers promoted matinees for 20¢ and night viewings for 50¢, showing films featuring stars such as Mary Pickford and Charlie Chaplin. It also advertised a Saturday afternoon show for "the benefit of the country folk." The man in the photograph at left may have been a ticket taker for the Star Theatre, though the club he carries in his right hand suggests that he may have been there for crowd control. Considering the popularity of the theater, he may have held dual jobs. (Both, courtesy of Sammy Beasley.)

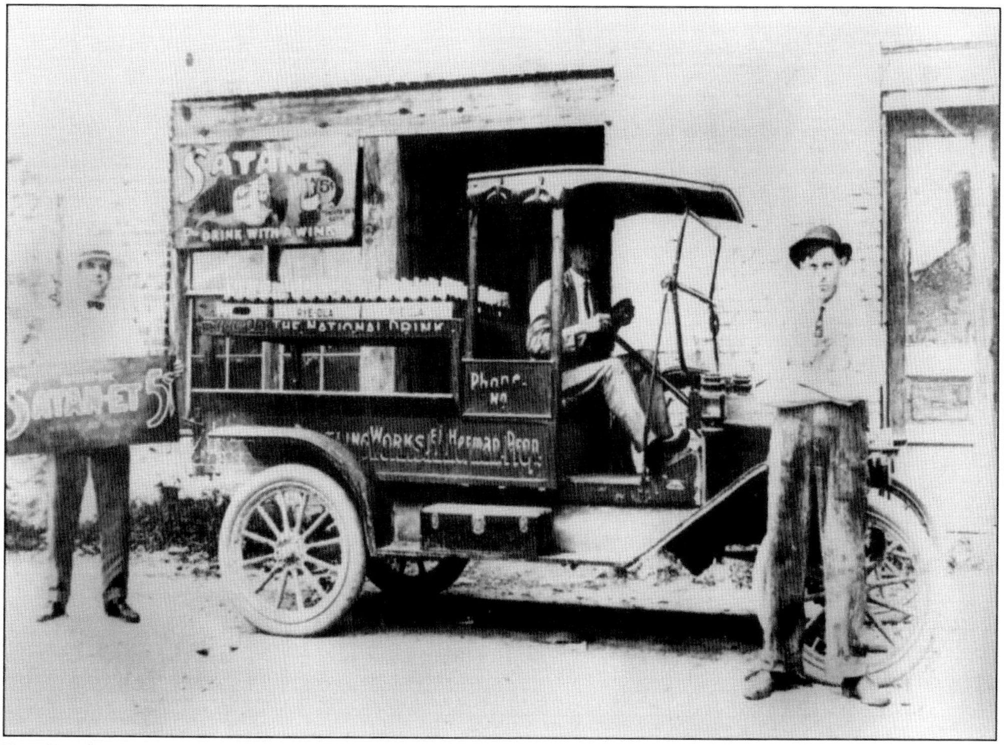

Fredrick Lee Herman (1885–1980) produced his nonalcoholic beverages at the Louisburg Bottling Works, in the building at the junction of Johnston and Church Streets. With the 1908 Prohibition vote, the market for alternative beverages was booming, and by 1910, the county also boasted bottling plants in Youngsville and Franklinton. Herman's sign advertises Satan-Et for 5¢, and the truck is loaded with "Rye-Ola, The National Drink." (Courtesy of Freddie Edwards.)

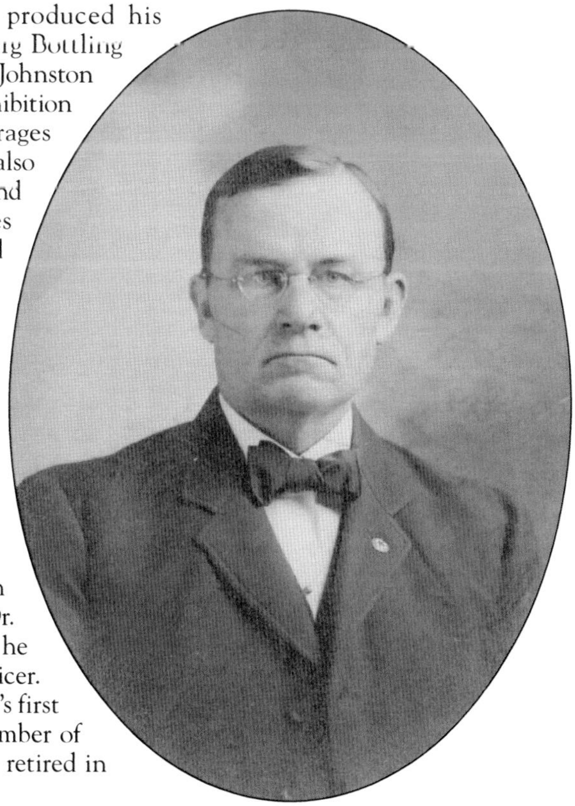

Dr. Samuel Perry Burt (1870–1955) received his medical degree in 1893 from the College of Physicians and Surgeons in Baltimore. As a physician in Louisburg, Dr. Burt served from 1896 until 1943, when he was elected Franklin County health officer. He was responsible for hiring the county's first sanitation officer and was a charter member of the Franklin County Health Board. He retired in 1948. (Courtesy of Sammy Beasley.)

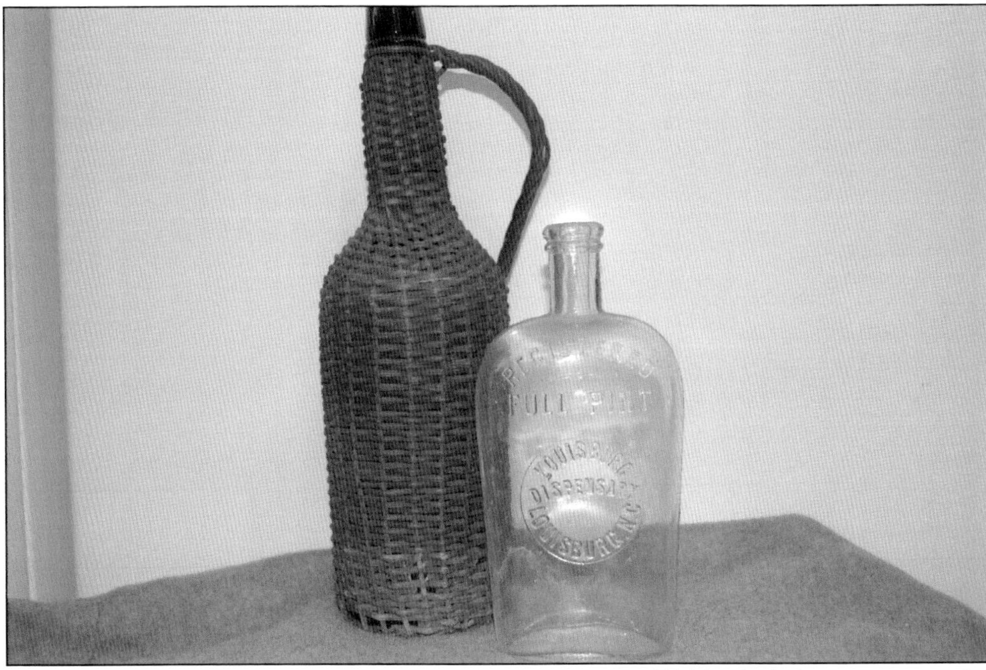

The demijohn and Louisburg Dispensary bottles above were refillable alcohol containers used in the early 1900s. The dispensary system allowed for state control of spirits, with each customer's name recorded. Dispensary bottles were embossed with the town's name, and their rarity makes them highly collectible today, selling at $200 and up. The Louisburg Dispensary, on East Nash Street, was run by James Redmond Collie (1871–1957) and operated until the beginning of Prohibition in Franklin County in 1908. Ephemera collectors will appreciate the November 3, 1905, receipt below, recording the purchase of 552 half-pint bottles and 75 pint bottles for a mere $12.96. Another receipt found noted payment of $8 to Griffin and Beasley to pick up and bury 100 bottles in June 1906; however, to the chagrin of today's collectors, no burial site was listed. (Both, author's collection.)

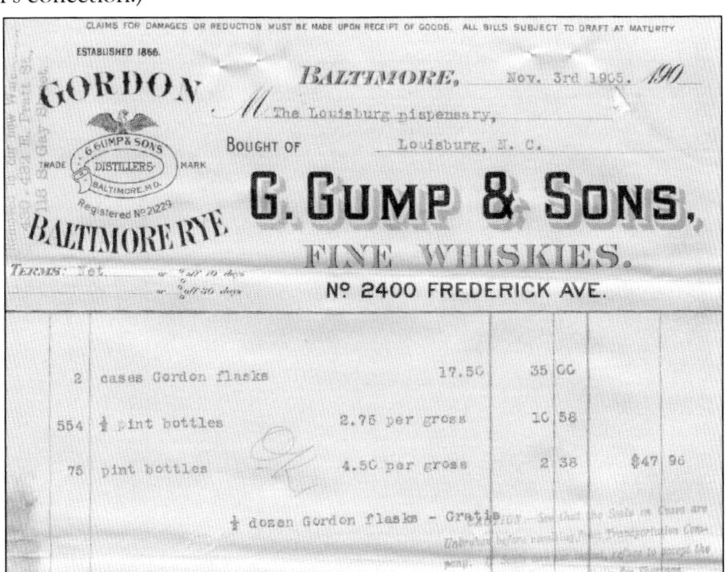

CLAIMS FOR DAMAGES OR REDUCTION MUST BE MADE UPON RECEIPT OF GOODS. ALL BILLS SUBJECT TO DRAFT AT MATURITY

ESTABLISHED 1866.

GORDON

G. GUMP & SONS DISTILLERS BALTIMORE, MD. TRADE MARK Registered No 21229

BALTIMORE RYE

BALTIMORE, Nov. 3rd 1905. 190

M The Louisburg Dispensary,

Louisburg, N. C.

BOUGHT OF

G. GUMP & SONS,

FINE WHISKIES.

No 2400 FREDERICK AVE.

TERMS: Net

2	cases Gordon flasks	17.50	35 00	
554	½ pint bottles	2.75 per gross	10 58	
75	pint bottles	4.50 per gross	2 38	$47 96
	½ dozen Gordon flasks - Gratis			

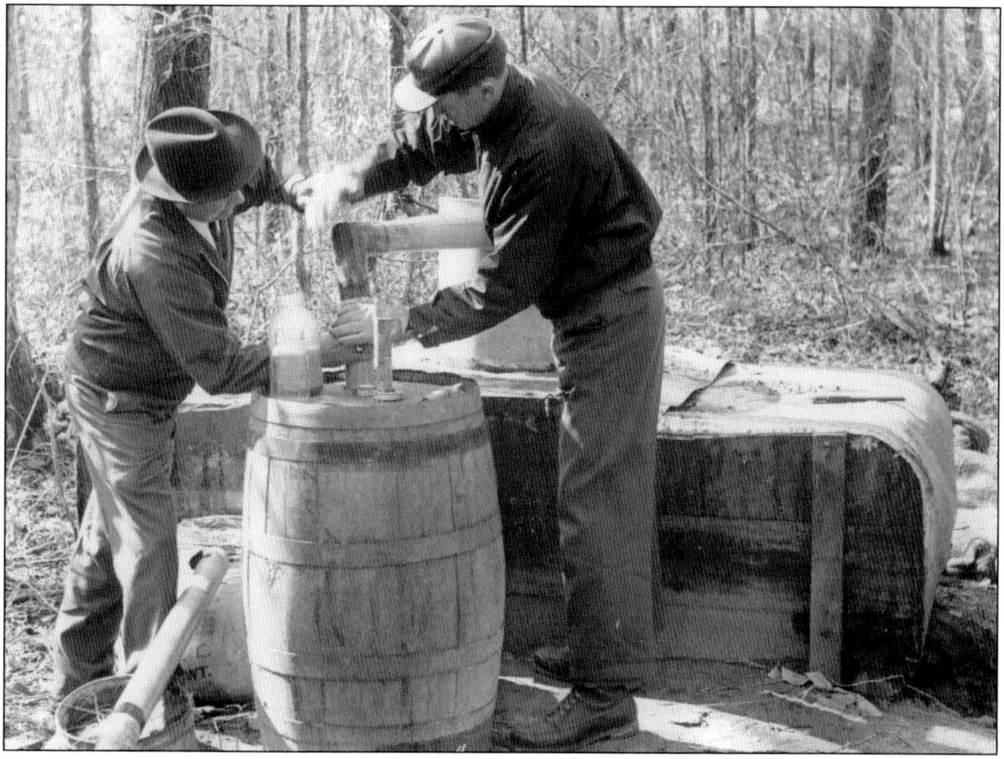

Not all businesses are of the legal kind. The stills in these crime scene photographs were for the illegal production of spirits, also known as white lightning, corn liquor, rotgut, or moonshine. Law enforcement in the 1950s and 1960s destroyed an average of one still per day, with units devoted entirely to their search and seizure. In February 1959, a still containing 10,000 gallons of illegal beer and several hundred gallons of whiskey were intentionally dumped and the runoff ended up in Franklinton's water supply. For weeks, faucets ran with the aroma of alcohol, prompting news coverage across the country. (Both, courtesy of Franklin County Sheriff's Department.)

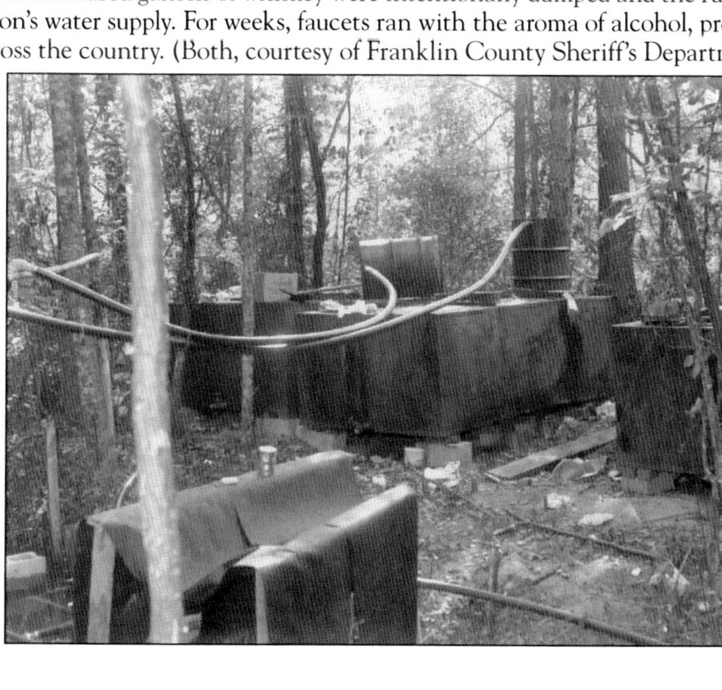

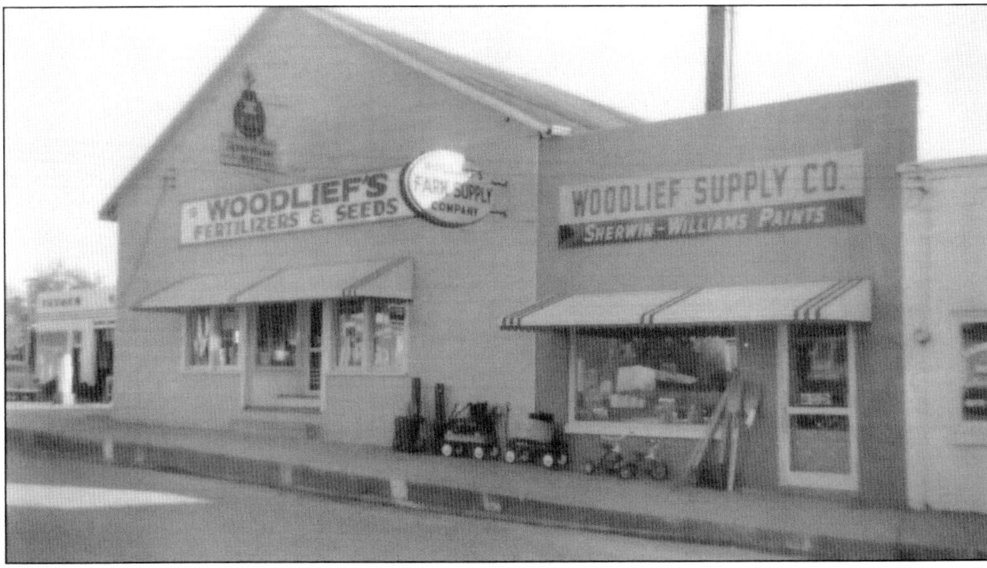

William Maurice Woodlief (1902–1964) bought the Old Eagle Tobacco Warehouse building and opened his farm supply store, which became the oldest continuously run business in Franklin County. Located on Main Street in Youngsville, the store now sells antiques and collectibles and is run by Woodlief's grandson Thomas Dement, whose knowledge of Youngsville's history rivals none. (Courtesy of Youngsville Town Hall.)

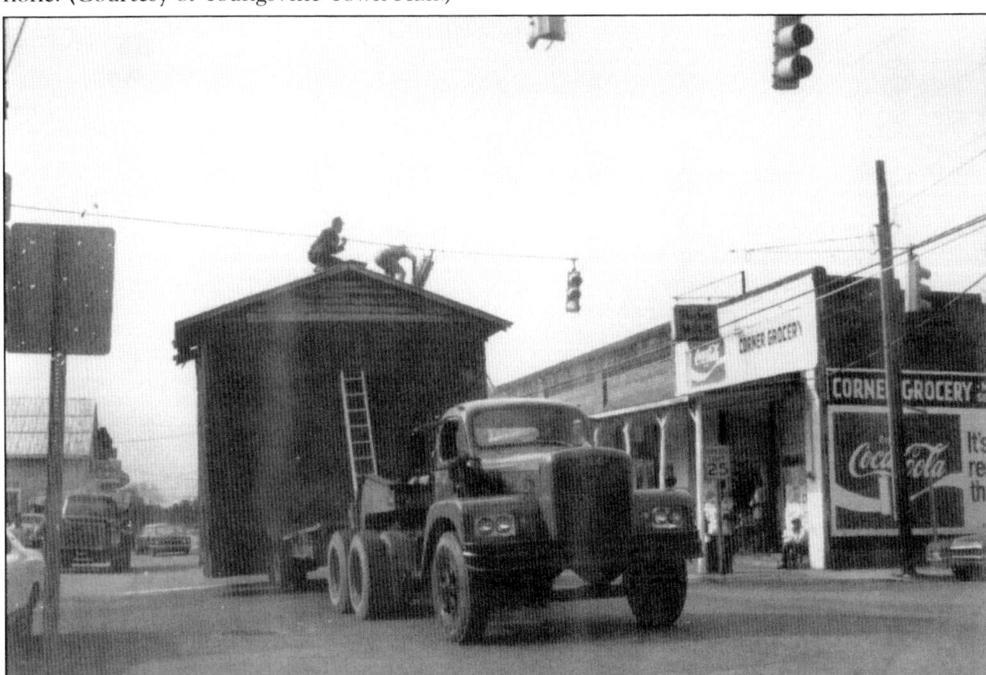

Chief of police Jack Stroud assisted movers as they navigated the busy intersection of Main and Cross Streets in Youngsville while moving this barn to a farm east of town. Urban sprawl and progress makes it necessary to move these old structures for preservation rather than destroying them. On the left is Woodlief's Store, and the Corner Grocery is to the right. (Courtesy of Franklin County Library, Lib Cheatham Collection.)

Dr. Charles A. Bland (1910–1953) opened a clinic in 1947 on the first floor of his home, at 304 North Main Street in Louisburg. Before Franklin County had a hospital, Bland's clinic had examining, operating, and delivery rooms; a laboratory; X-ray capability; a nursery; and waiting rooms, as well as overnight services. Bland practiced medicine until his death in 1953, and his wife sold the house in 1963. (Courtesy of Charles E. Bland.)

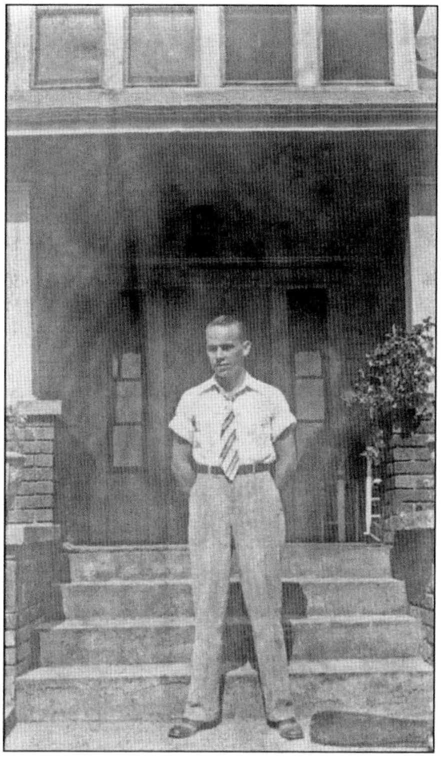

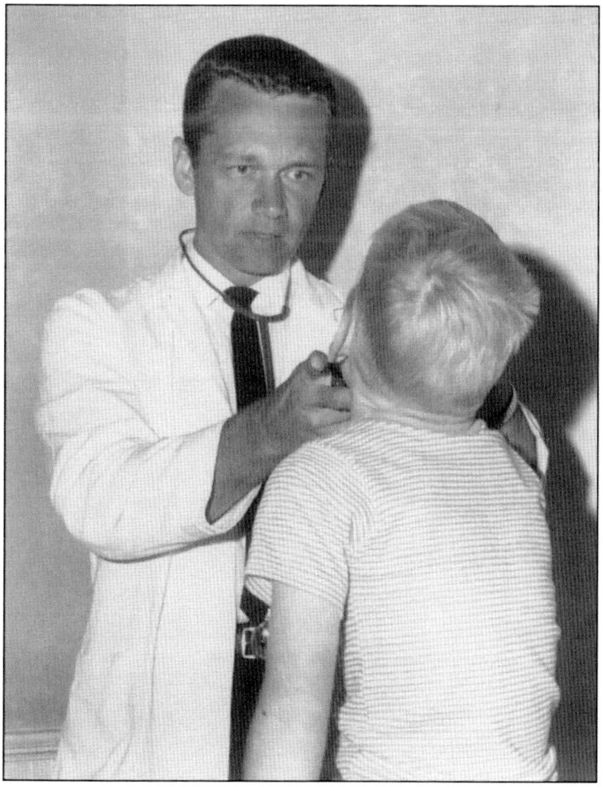

Dr. Albert N. Corpening (1930–2010) delivered over 1,000 babies during his career as a family physician in Youngsville. After graduating from Wake Forest College and serving two years as a naval medical officer, Corpening and wife, Mary C. Patterson, ran his 45-year practice from the 1911 Patterson House. They continued to support the community when they donated the land for the Youngsville library. (Courtesy of Youngsville Town Hall.)

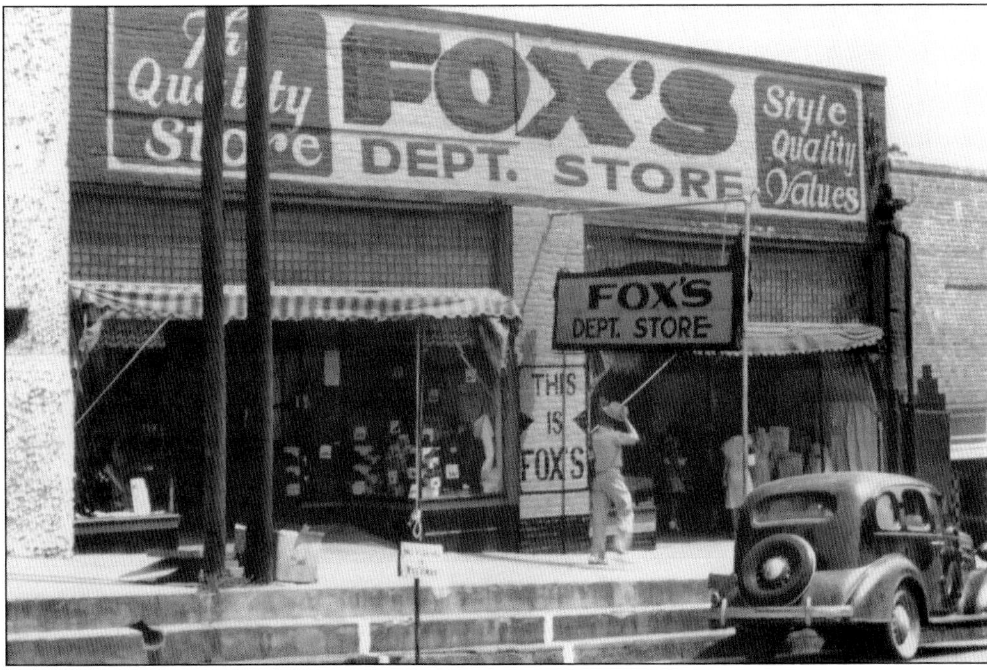

Fox's Department Store, on Nash Street, was a popular shopping stop for many years in downtown Louisburg. In June 1945, the plate-glass windows of Fox's were blown out when the Opera House across the street was hit by lightning and destroyed by the ensuing fire. Louisburg's annual sidewalk sales, first organized by Marvin Dodson Dickerson (1938–2012), the chamber of commerce president and the longtime manager of Fox's, were well attended, attracting many customers to downtown. The photograph below shows customers looking for bargains at a sidewalk sale along Nash Street. A 1970 advertisement in the *Franklin Times* announced Fox's sale items as men's dress shirts for $1, ladies' shoes for 50¢, and hosiery for 15¢ a pair. Other Louisburg department stores over the years included Hick's, Leggett's, Pope's, Roses, and Tonkel's. (Both, courtesy of Louisburg Town Hall.)

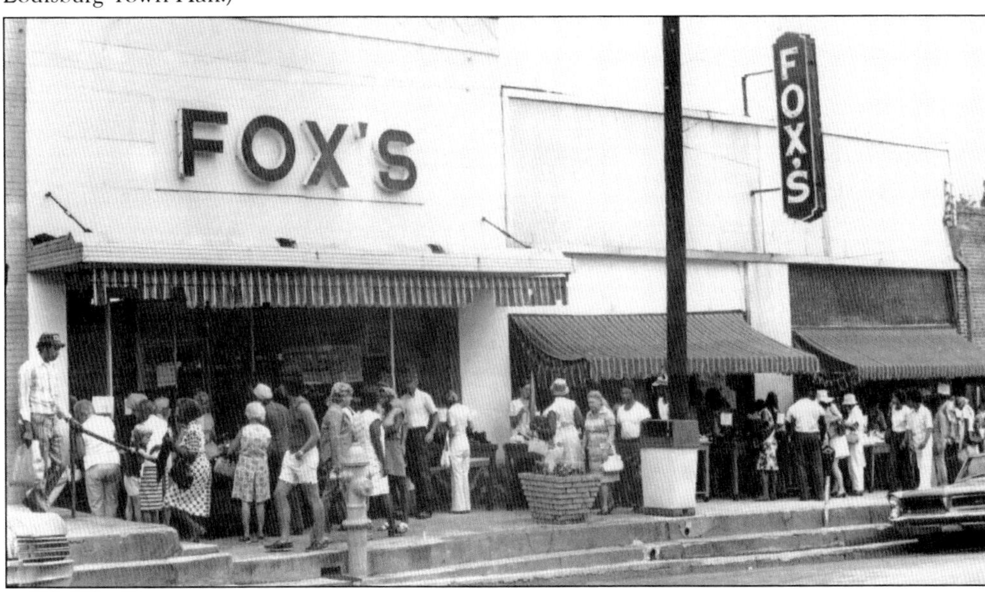

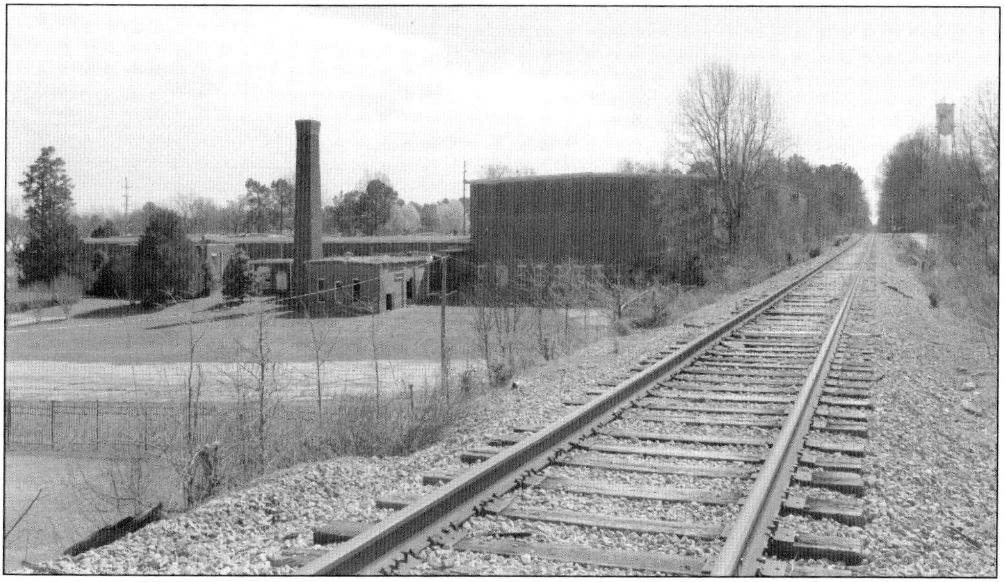

Samuel C. Vann (1852–1924) opened the Sterling Cotton Mill in 1895; by 1940, it employed over 400 workers. Union Underwear Company bought the mill in 1970 and produced products for Fruit of the Loom. After closing in 1991, the building was added to the National Register of Historic Places in 1996. (Author's collection.)

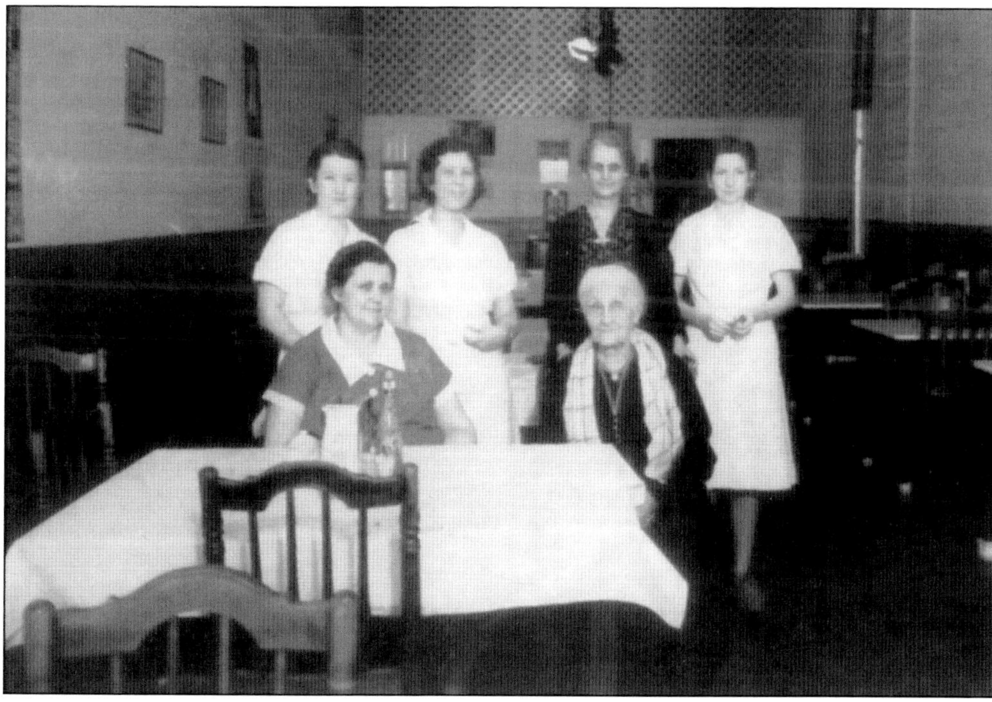

In 1940, Gladys Poythress Beasley (1902–1992), seated on the left, ran a café and boardinghouse on East Nash Street in Louisburg. The café was on the first floor, and her residence and boarders' rooms were on the floors above. It was known as Mrs. Beasley's, and she opened at least three locations before retiring in the mid-1950s. Also identified here are sisters Pauline and Gladys, standing to the right. (Courtesy of Sammy Beasley.)

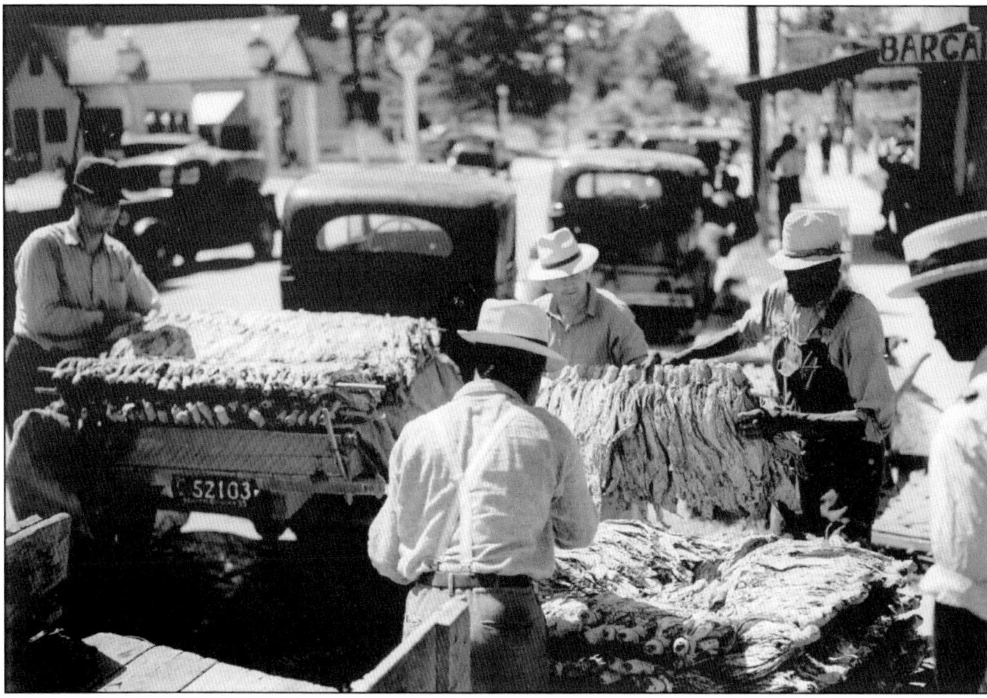

The aroma of cured tobacco once permeated downtown Louisburg when the town's many tobacco warehouses opened each year for the tobacco market auctions. As seen above in August 1939, with World War II raging in Europe, growers were forced to rush their crops to auction due to the withdrawal of British buyers from the market. Farmers are unloading their crops at the Union Warehouse, which once stood on South Main Street where Johnston Street now runs next to the courthouse annex. Other warehouses in Louisburg once included Riverside, on Market Street; Planters; Farmers Meadows; and Harris, on Nash Street. (Both, courtesy of the State Archives of North Carolina.)

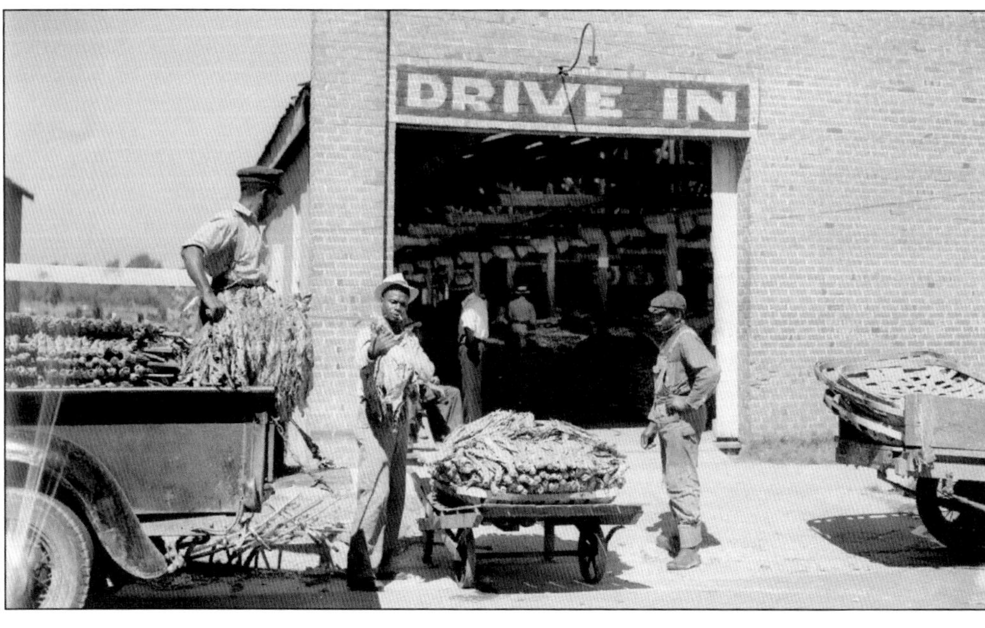

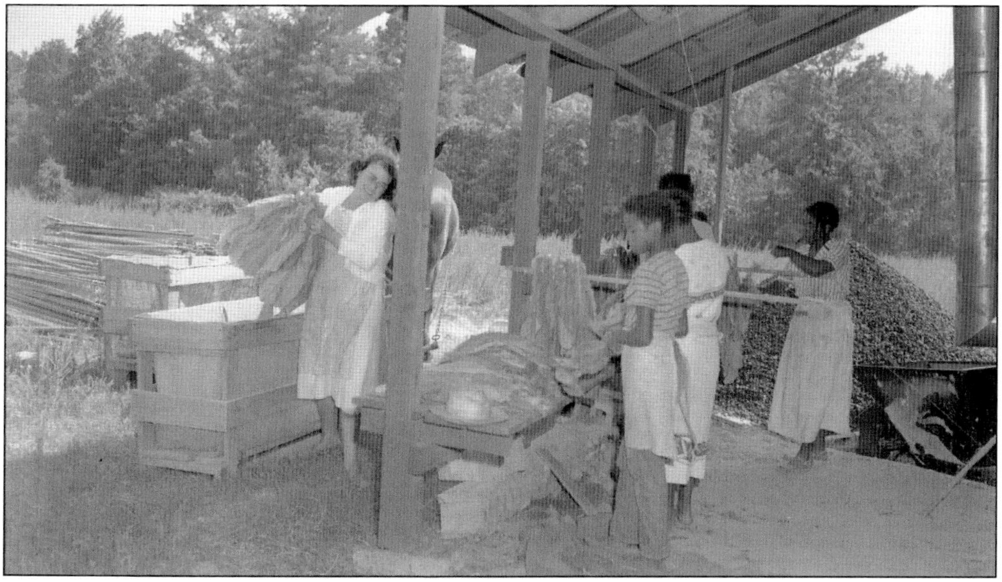

Tobacco "barning" was once a family-run industry, with each member having a job to do. Those with strong backs were in the fields, while the women and the young prepared the crop at the barns. On this Franklin County farm in 1951, tobacco leaves have been harvested, placed in horse-drawn trailers, or "slides," and brought to the barns to be strung on sticks for curing. (Courtesy of the State Archives of North Carolina.)

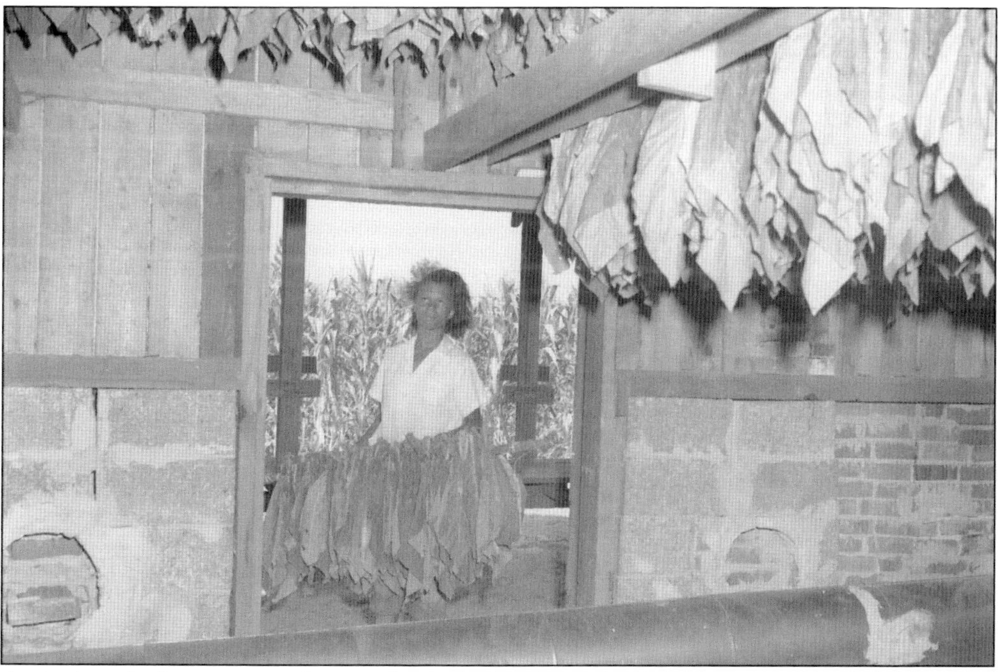

At day's end, the weary workers took on the hardest job of the process, hanging the strung tobacco sticks in the barns. The strongest straddled tiers in the four-to-six-story high barns and were handed the sticks through an assembly line of women and children. The flue-cured tobacco was then heated to a golden yellow and stored until the markets opened in August. (Courtesy of the State Archives of North Carolina.)

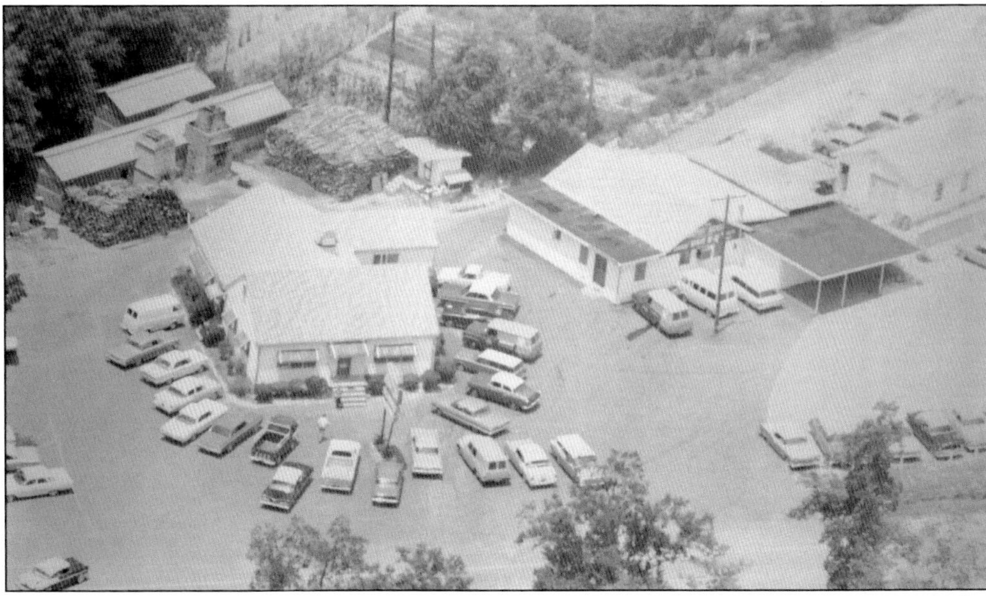

This early-1960s aerial view of the Murphy House shows the popular barbecue restaurant before Johnston Street intersected with Bickett Boulevard. George Herman Murphy opened his restaurant in 1951, and it became the favored choice for Sunday dinner, family outings, and community gatherings. When it was sold and consequently closed in 2010, the building was razed and replaced with a Sheetz convenience store. (Courtesy of Johnny Sledge.)

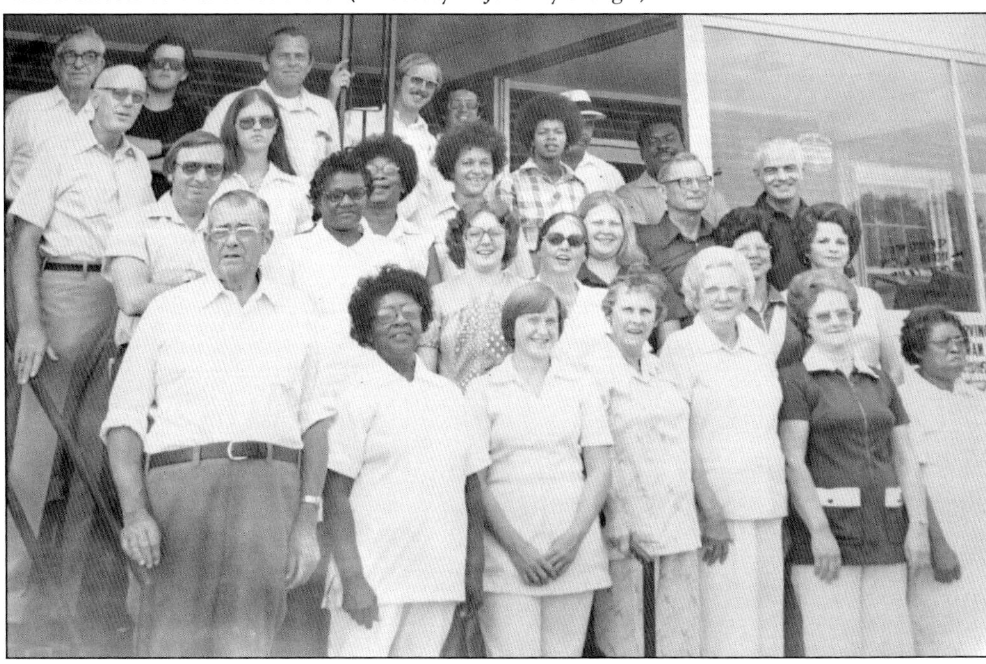

The Murphy House family poses on the restaurants steps in this late-1970s photograph. Diners knew them by name and usually had a favorite server, as well as a favorite booth or table. There are few Franklin County residents who cannot relate a personal memory of lively conversations over mouth-watering hush puppies and sweet iced tea. George Herman Murphy Sr. is seen here on the far left of the first row. (Courtesy of Johnny Sledge.)

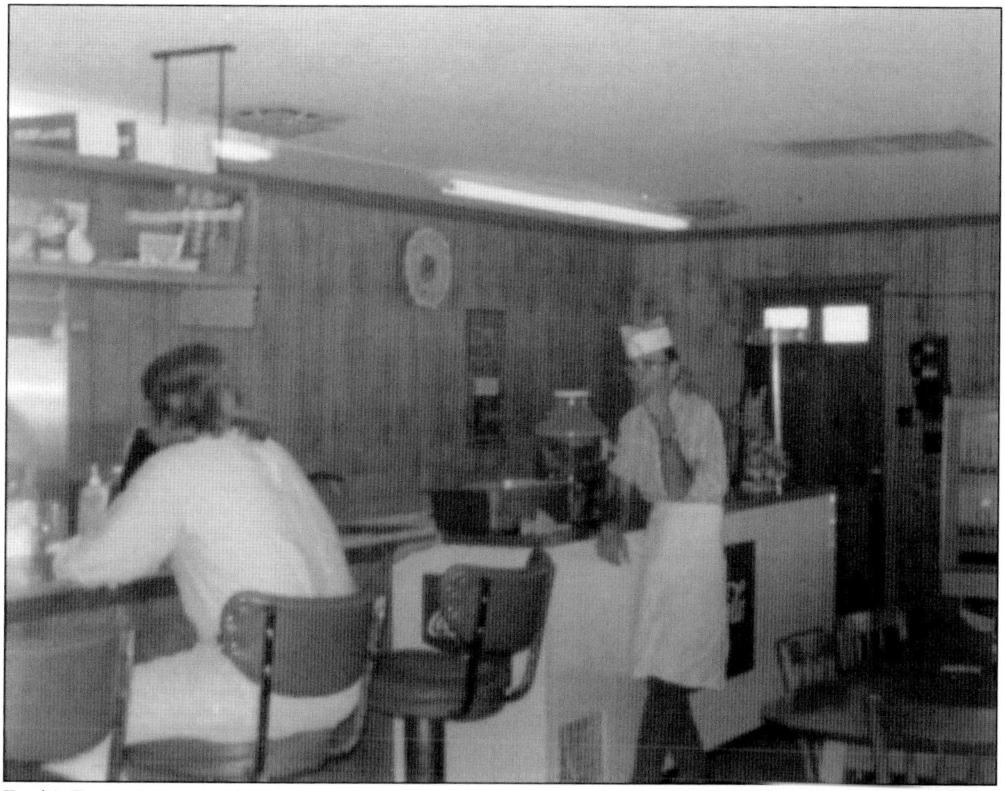

Dick's Drive-In on Bickett Boulevard in Louisburg was typical of the 1950s diner of the south. Red vinyl booths lined the large windows and swivel bar chairs allowed for counter service. While Dick's specialty was hot dogs, cheeseburgers and plate lunches were also on the menu. The restaurant was the place to be seen for the youth of the 1950s, for after-game celebrations and date-night dinners. Though the drive-in once offered the amenity, note that the window sign says, "No Curb Service." Richard "Dick" Collier (1923–1978) is seen standing in the photograph above. A March 4, 1958, advertisement in the *Franklin Times* announced that R.C. "Dick" Collier, a World War II veteran with seven years experience as a police officer and constable of the Louisburg township, was running for sheriff. (Both, courtesy of Darrell Collier.)

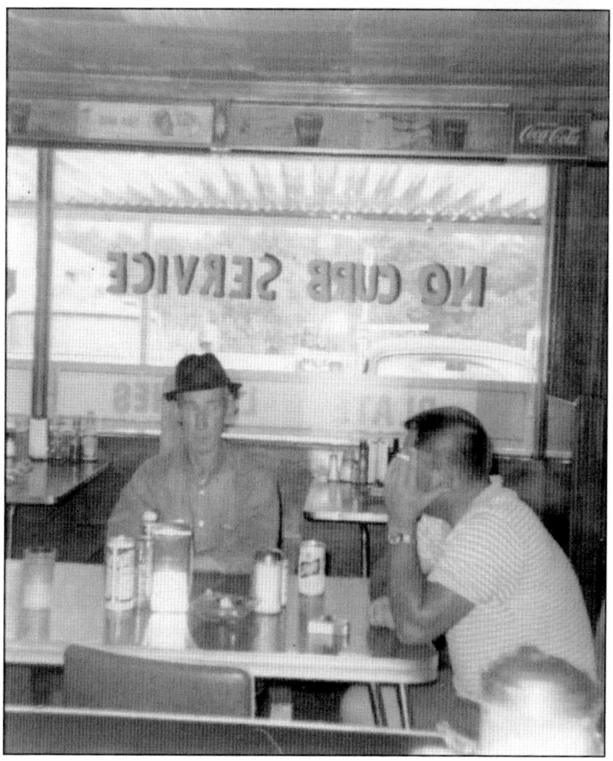

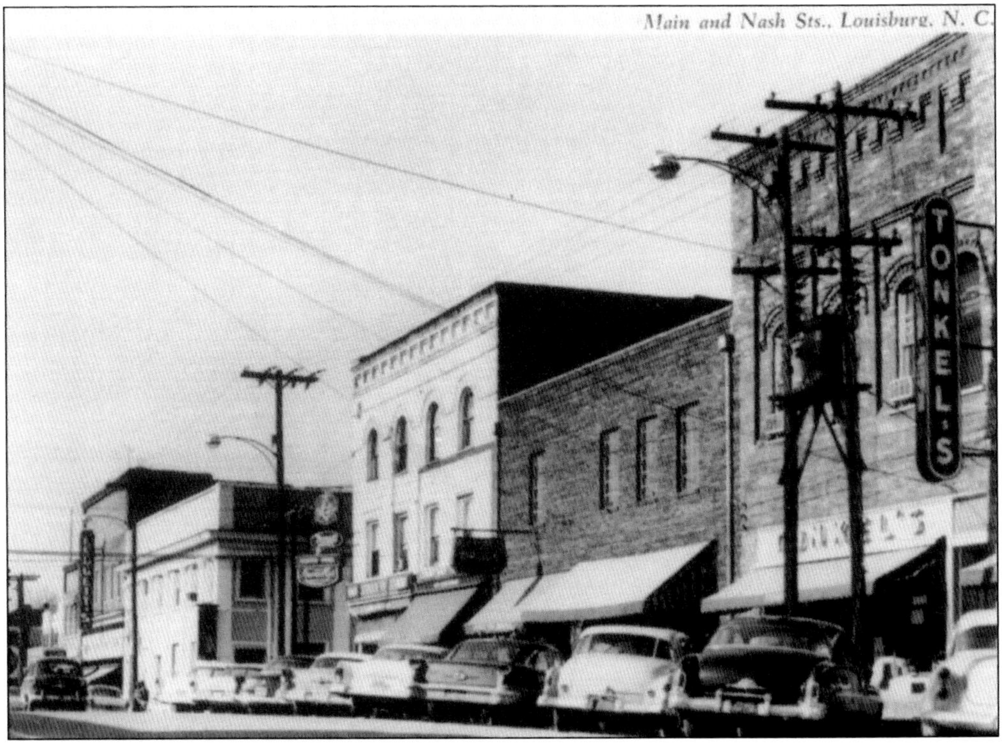

This 1950s postcard of Nash and Main Streets in Louisburg gives a view of Tonkel's Department Store, on the right, and Leggett's, across Main Street on the left. First Citizens Bank, with its well-known clock, stands on the far corner. Cars are diagonally parked along Nash Street, where the parking is limited to parallel today. (Courtesy of the Raymond and Barbara Burnette collection.)

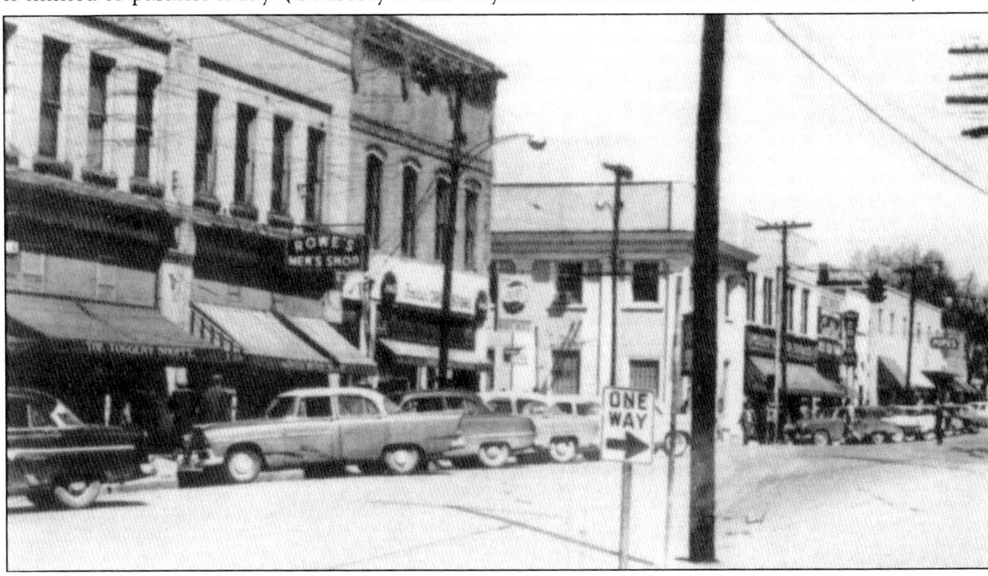

The sign for Rowe's Men's Shop, on North Main Street, hangs between the Toggery Shoppe and Boddie's Drug Store in this 1950s postcard. The Toggery was a women and children's ready-to-wear shop. In the distance, beyond the stoplight, are Roses and Pope's Variety Store. (Courtesy of the Raymond and Barbara Burnette collection.)

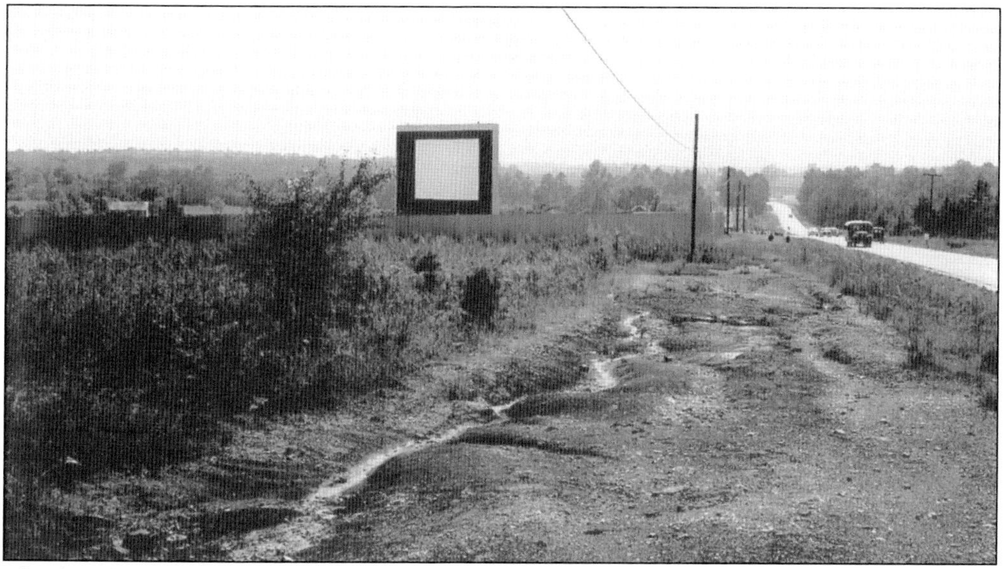

The first showings at the Car-View Drive-In Theatre on March 25, 1955, were *Riding Shotgun*, with Randolph Scott, and *Gentlemen Prefer Blonds*, with Marilyn Monroe. With a one-screen, 275-car capacity, the owners offered free popcorn, gave the first 10 cars free admission, and gave away 50 free gallons of gasoline on weekends. The Car-View was located on Highway 56 West on what is now the Walmart plaza. (Courtesy of the State Archives of North Carolina.)

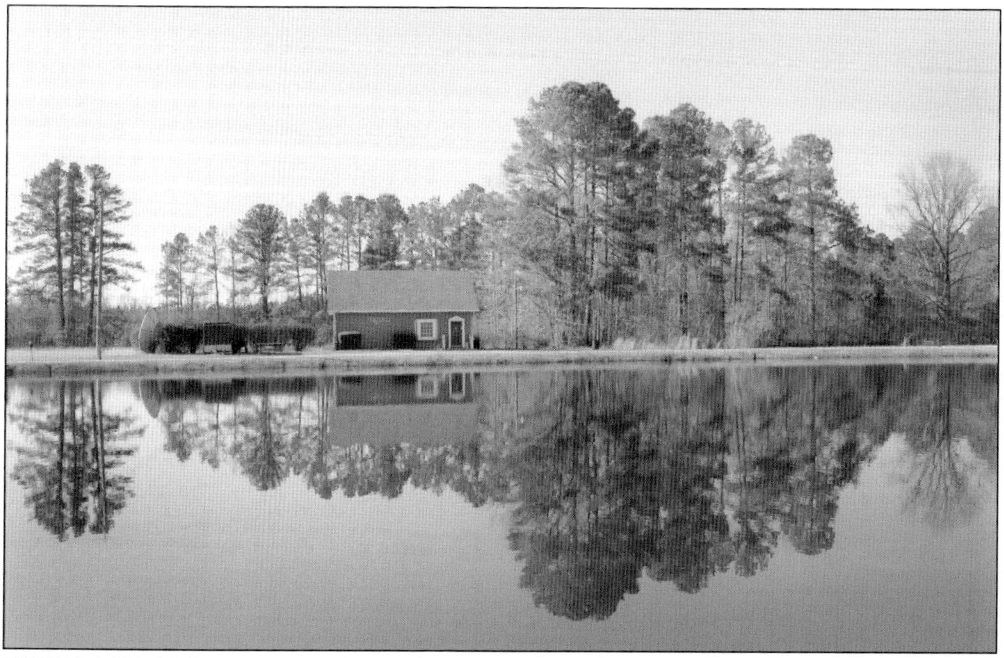

WYRN 1480-AM went on air September 12, 1958, with co-owners Joseph Lane and George Peterson broadcasting local news, country farm reports, and Sunday church services. In 1969, ownership turned over to employees Euland McBride, Asher Johnson, and Molly Evans, who added a breaking news cruiser. Following Johnson's 1981 departure and McBride's 1992 death, Evans sold her controlling interest in 2003, and the station went quiet in 2010. (Courtesy of Molly Burnette Evans.)

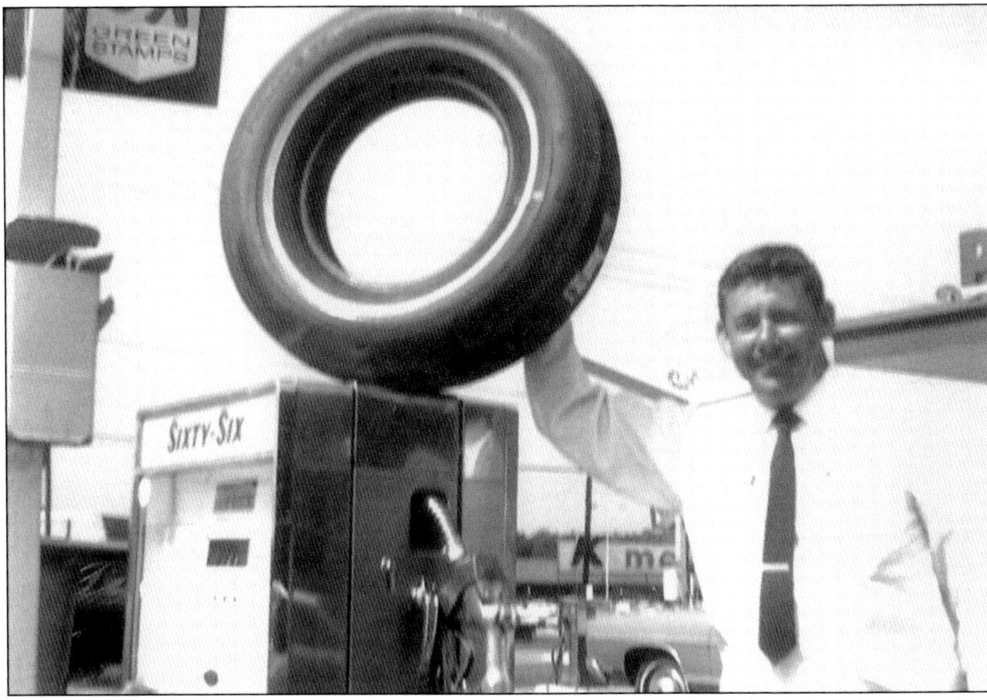

In 1957, White Level resident and farmer Robert Lee Swanson (above) opened the first of his six Raleigh service stations on the corner of Wake Forest and Six Fork's Roads. By 1965, he had expanded his holdings to country convenience stores in Franklin County. Swanson's store in the photograph below was located on Highway 56 at Edward Best High School. Note the S&H Green Stamps sign above and the telephone booth below, both relics of days gone by. Swanson entered politics in 1976, when he was first elected county commissioner. He served the people for 36 years before retiring in 2012. (Both, courtesy of Robert Lee Swanson.)

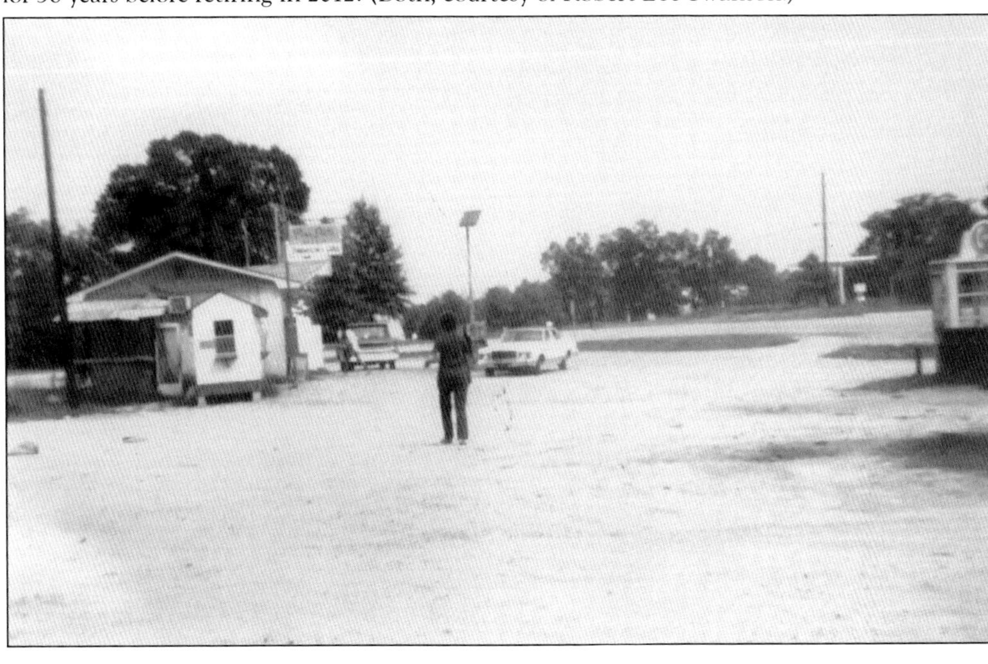

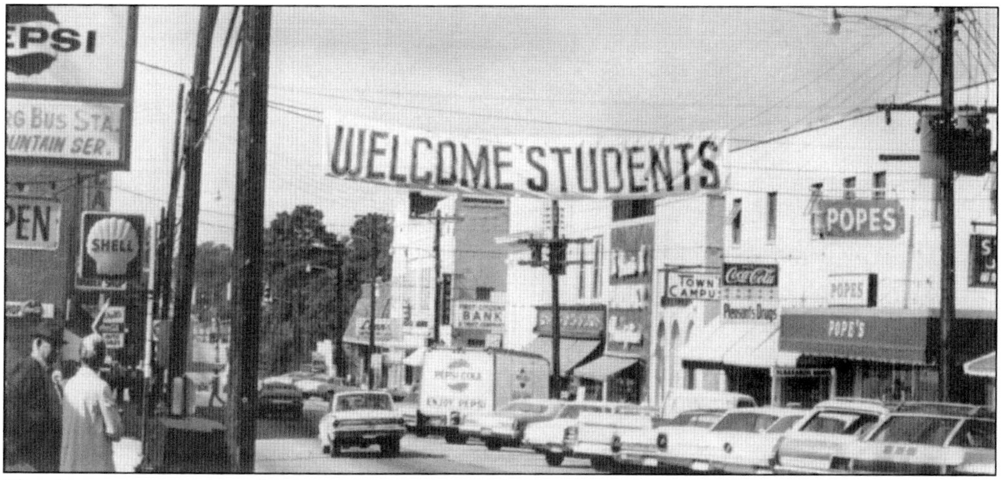

This banner across North Main Street in Louisburg welcomes students back to town for a new session at Louisburg College in the 1960s. Businesses along Main Street included Stewarts Jewelers, Pope's, Pleasants Drugs, Town N Campus, Harris Pharmacy, Roses, and First Citizens Bank. The Shell station and Louisburg bus station signs can be seen on the left. (Courtesy of Cecil W. Robbins Library.)

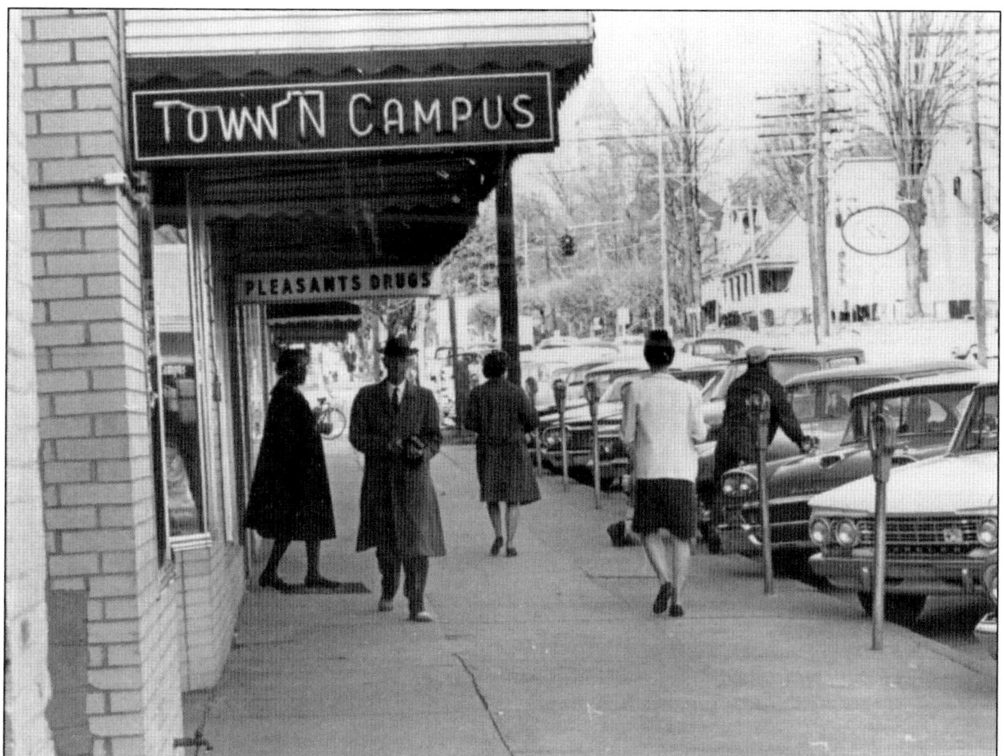

The Town N Campus clothing store opened in the 1960s and catered primarily to college students and young professionals. Parking meters were still in use in this photograph and were a necessary control for the heavy traffic in the downtown streets of Louisburg. (Courtesy of Cecil W. Robbins Library.)

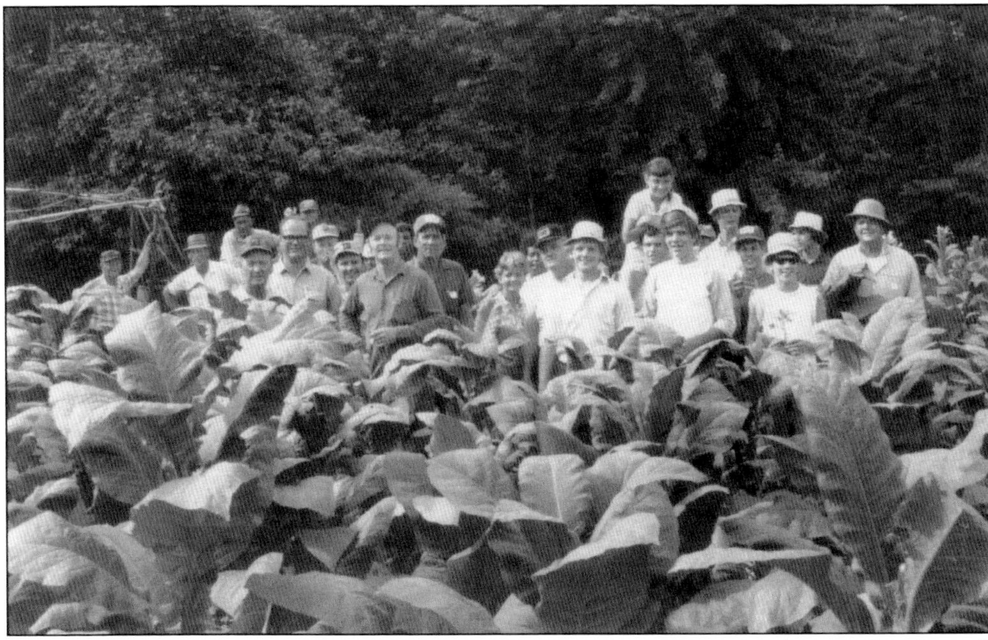

Friends and neighbors along Tarboro Road in the Youngsville community volunteered in the early 1970s to help an ailing farmer in need. When Haywood Holmes was hospitalized due to a heart attack, some 30 men, women, and children pitched in to top 14 acres of tobacco and provide the labor and machinery necessary to get the crop in on time. (Courtesy of Franklin County Library, Lib Cheatham Collection.)

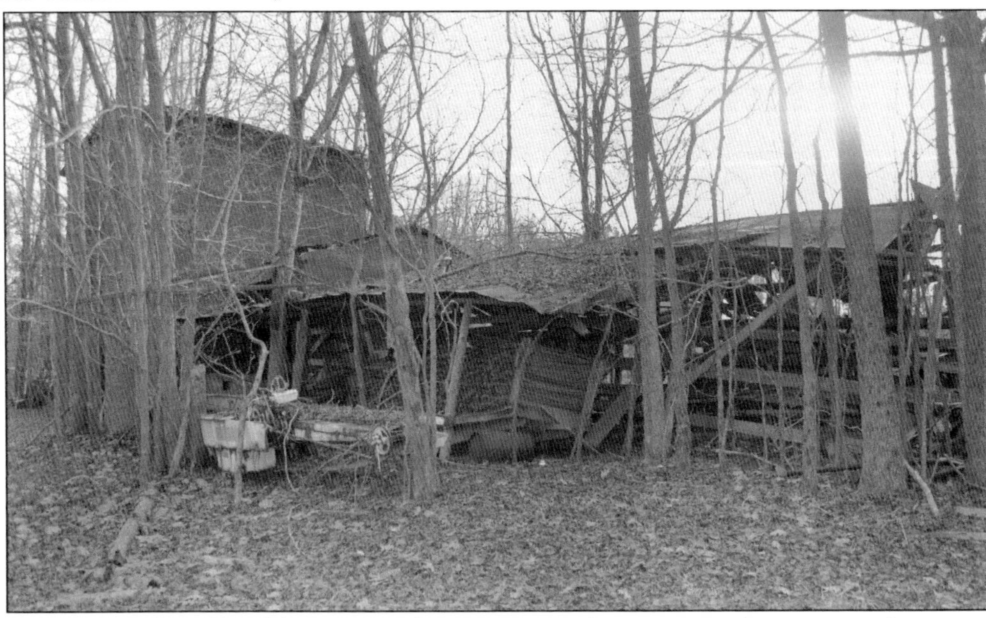

These aging relics of Franklin County's farming past can be seen in rural areas across the county. The tobacco barns were once the center of activity on the farm and were used for both work and play. Many family gatherings, reunions, and social events were held under the shaded shelters. This barn, located on the Bridges farm in Youngsville, still smells of cured tobacco and barbecue. (Author's collection.)

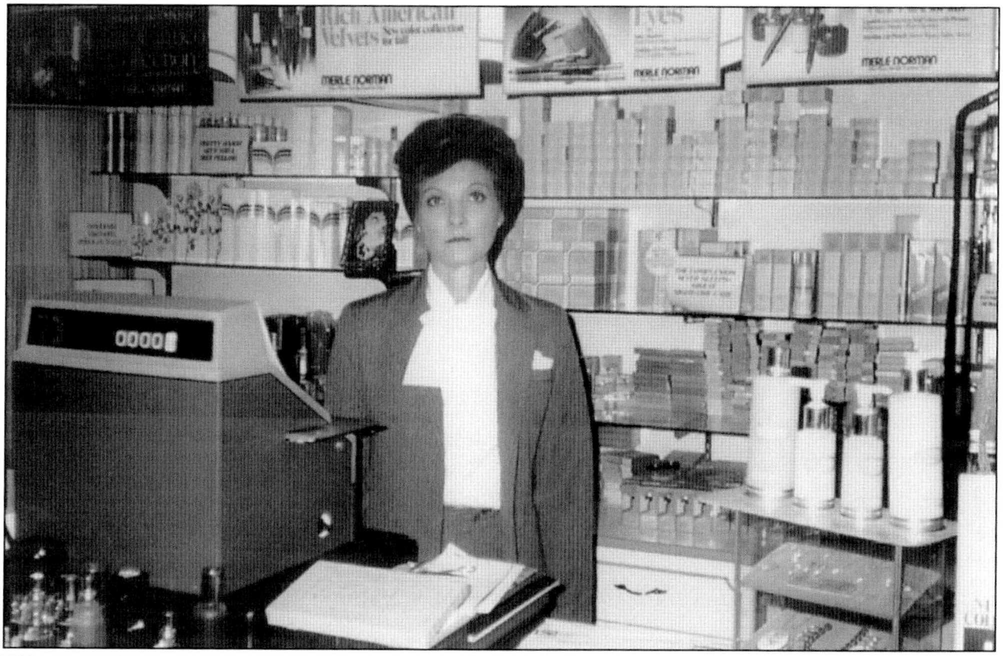

Whether the event was a wedding, prom, school pictures, or just a big date, few young ladies missed a visit to Vogue Hairstyling and the expert stylings offered by Barbara Foster Burnette (1937–2012). Opened on Bickett Boulevard in 1970, the Vogue was a full-service salon providing hair, nails, and makeup, as well as the charm and grace of a truly impeccable lady. (Courtesy of the Raymond and Barbara Burnette collection.)

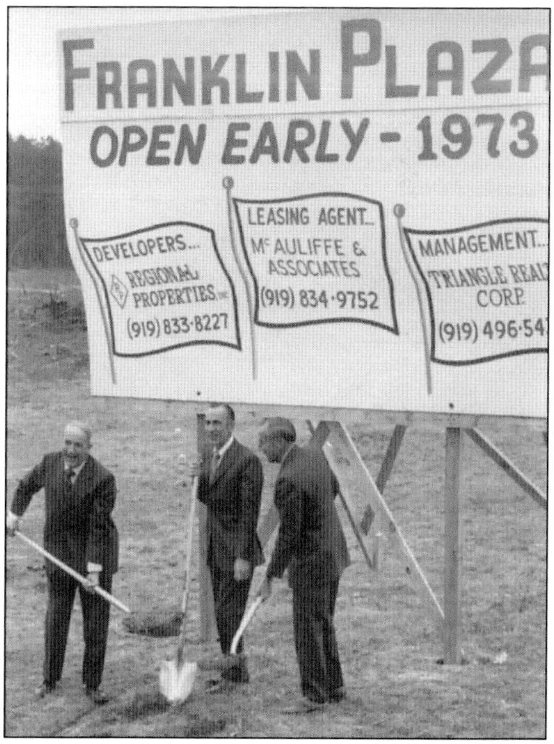

Seen here in 1973, from left to right, developer Seby Brown Jones (1915–2002), Mayor V.A. Peoples (1927–2001), and realtor Raymond Earl Burnette (1929–2007) break ground on the Franklin Plaza shopping center, on Bickett Boulevard. The strip mall became the home to the first Walmart in Franklin County. Jones was instrumental in the construction of Crabtree Valley Mall in Raleigh and also served as the city's mayor in 1969. Louisburg College's Seby B. Jones Performing Arts Center is dedicated in his honor. Peoples was the mayor of Louisburg from 1963 to 1985 and, with partner Hillman Cash, operated C&P Music Company. Raymond Burnette was responsible for bringing numerous businesses to the county, including the Community Bank, Sunrise Biscuits, and Food Lion, as well as improving the county's water supply as head of the Water and Sewer Authority (WASA). (Courtesy of the Raymond and Barbara Burnette collection.)

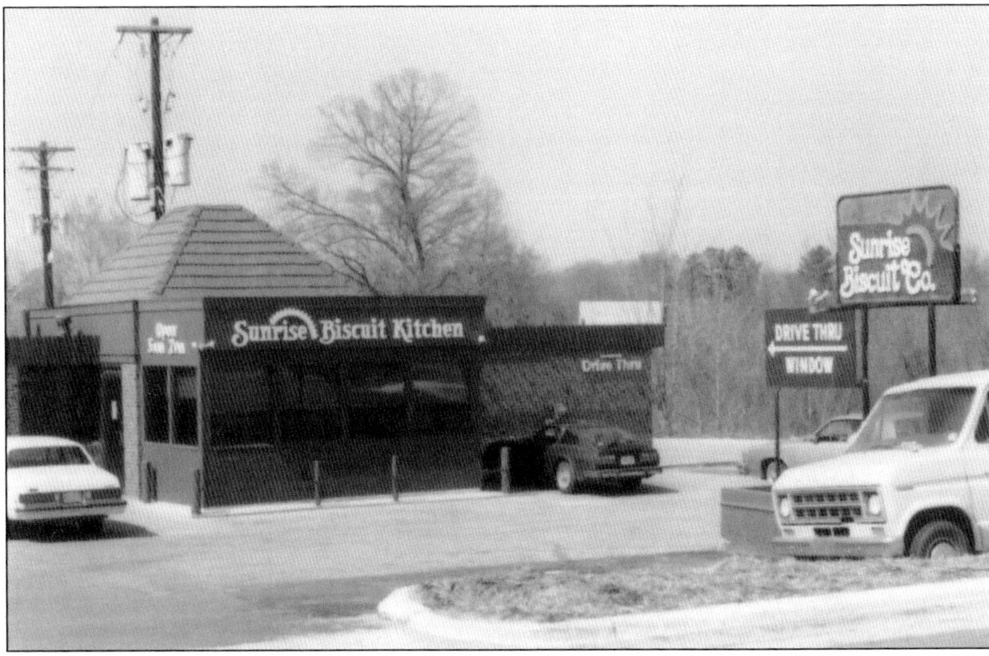

Using his grandmother's recipe, David Allen opened Sunrise Biscuits with his partner John Carmondy in May 1978. For the past 35 years, Louisburg has awakened to the aroma of country ham, sausage, and made-from-scratch biscuits on Bickett Boulevard along the Tar River. Locals begin to gather at 5:00 a.m. for morning coffee, breakfast, and to discuss the news of the day. Over the second cup, discussions turn to days gone by as the sun rises over Louisburg. (Courtesy of David Allen.)

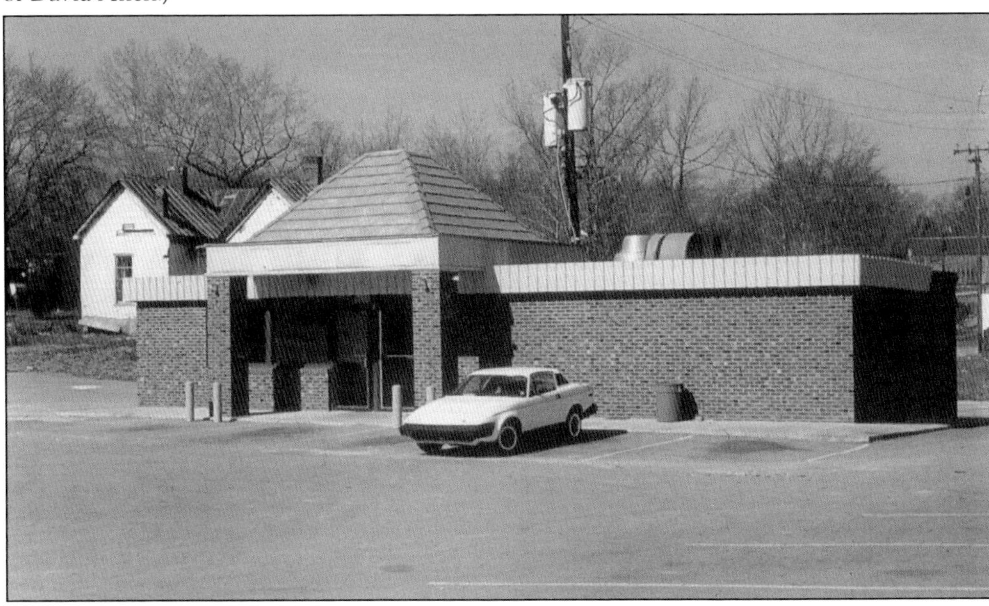

The building now occupied by Sunrise Biscuits was originally the Golden Skillet, serving fried chicken and fixings. Improvements have changed the facade and enhanced the curb appeal. A drive-through and dining area were later added to offer customers the choice of breakfast on the run or a leisurely opportunity to dine and read the morning paper. (Courtesy of David Allen.)

Four

Getting around Town, Visiting Neighbors

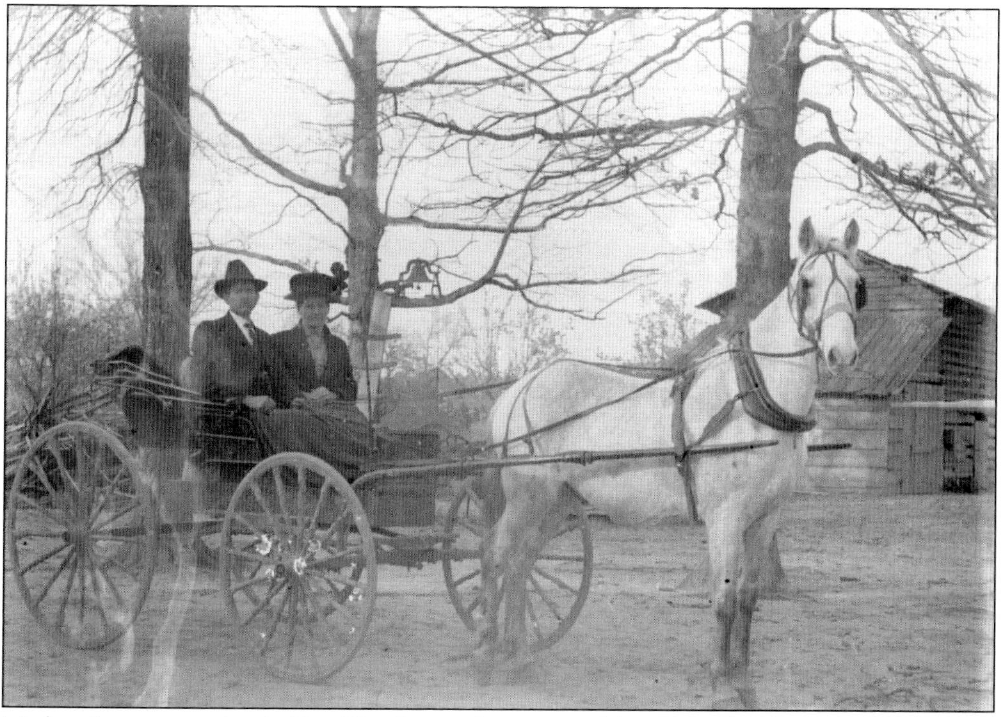

Modes of transportation in Franklin County have ranged from traveling by foot and horse and buggy to trains, planes, and automobiles. This unidentified couple's two-seater was perfect for a Sunday morning ride to church or a quick trip to town. Note the bell in the background, which was once a standard form of communication in rural areas of the county. (Courtesy of the State Archives of North Carolina.)

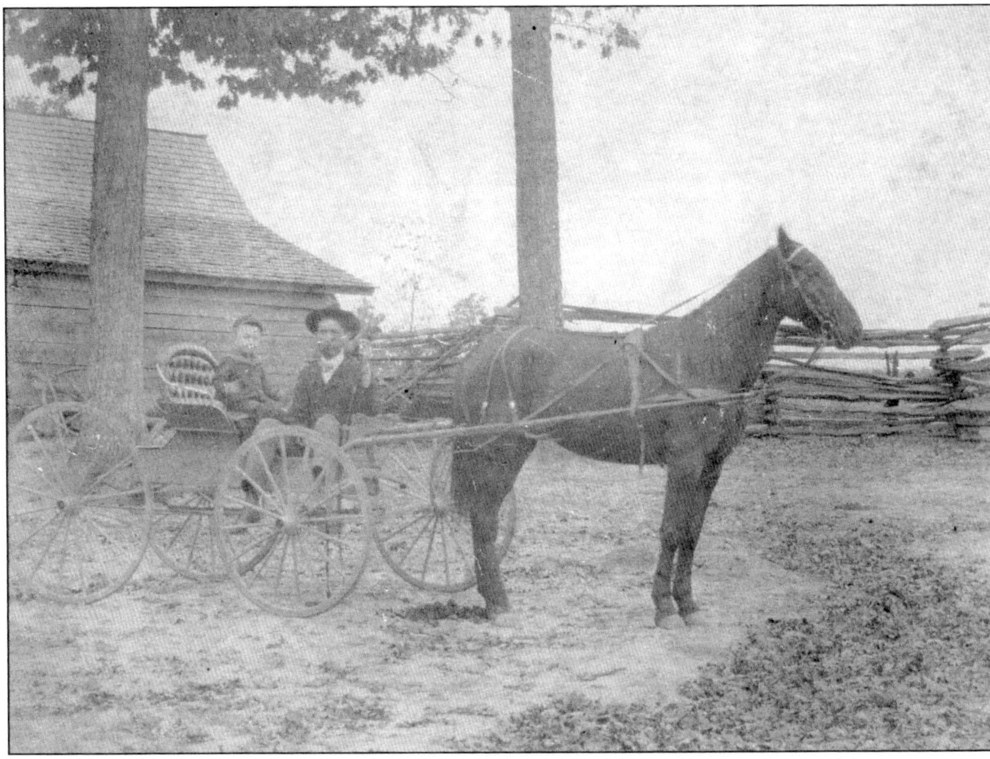

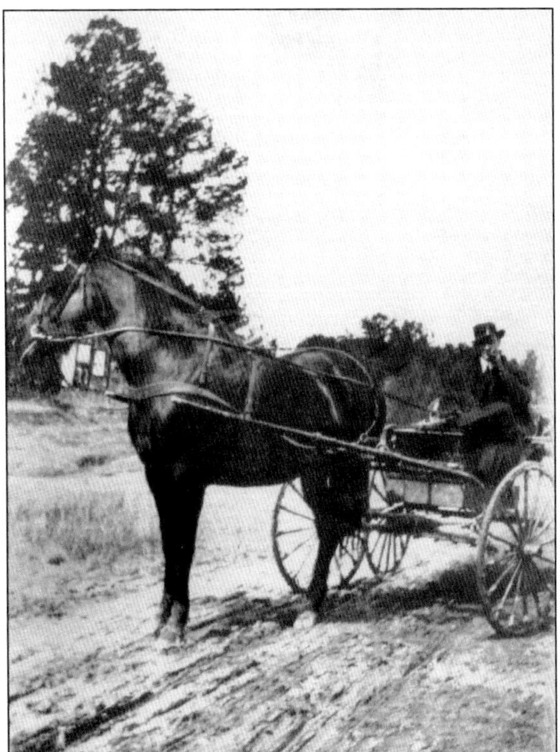

Eugene Merritt and Buddy Tharrington pose in a two-seat buggy with rolled and pleated upholstery, which surely aided in softening the bumpy ride. The setting suggests a rural farm, with a barn and cross-stacked rail fencing in the background. Rail fences were popular in those days, costing only the farmer's labor to erect. (Courtesy of Dianne Cottrell Dickerson.)

This finely attired Louisburg man with his groomed horse suggests a businessman out for a country ride. Horses in town were housed in stables such as Hayes & Fuller Livery, Feed, and Sales; Allen's Sales and Exchange; and Lancaster's Stables, all located along Nash Street. The horse exchange allowed a traveler to ride into town on a tired horse and continue on with a fresh steed. (Courtesy of Sammy Beasley.)

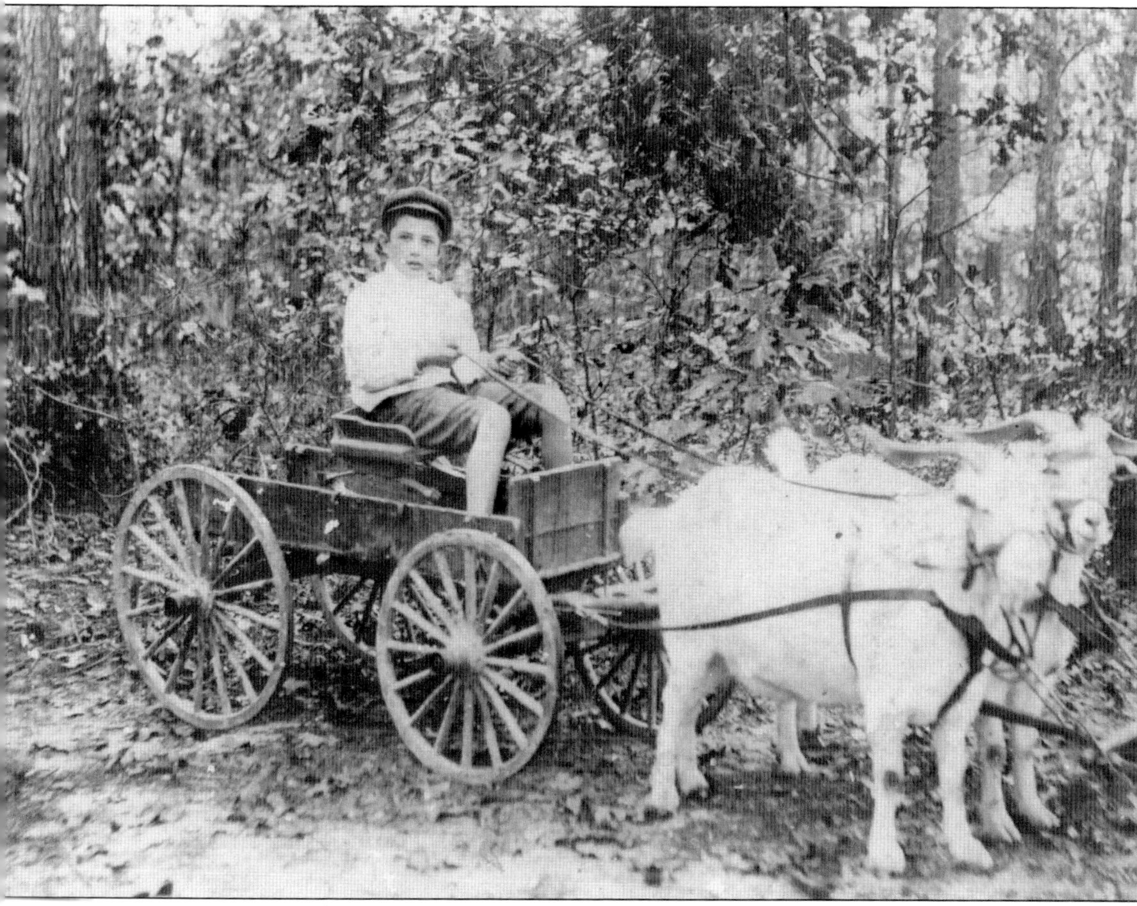

William Elias Beasley Sr. of Louisburg hitched his wagon to a pair of goats. In fact, goats were a very common form of transportation at the turn of the 20th century for young and old alike. Goat carriages were even used along with the horse-drawn type for tours around New York's Central Park from the early 1800s to the early 1900s. (Courtesy of Sammy Beasley.)

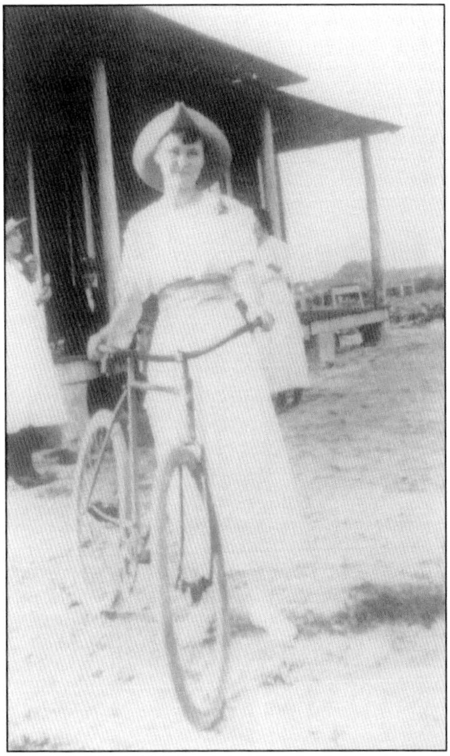

On this day in 1916, Mamie Lee Dent's (1901–1990) transportation was her bicycle. The bicycle was the first acceptable means of independent travel for women. As riding became a more common means of travel, ladies chose outfits containing less volume for ease of riding, and their large skirts were traded for bloomers or the divided skirt. Mamie married Dewey Russell Ayscue (1901–1959) in December 1918. (Courtesy of Cindy Hunt Carroll.)

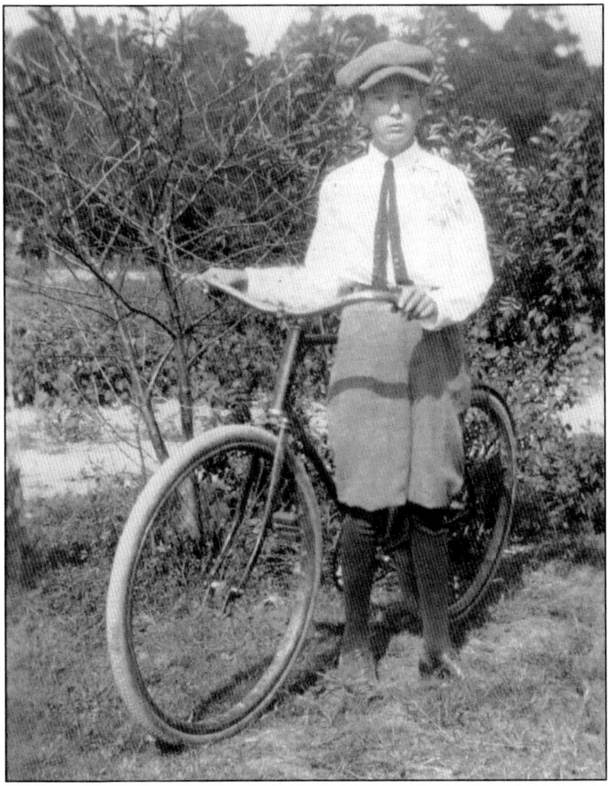

Samuel Perry Burt Beasley (1910–1980) could ride his bicycle to Mills School, on Main Street, from his home, located on what is now the intersection of Highway 56 East and Bickett Boulevard. In this 1920 photograph, a 10-year-old Beasley appears dressed in a schoolboy's uniform of knickers, white shirt, and tie. Beasley grew up to be a community leader and successful businessman. (Courtesy of Sammy Beasley.)

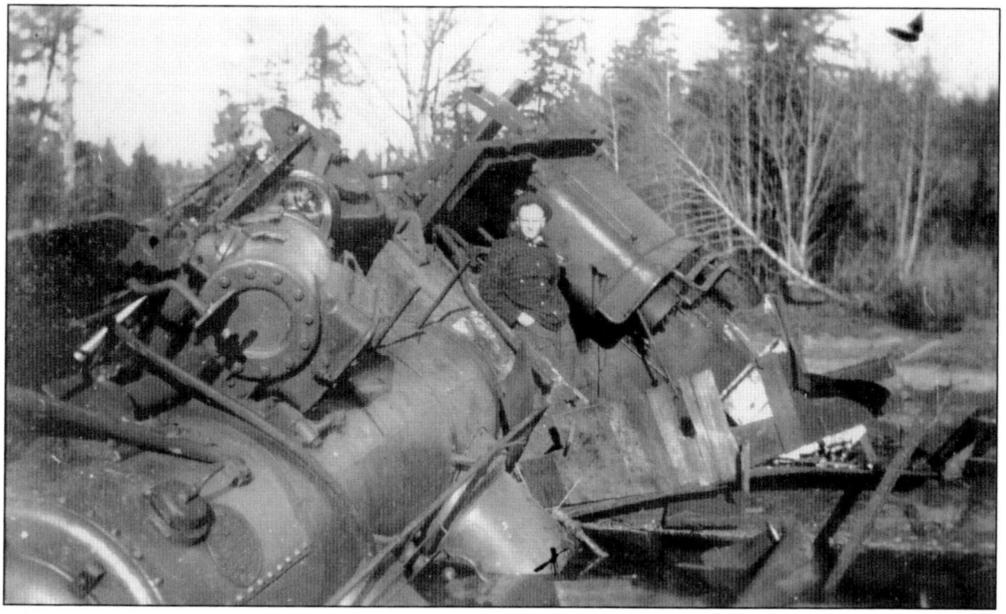

This photograph was labeled by the North Carolina State Archives as a "1918 train wreck in Franklin County." No data was found for such a wreck in 1918; however, a February 15, 1916, collision of a Seaboard Air Line freight train and a passenger train from Raleigh occurred in Franklinton, resulting in multiple injuries and the death of fireman James Holloway (1891–1916). Investigators attributed the accident to a switching error. (Courtesy of the State Archives of North Carolina.)

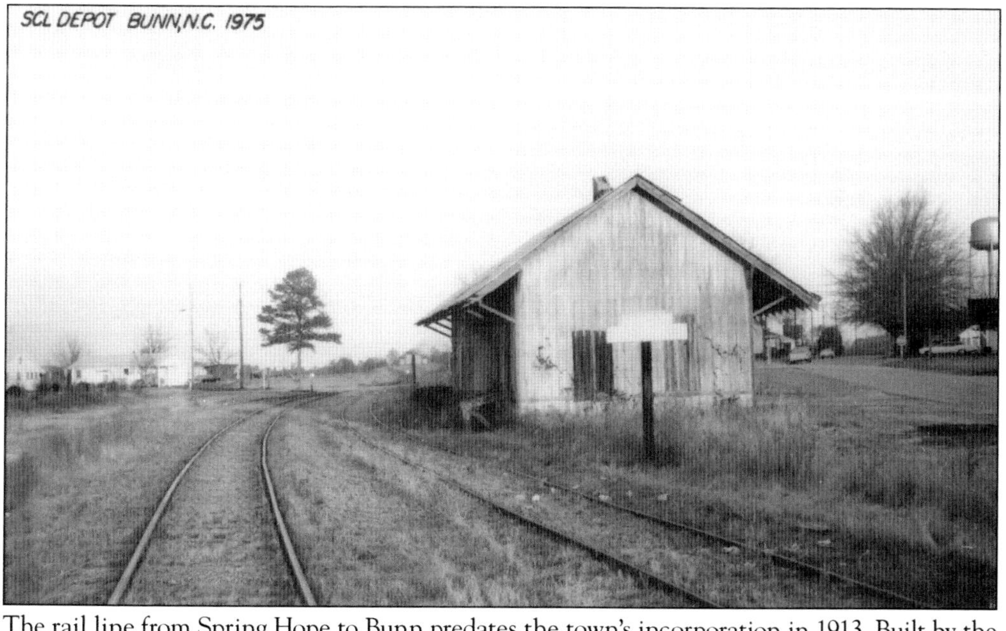

The rail line from Spring Hope to Bunn predates the town's incorporation in 1913. Built by the Montgomery Lumber Company to haul timber and supplies, the line moved in 1916 to include passenger travel. As the town grew, the Atlantic Coast Line Railroad took over the tracks, followed soon after by the Seaboard Coast Line Railroad. (Courtesy of the State Archives of North Carolina.)

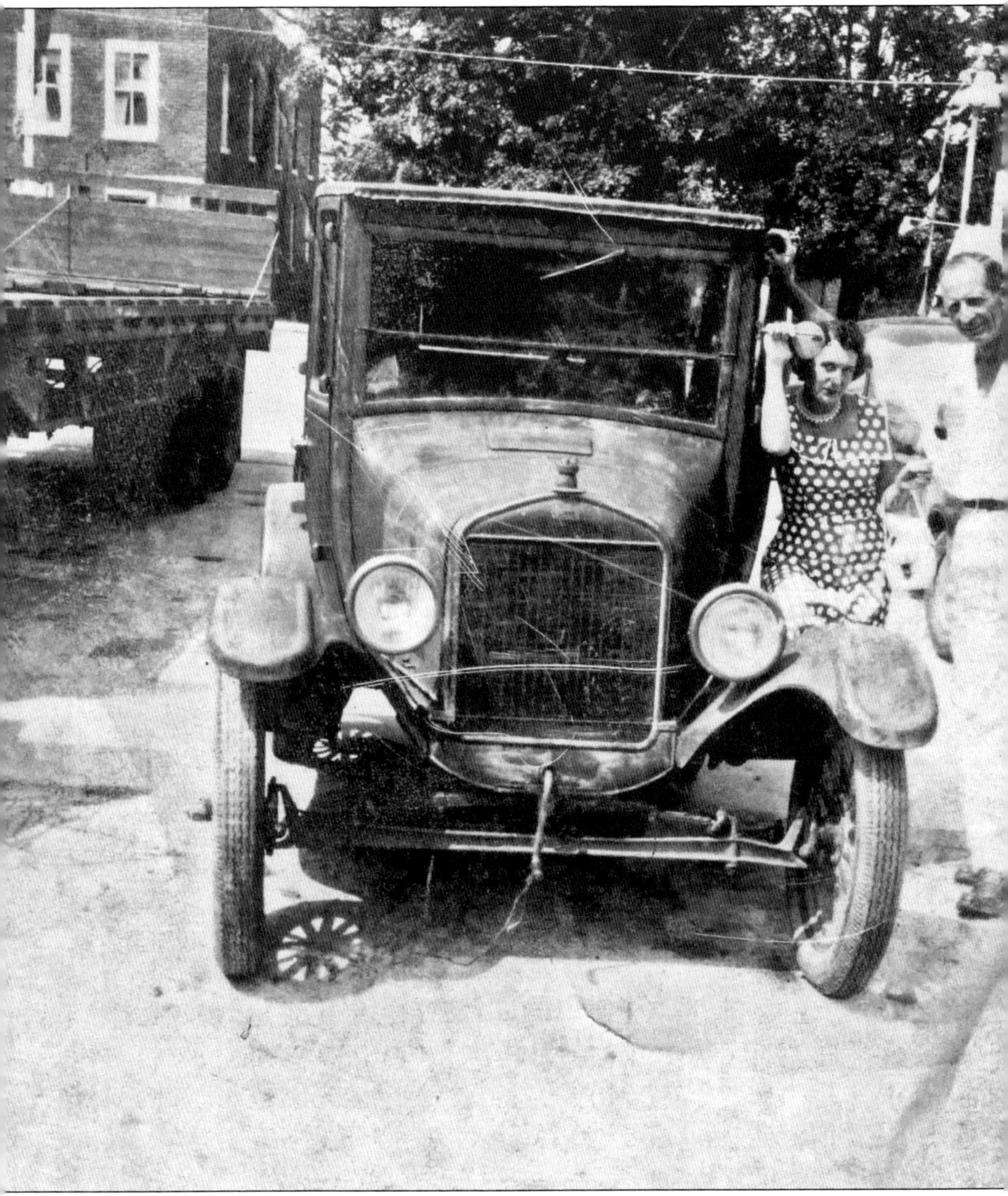

Mary Johnson Bland Champion (1913–1981), wife of Dr. Charles A. Bland (1910–1953), has a conversation with an unidentified friend. Automobiles were becoming more popular and, in 1925, Franklin County had licensed 2,497. Improved roads also made it easier for local doctors to make house calls to the countryside. (Courtesy of Charles E. Bland.)

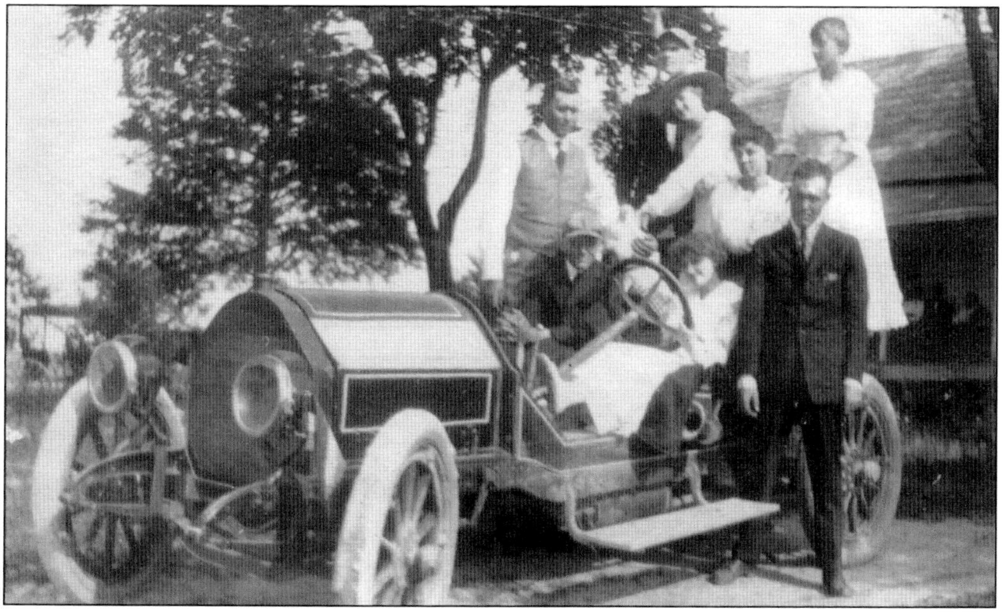

Priscilla (last name unknown) is happy to offer all of her friends a ride in her new 1915 Studebaker Speedster. Studebaker, manufactured in South Bend, Indiana, first opened in 1902 with an electric car and was marketing gasoline engines by 1912. Note the old carriage in the back left, which Priscilla most likely retired on this day. (Courtesy of Sammy Beasley.)

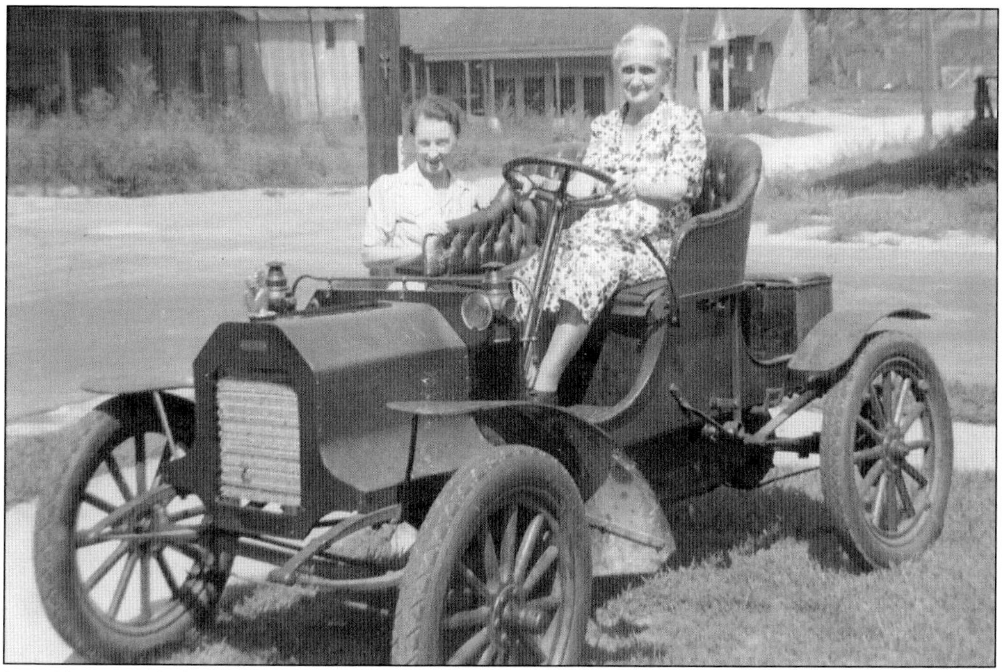

Inez Sloan McFarland (1902–?) gives Ella Bailey Dennis (1870–1947) a chance at the wheel of her roadster. McFarland's husband, Ernest Holt McFarland (1891–1973), was an automotive mechanic, so the odds are that the car was in top condition for the test drive. Ella Dennis and her husband, William Dennis (1865–1921), arrived in Louisburg from Maryland via train in 1903 and made their home in Cedar Rock. (Courtesy of John and Hallie Hearn.)

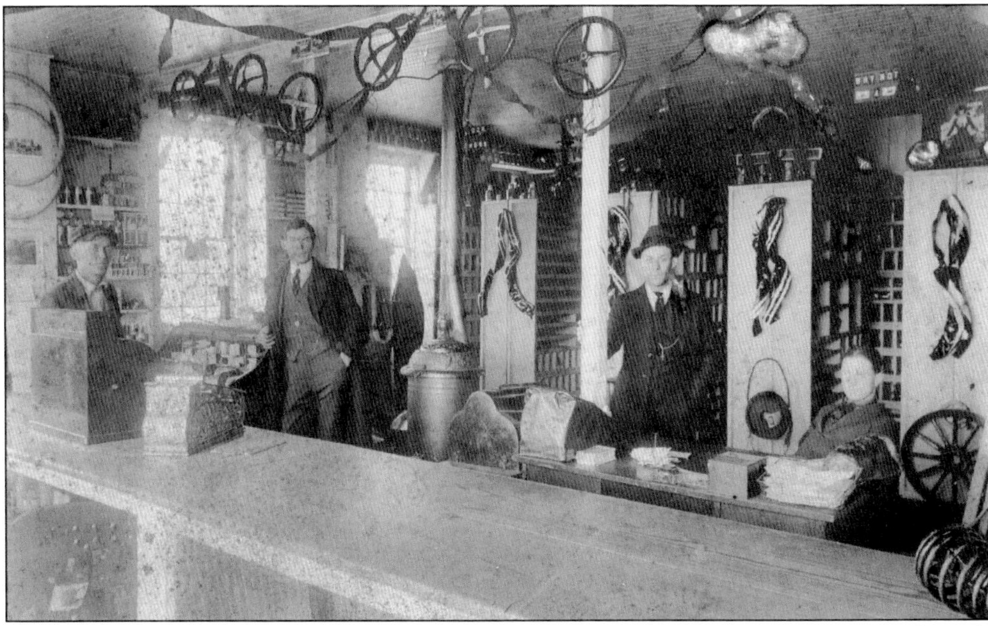

This photograph gives no clues to the location or the name of the store, but it is thought to be located in Youngsville. The headlights in the display case, the steering wheels hanging from the ceiling, and the parts bins in the background suggest it may be the office to the garage below or an attached car parts store. (Courtesy of Youngsville Town Hall.)

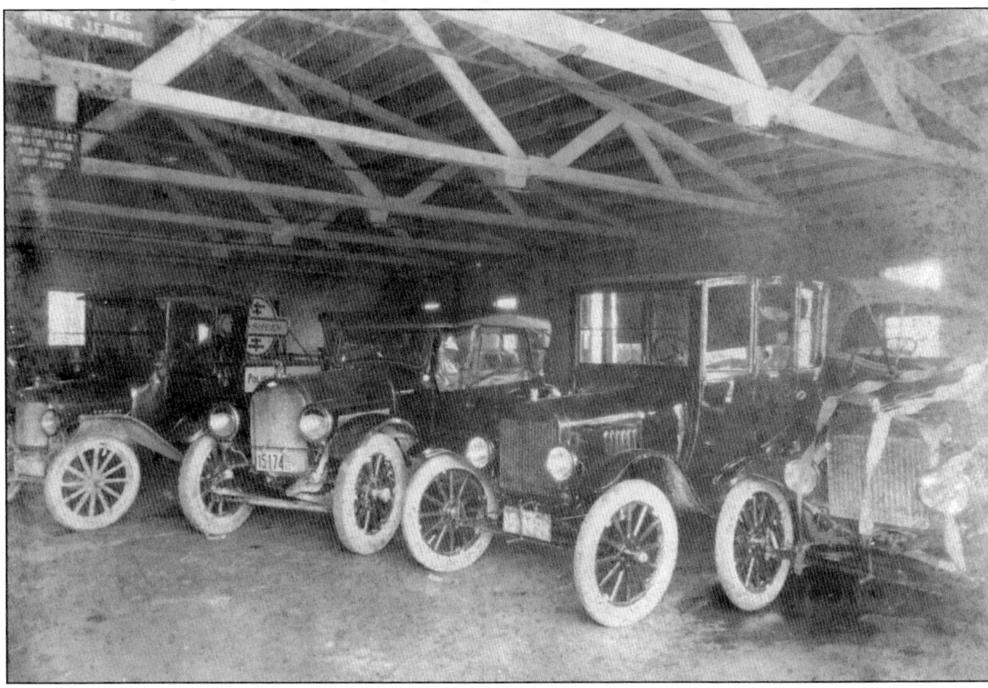

The sign in the upper left of this photograph says, "Cars stored at owner's risk, Keep hands off cars." Above that, it directs the reader to the office of J.F. Brown. The exact location of this garage is unknown, but it is believed to have been in Youngsville. If the garage and the 1920s cars were still there today, they would be worth a small fortune. (Courtesy of Youngsville Town Hall.)

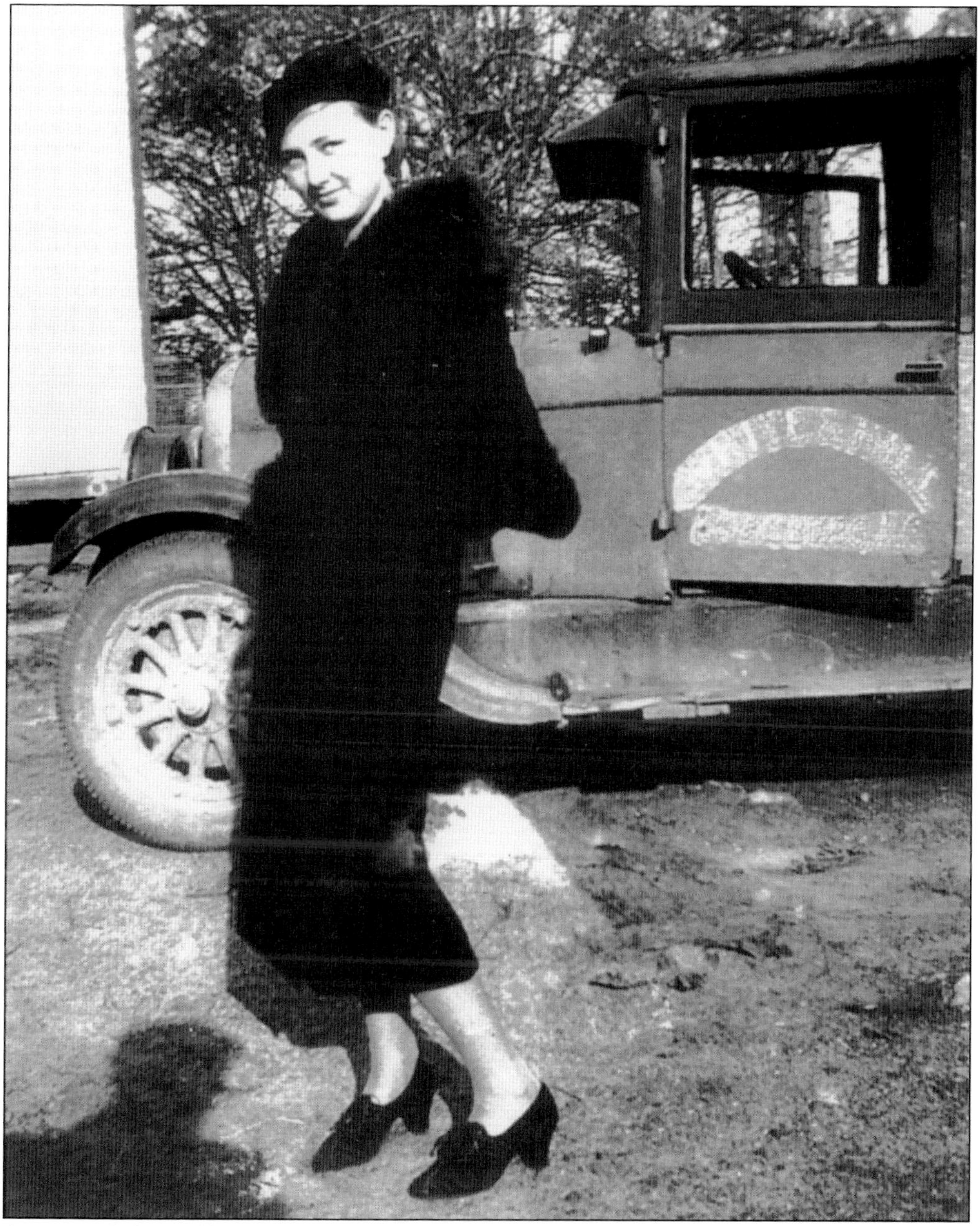

A very stylish Lucille Foster Bobbitt (1917–2004) stands before a White & Hill delivery truck around 1937. White & Hill was operated by William E. White Jr. (1902–?) and opened between 1930 and 1940. William was the son of William Edgar White Sr. (1871–1938), who ran the W.E. White Furniture Company and Funeral Home on North Main Street in Louisburg. The funeral home was originally located above the furniture company in 1896. In 1936 or 1937, the large two-story house located at 125 North Main Street was moved to Franklin Street to make room for the new post office, and it became White Funeral Home. The name changed with new owners, and it eventually became Strickland Funeral Home and Crematory. Bobbitt's demeanor gives no clues as to whether the delivery was from the furniture or funeral side of White's business. (Courtesy of Wendy Shearin Taylor.)

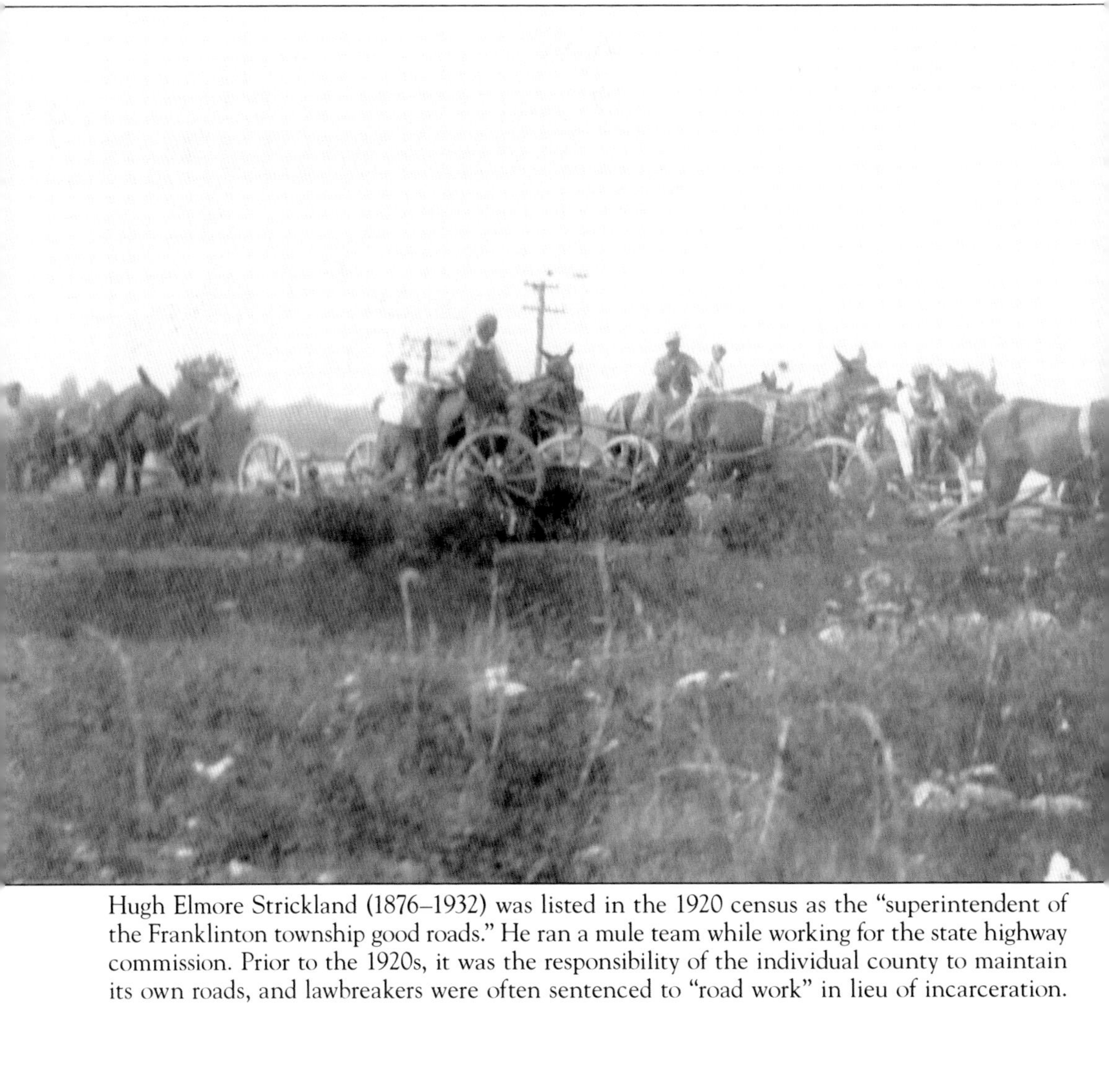

Hugh Elmore Strickland (1876–1932) was listed in the 1920 census as the "superintendent of the Franklinton township good roads." He ran a mule team while working for the state highway commission. Prior to the 1920s, it was the responsibility of the individual county to maintain its own roads, and lawbreakers were often sentenced to "road work" in lieu of incarceration.

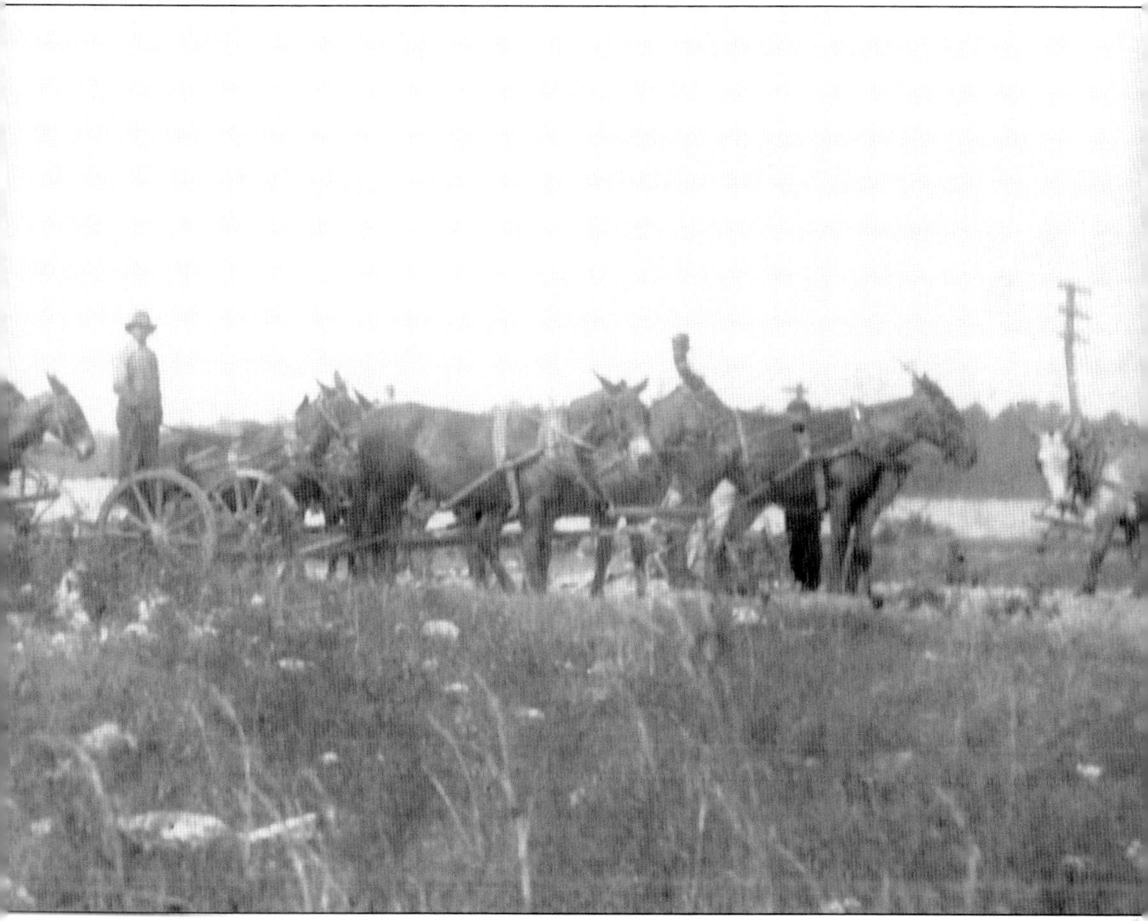

Depending on the severity of the crime, the penalty could range from days to weeks or months of the backbreaking labor. Strickland's mule team here may have been working to clear Highway 56, known then as the Franklinton to Louisburg road. (Courtesy of Carrie Daniels.)

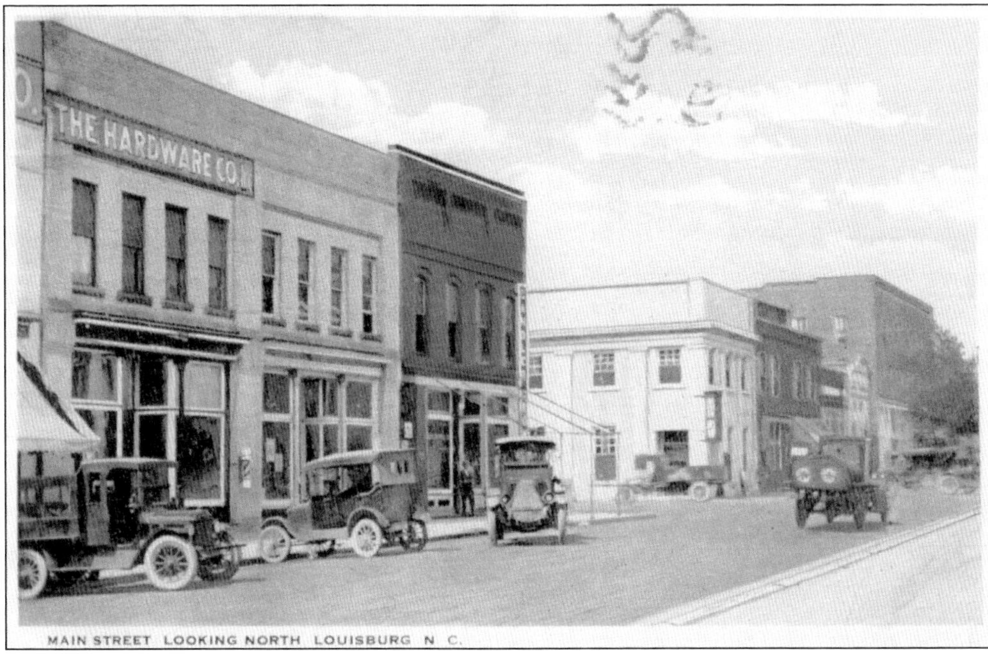

These two postcards, depicting Louisburg's North Main Street (above) and the Tar River Bridge (below), herald the increased use of the automobile in the 1920s. Streets appear wide and even have curbing and sidewalks. Louisburg began paving its streets in 1917, as more and more citizens moved away from the use of the horse and carriage to this more modern form of transportation. In 1920, North Carolina reported over 100,000 registered automobiles, with the majority of the owners being rural farmers. Note that stoplights, parking lanes, and road lines were not represented on these postcards. (Both, courtesy of Freddie Edwards.)

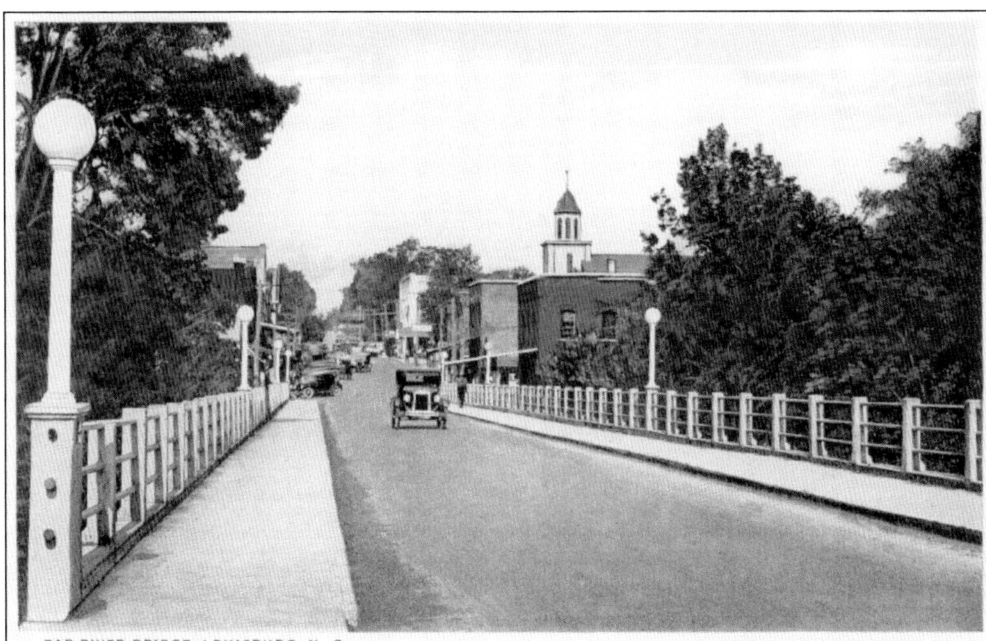

In this 1930s photograph, man's best friend catches a ride with William Norwood Fuller (1890–1941). In those days, higher tires were required to maintain clearance off rough and muddy roads, making the running board a necessary step up into the automobile. It also provided the perfect platform for this German shepherd. As roadways improved, tire diameters decreased and running boards were phased out. (Courtesy of Franklin County Courthouse.)

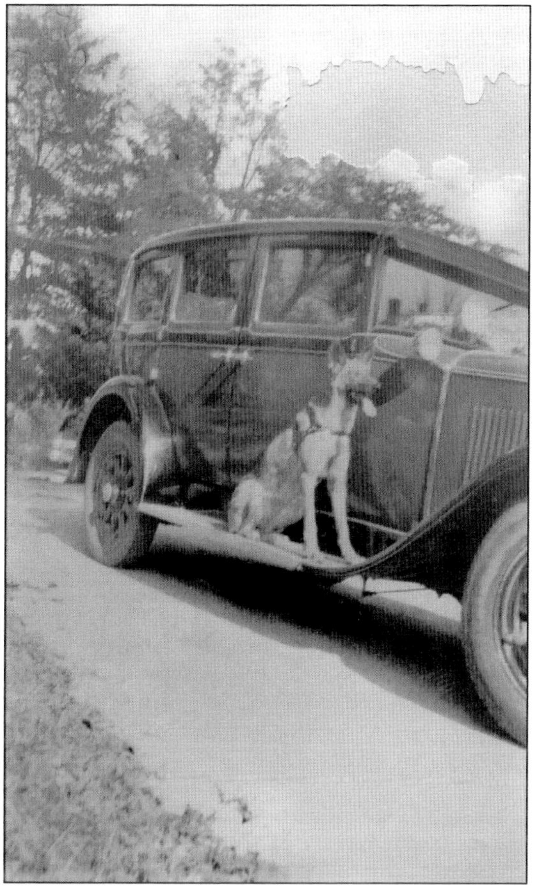

When the Youngsville Baptist Church sent a group to Ridgecrest Baptist Assembly in the 1930s, Ernest Hart (sitting on the front bumper) volunteered to drive his truck. Connor Jeffreys is standing to the right of the truck, and some of those identified are, in no particular order, Clellie Mae Croom, Gertrude Holden, Frances Winston, Nancy Winston, Martha Holden, Charlie Raymond Edwards, Arlene Hart, Eldred Pearce, and Frances Allen. (Courtesy of Youngsville Town Hall.)

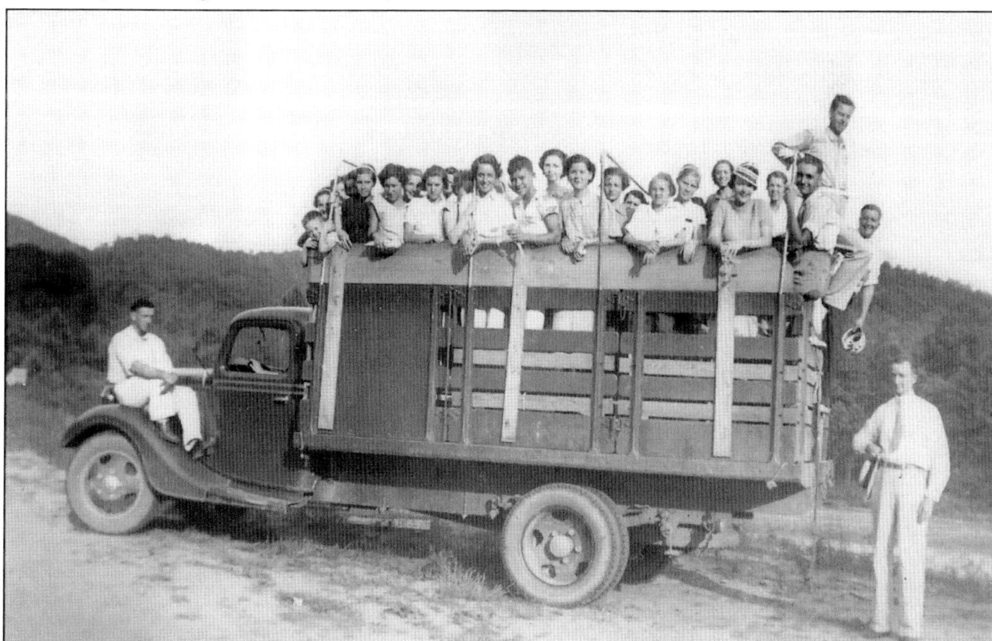

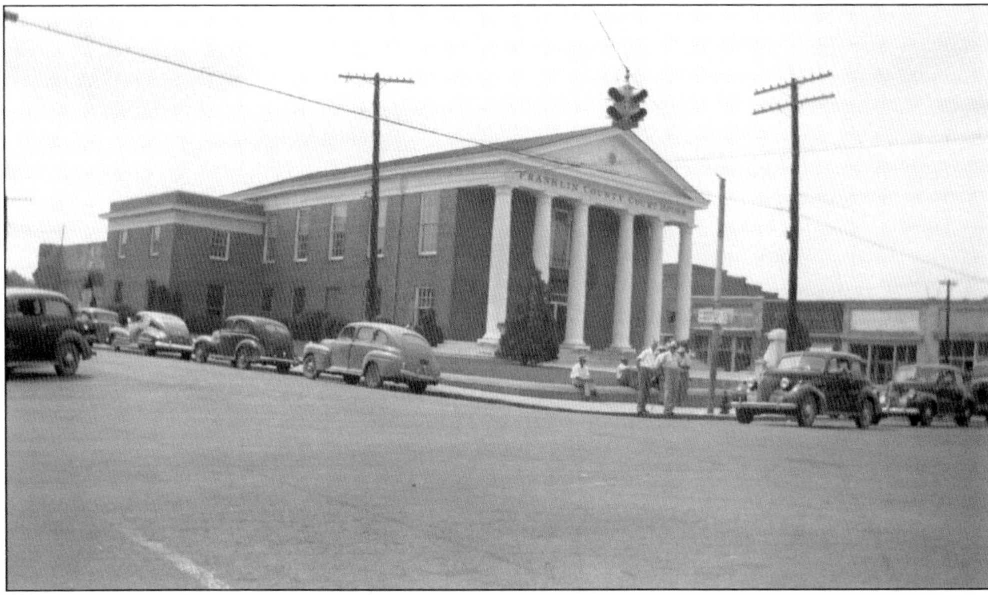

This photograph of the intersections of Main and Nash Streets in Louisburg was dated July 23, 1948, and shows the usual activity surrounding the courthouse. The streets are lined with 1940s automobiles while men gather on the courthouse steps. On the left are the remains of the burned Opera House. (Courtesy of Franklin County Courthouse.)

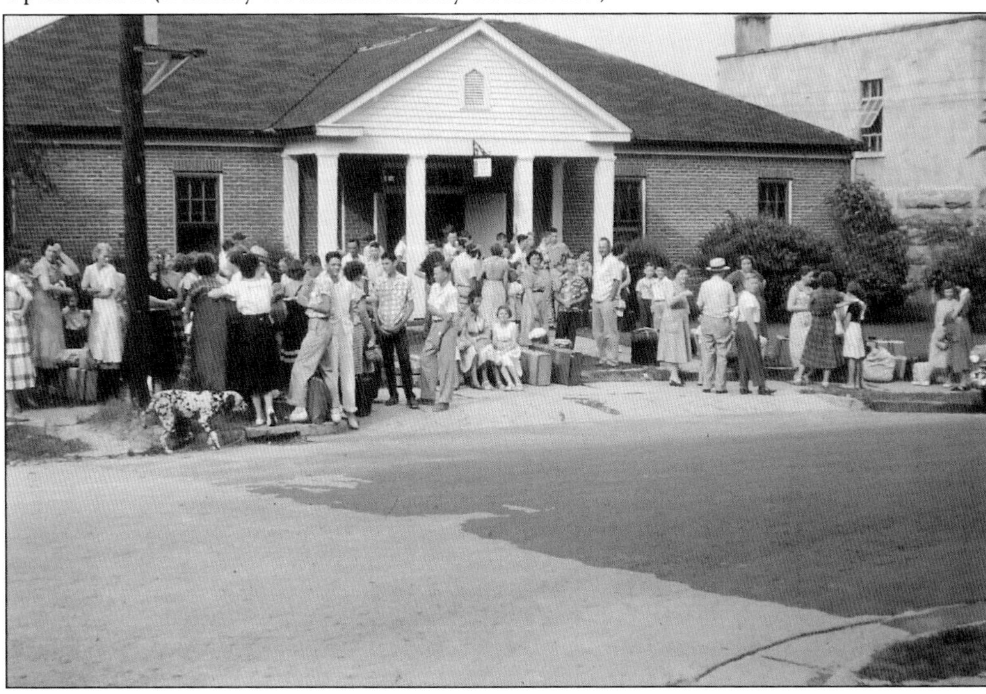

In 1958, Franklin County youth gathered on East Nash Street in Louisburg to await their ride for a group trip to Roanoke, Virginia. Group leaders and counselors chaperoned over 40 children during the three-day adventure. The Extension Building shown here in the background still stands next to the old jail on Nash Street, though the front facade has changed. (Courtesy of Martha Leonard Mobley.)

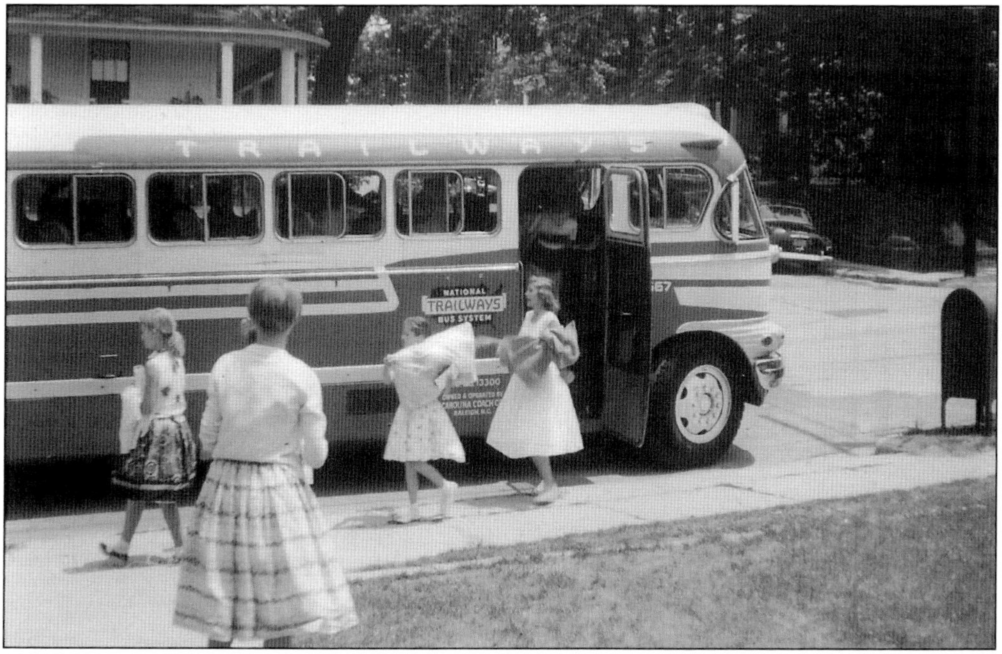

A Trailways bus from the Carolina Coach Company arrives on East Nash Street to take the 4-H group on their three-hour trip to Manteo. Carolina Coach was formed in 1925 and was North Carolina's first successful intercity carrier. By 1940, it had grown into the nation's largest regional bus company. Their distinctive cream-and-crimson buses were headquartered on Blount Street in Raleigh. (Courtesy of Martha Leonard Mobley.)

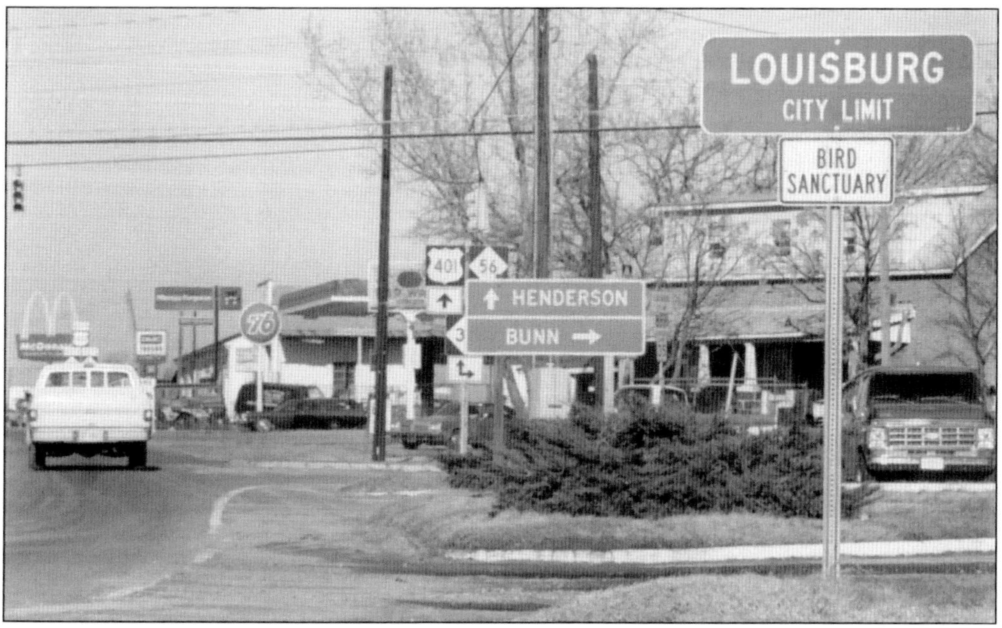

The late 1970s saw Bickett Boulevard grow into a major artery with the addition of fast food restaurants, service stations, automobile supply shops, and shopping centers. In the background of this photograph are the golden arches of McDonald's, which was built in 1977. (Courtesy of Cecil W. Robbins Library.)

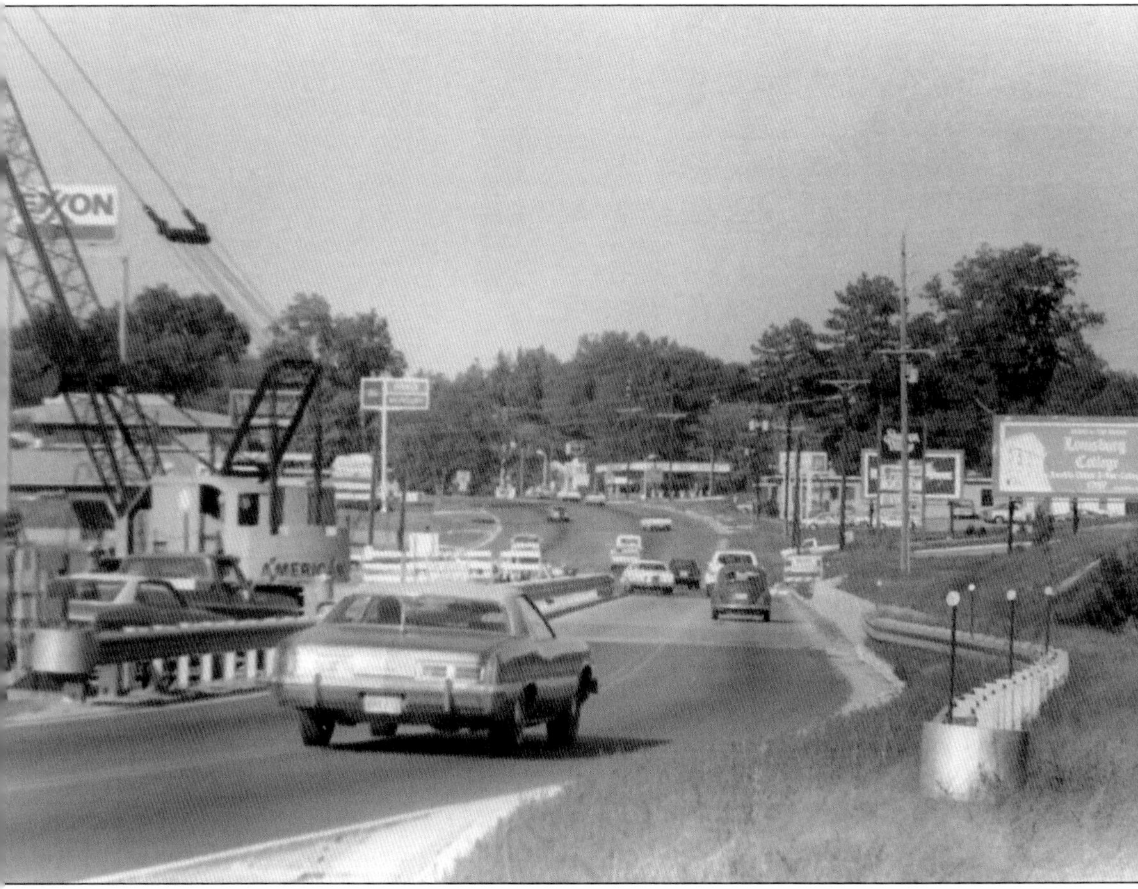

Increased traffic through Louisburg prompted the widening of Bickett Boulevard and the addition of lanes to the Tar River Bridge, requiring a slight traffic shift. The Shannon Village sign to the right lists Winn-Dixie and TG&Y as two of the strip mall's occupants, and behind the crane to the left, the Pizza Hut and Hardees signs are barely visible in this late-1970s photograph. (Courtesy of Cecil W. Robbins Library.)

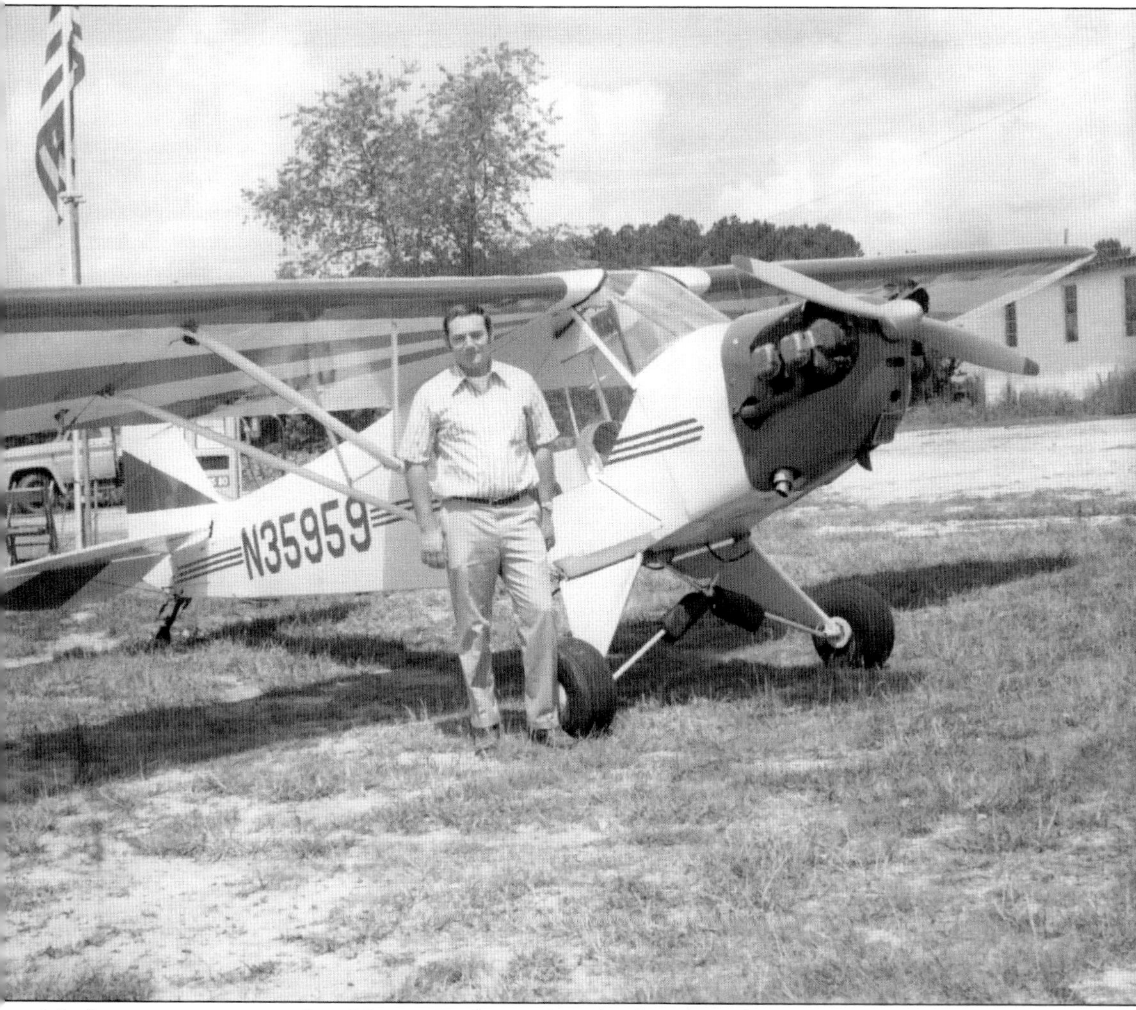

Moulton community resident Vernon Dickerson bought this clipped-wing cub in 1968 before he learned to fly. He was soon in the air thanks to his personal flight instructor, his uncle Joseph Kearney Ball Jr. Dickerson went on to a career as a crop duster from 1974 to 1984. He still flies out of Ball's Airport, where he maintains his family's legacy. (Courtesy of Vernon Dickerson.)

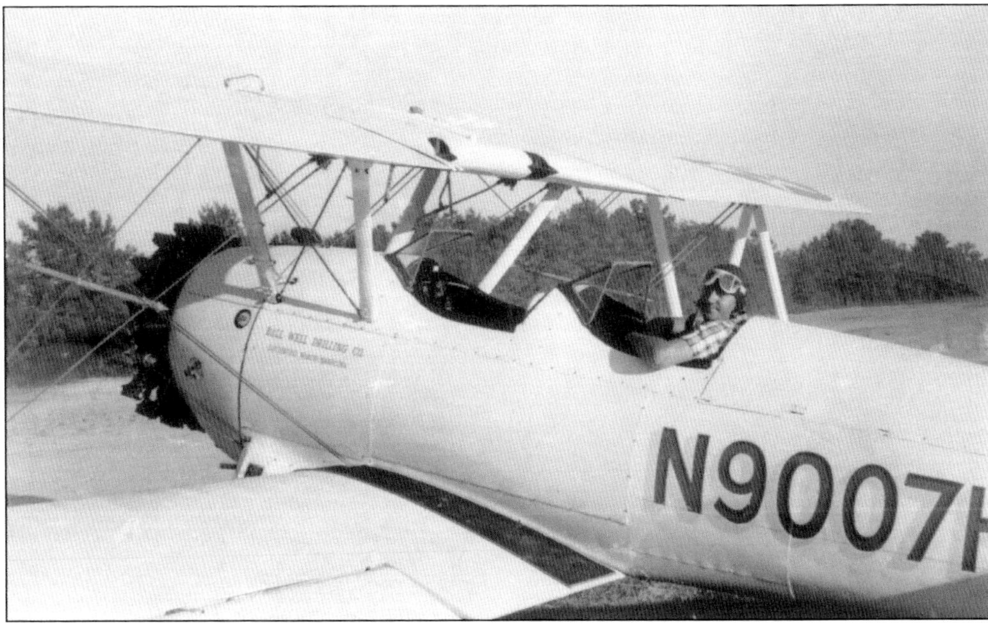

Above, the Stearman that belonged to Joe Ball Jr. (1924–1995) stops by the hanger at Ball's Airport, off Moulton Road in Louisburg. Ball was one of Franklin County's many storied pilots whose legendary exploits have continued to live on long after their final flights. Ball, along with pilots Floyd Griffin, Linwood Gupton, and James Cooper, worked as civilian instructors for Army pilots during the 1940s. Back home, Joe and brother Clyde Hillman Ball (1932–2013) worked as crop dusters from the field that would one day become Ball's Airport. Long after his passing, friends, family, and fellow pilots continue to meet every October for a fun day of flying at the annual Ball's Fly-In, celebrating his birthday. In the photograph below, Aubrey Nicole Taylor poses with Ball's plane. (Above, courtesy of Vernon Dickerson; below, author's collection.)

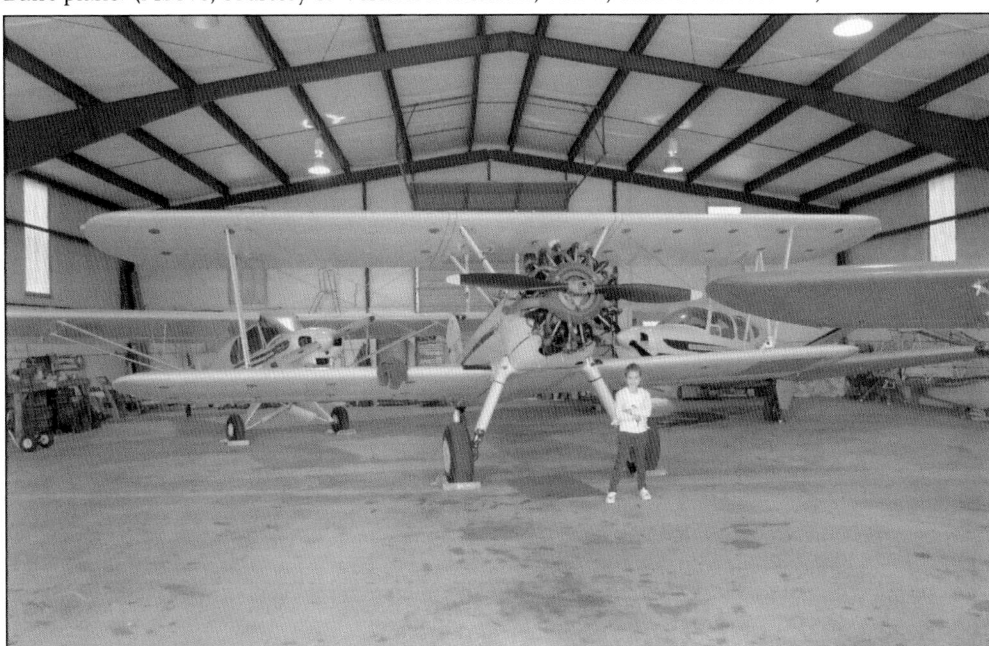

Five

Nurturing the Mind, Feeding the Soul

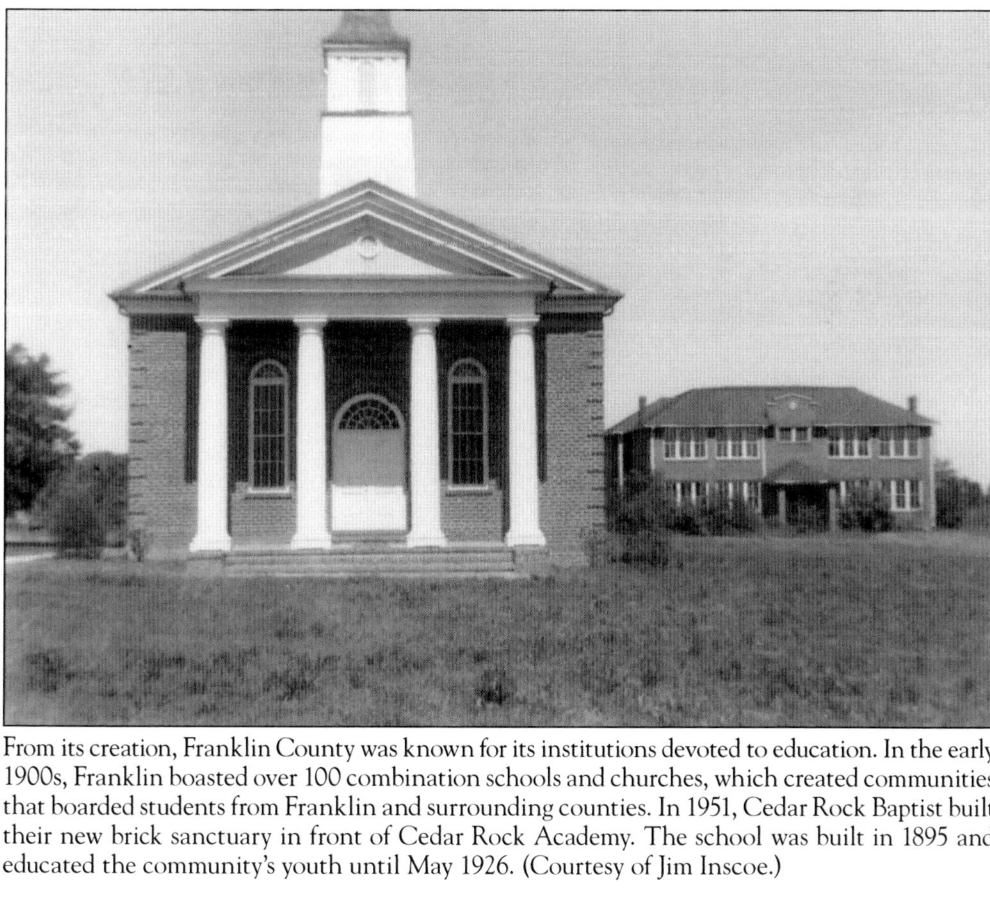

From its creation, Franklin County was known for its institutions devoted to education. In the early 1900s, Franklin boasted over 100 combination schools and churches, which created communities that boarded students from Franklin and surrounding counties. In 1951, Cedar Rock Baptist built their new brick sanctuary in front of Cedar Rock Academy. The school was built in 1895 and educated the community's youth until May 1926. (Courtesy of Jim Inscoe.)

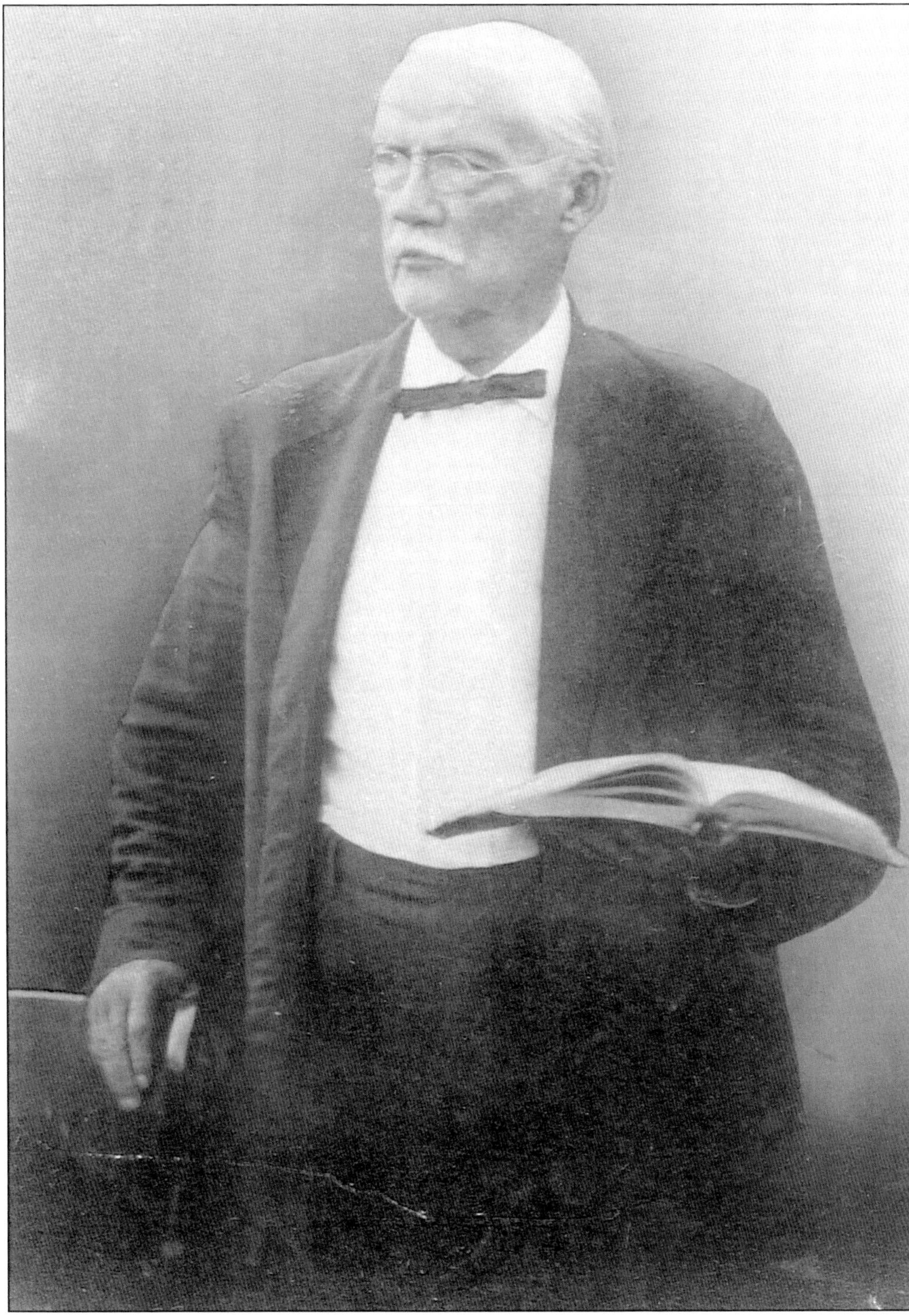

George M. Duke (1845–1918) was born in Warren County but spent most of his life serving the churches of Franklin. He preached at Cedar Rock, Maple Springs, Sandy Creek, and Poplar Springs and served as pastor at Maple Springs and Mount Zion for over 40 years each. Duke Memorial Baptist Church was named to honor Pastor Duke in 1924. (Courtesy of Karen Phelps Fuller.)

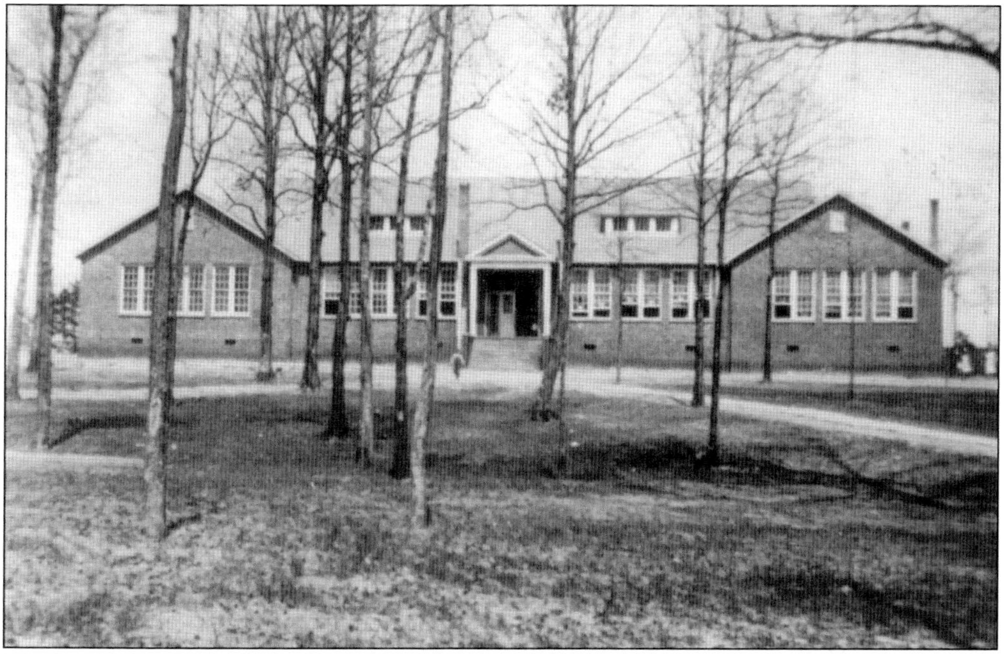

The Wood Academy was built in 1905 behind Wood Baptist Church, off Highway 561. In 1928, this brick building was added, featuring seven classrooms and a large auditorium. When attendance waned in 1946, students moved to Gold Sand High School, the school closed, and the building became part of Wood Baptist Church. (Courtesy of Sammy Beasley.)

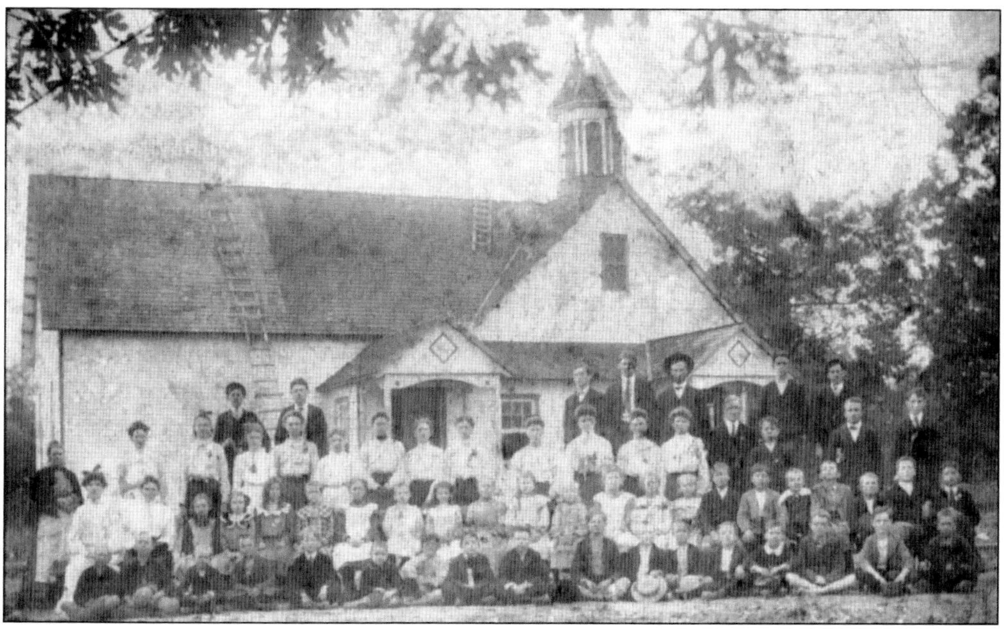

In this photograph, a large class of students and teachers pose in front of the Ingleside School around 1900. The only person who can be identified is Peter Stapleton Foster (1892–1950), seated third from the right, whose family owned Locust Grove Plantation, on Old Stage Road towards Warrenton. (Courtesy of Bill Harris.)

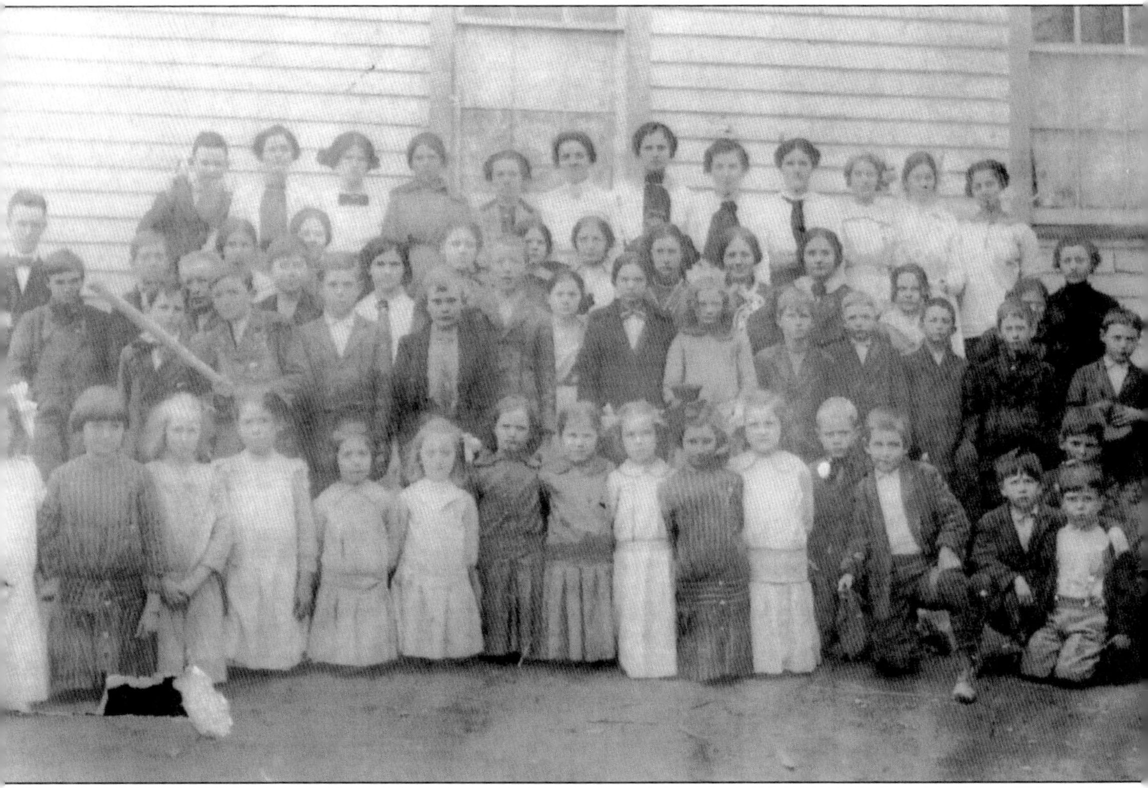

This 1912 photograph shows the Sandy Creek School, which was once located in front of the church. Many of the descendants of these students comprise the congregation of Sandy Creek Baptist Church today. Though the school burned, the church remains one of the oldest in the county. From left to right are (first row) Antha Joyner (Burnette), Violet Brewer (Mullen), Carlell Allen (Cannon), Beulah Nelms (Burnette), Alta West (Collier Radford), Eula Gupton (Joyner), Lena House (Burnette), Sarah Davis (Hamlet), Magnolia Burnette (Wiggs), Zena Brewer (Alford), Curtis Gupton (Lancaster), Clarence Gupton, Maurice Nelms, Reuben Allen, Marvin West, Thurston Brewer (behind West), and Graham Nelms (sucking his thumb); (second row) Caleb Allen, Victor Joyner, Tollie Brewer (holding large stick), Clinton Nelms, Brooks Parrish, Clyde Leonard, Lola Parrish (Allen), Maggie Allen (Osborne), Tempie Davis (Tensy Fuller), Bruce Harper, Eddie Evans, Henry Leonard, Kirby Gupton, and Ira Gupton; (third row) Howard Johnson, Otis Parrish, Gorman Leonard, Dewey Gupton, Minta Parrish (behind Dewey Gupton), Pattie Lou Gupton, Myrtle Gupton Clark, Annie Mae Gupton (Griffin), Lola Leonard (Stallings), Minnie Burnette (Gray), Ida Parrish (Ricks), Mittie Lou Parrish (Foster), Beatrice Aycock (Harper), Tempie Burnette (Hamlet) and Maggie Johnson; (fourth row) Forest Joyner, Monnie Gupton (Griffin), Mammie Gupton (Murphy), Blanche Davis (Pearce), Alma Parrish (Fuller), Pauline Pleasants (Duke), Lillie Gupton (West), Annie Gupton, Lizzie Gupton, Bertha Brewer (Mullen), Vallie Joyner (Dennis), and Linnie Nelms (Cheatham). (Courtesy of Gerald Leonard.)

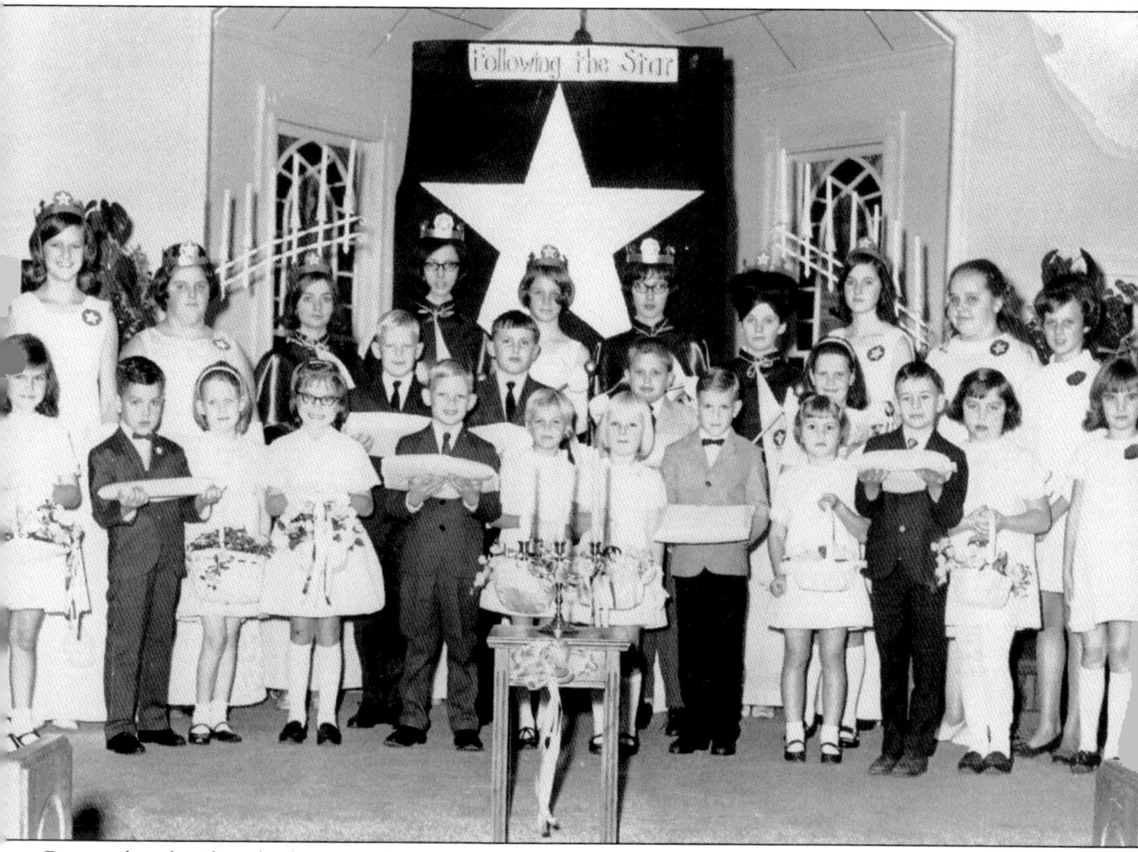

Pictured at the church altar in 1968, the Sandy Creek Church Girls in Action held a Recognition Service to award crowns, scepters, capes, or badges to those accomplishing varying levels of achievement in Mission in Action projects. From left to right are (first row) Deborah Gupton (Coley), Wayne Gupton, Karen Hunter, Brenda Aycock (Fuller), Alan Elam, Amy Burnette (Dickens), Georgette Foster (Baker), Carlton Burnette, Tammy Dickerson (Bennett), Stan Harper, Rachel Ann Ballinger, and Betsy Burnette (Hunt); (second row) Wesley Elam, Michael Jay Aycock, Greg Byrd, and Lisa Burnette (Baker); (third row) Becky Shearin (Allen), Lydia Murphy (Stallings), Gloria Bartholomew (Horton), Kathy Leonard (Gupton), Vicky Joyner, Beth Dickerson (Gordon), Becky Burnette (Leonard), Skeet Shearin (Shearin), Sarah Lynn (Ballinger), and Cecilia Burnette (Nash Boone). (Courtesy of the Raymond and Barbara Burnette collection.)

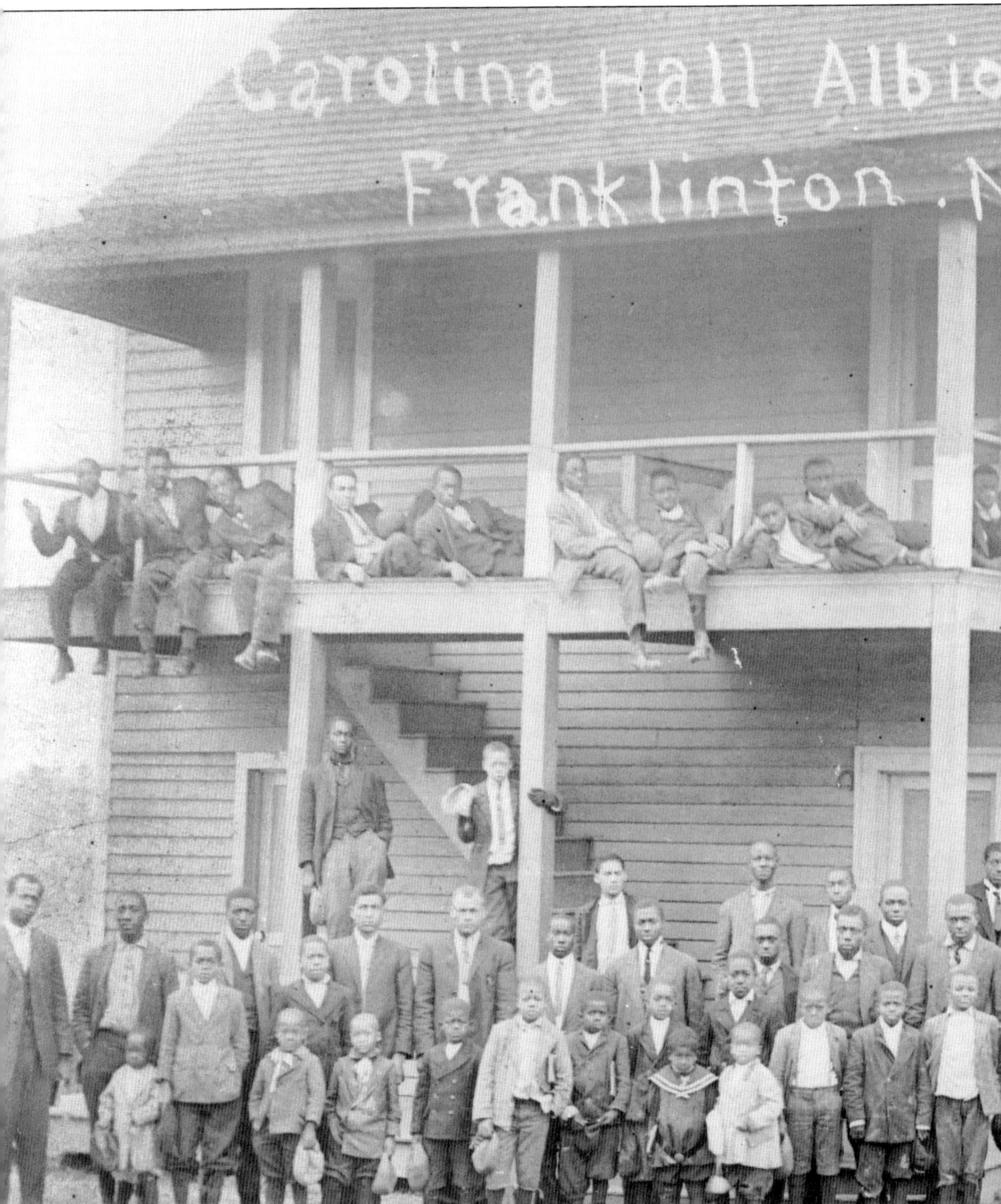

Located on East College Street in Franklinton, Albion Academy was once known to be one of the best black high schools in the state. Founded in 1879 by Dr. Moses Aaron Hopkins (1846–1886) and sponsored by the Northern Presbyterian Church, Albion grew from a two-acre campus to include 10 buildings on 60 acres before closing its doors in 1933. Under the direction of principal Dr. John Anthony Savage (1857–1933), many of Albion's more than 500 students went on to

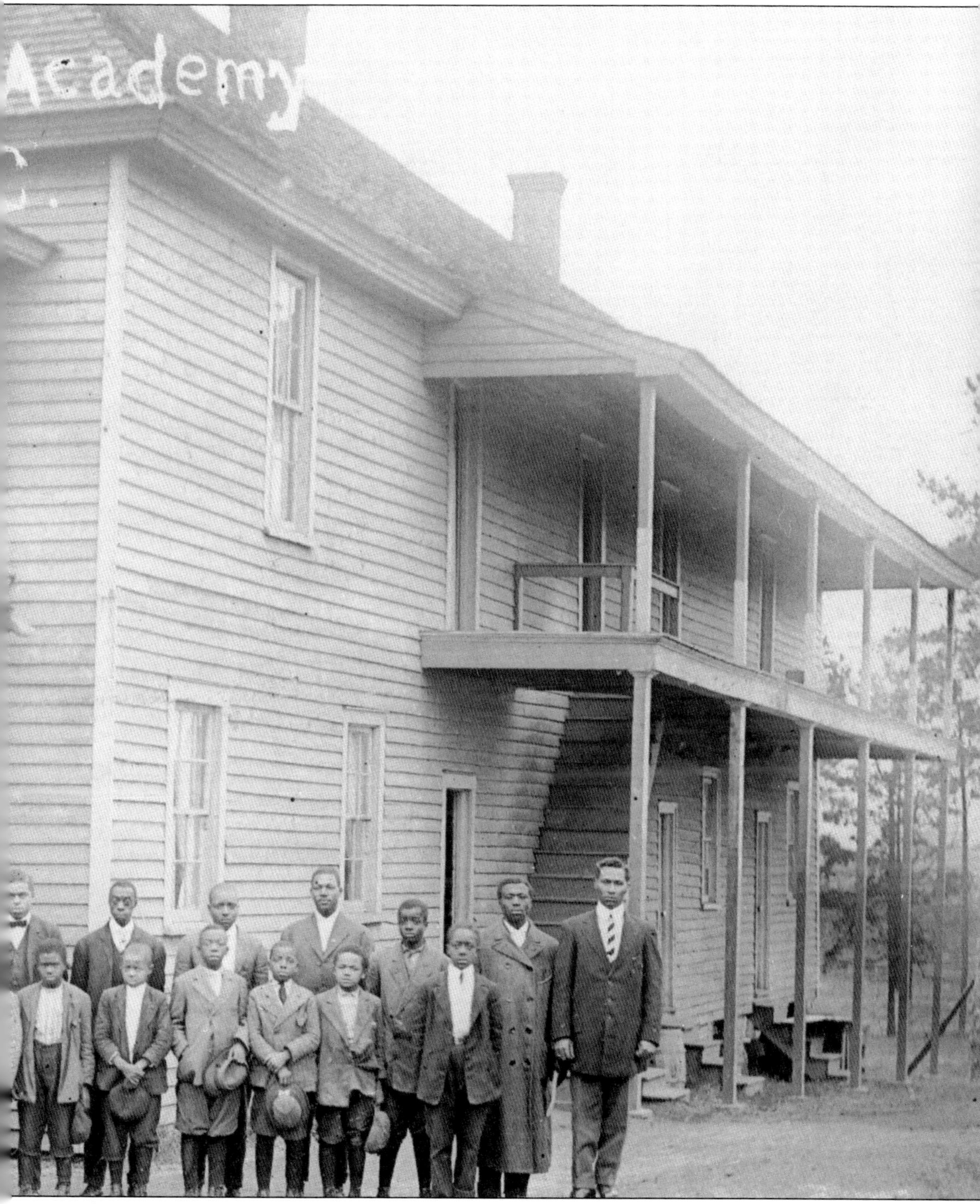

attend institutes of higher education and achieve degrees in medicine, theology, and education. Fire destroyed Albion Hall in 1925, and the only signs of the school that still remain are the stone pillars marking the entrance at College and Hawkins Street, where the Academy Village apartments now stand. (Courtesy of the State Archives of North Carolina.)

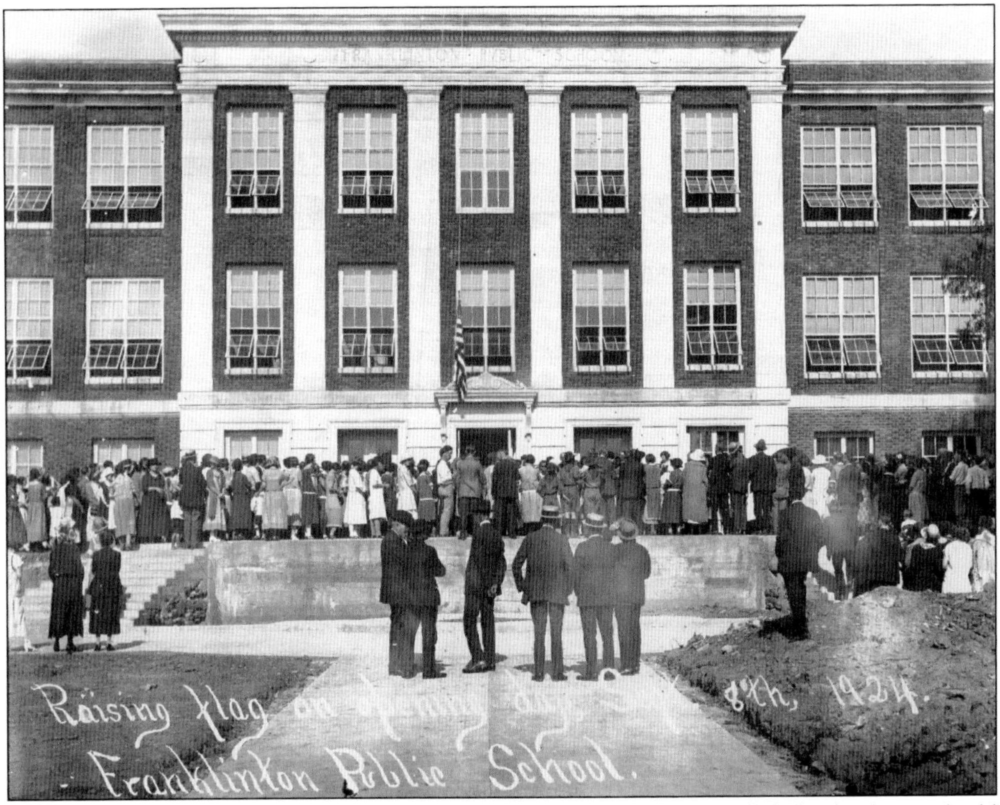

Samuel C. Vann (1852–1924), owner of the Sterling Cotton Mill, provided the funding to build the Franklinton Public School, dedicated here in September 1924. When laying the cornerstone in May 1923, Vann also provided some personal items, including his wife's Bible and a photograph, to be discovered by future generations. Sadly, Vann passed away on November 11, 1924, just two months after its opening. (Courtesy of Franklinton Town Hall.)

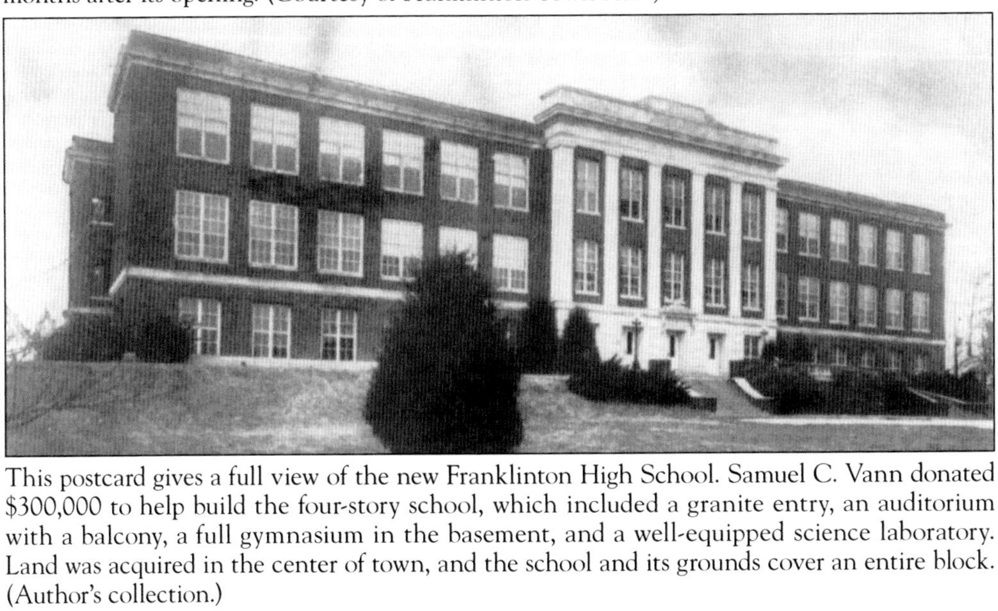

This postcard gives a full view of the new Franklinton High School. Samuel C. Vann donated $300,000 to help build the four-story school, which included a granite entry, an auditorium with a balcony, a full gymnasium in the basement, and a well-equipped science laboratory. Land was acquired in the center of town, and the school and its grounds cover an entire block. (Author's collection.)

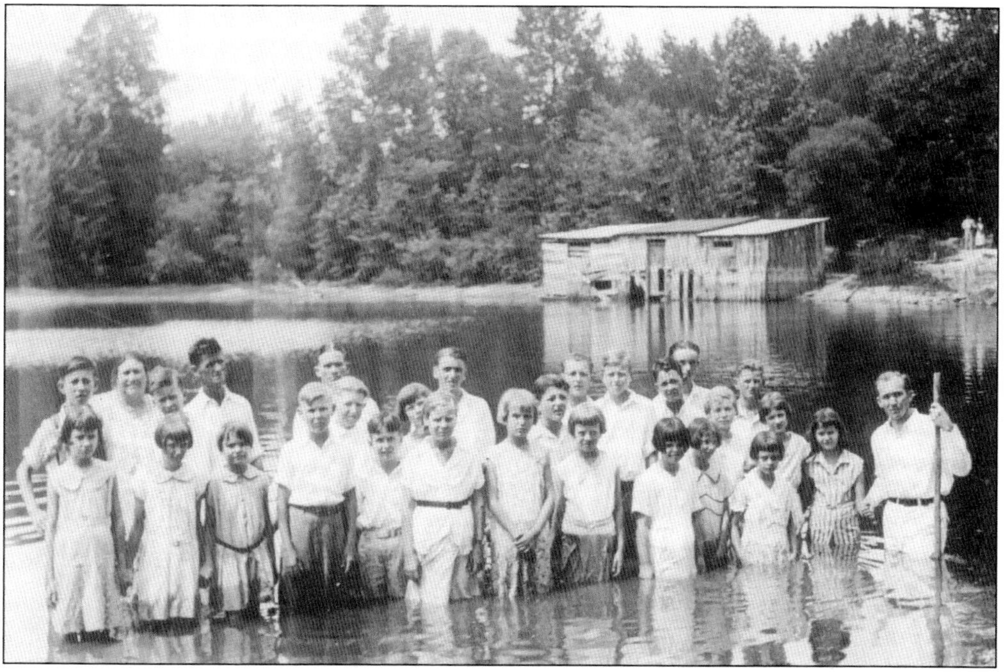

Members of Harris Chapel Church pose for the camera before getting baptized at Moore's Pond, on Moore's Pond Road in Youngsville. Mattie Gay Rogers Layton (1915–1994) is in the first row, second from left, and appears to be about 10 years old, dating the photograph to around 1925. Others identified are, in no particular order, Jean Harris Winn, Furney Carter, and Charles Barrett (holding the stick). (Courtesy of Cathy Loy.)

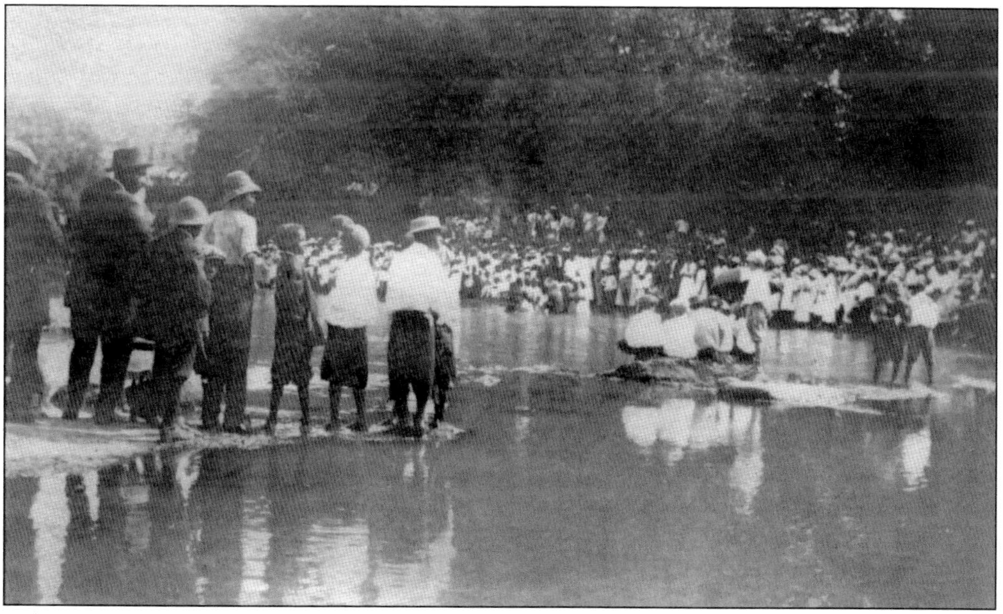

A large and diverse group line the Tar River in Louisburg to witness a baptism. River baptisms were popular in the late 1800s and early 1900s in the South. These public displays of faith drew large crowds and were often used to promote mass revivals and encourage church attendance. (Courtesy of Sammy Beasley.)

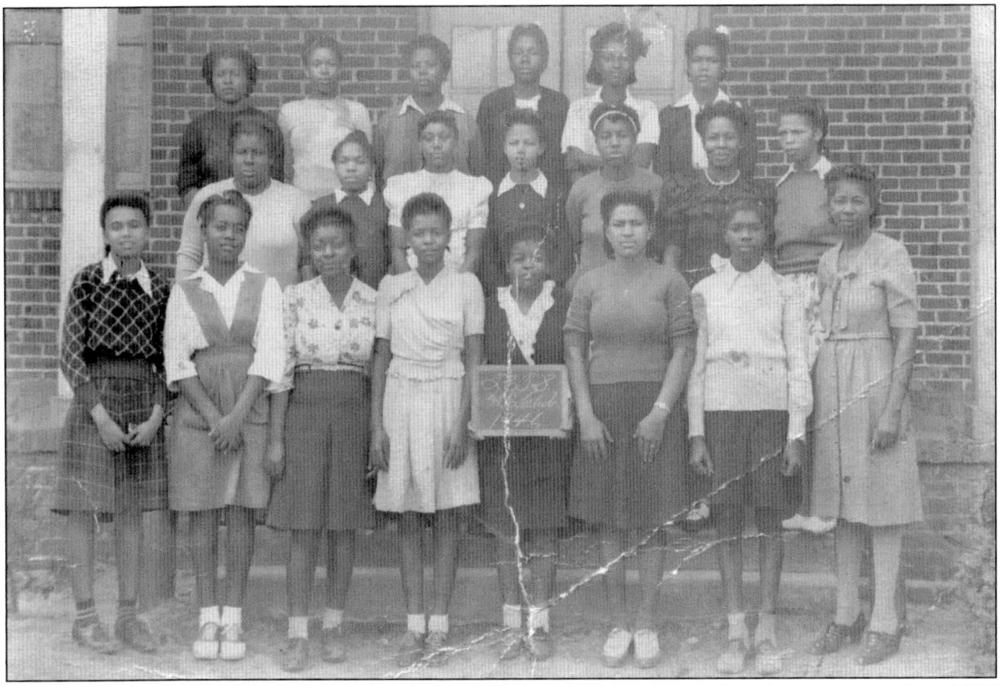

The Franklin County Training School, on Louisburg's West River Road, was opened in 1928 with support from Sears, Roebuck & Co.'s Rosenwald Fund. Through the efforts of Frank Fogg (1870–1953) and John Sills, the board of education worked together with the African American community to fund the expansion of the existing school to create the new seven-classroom school. Pictured here is the 1946 H.E. Club. (Courtesy of Annie Brodie Harris.)

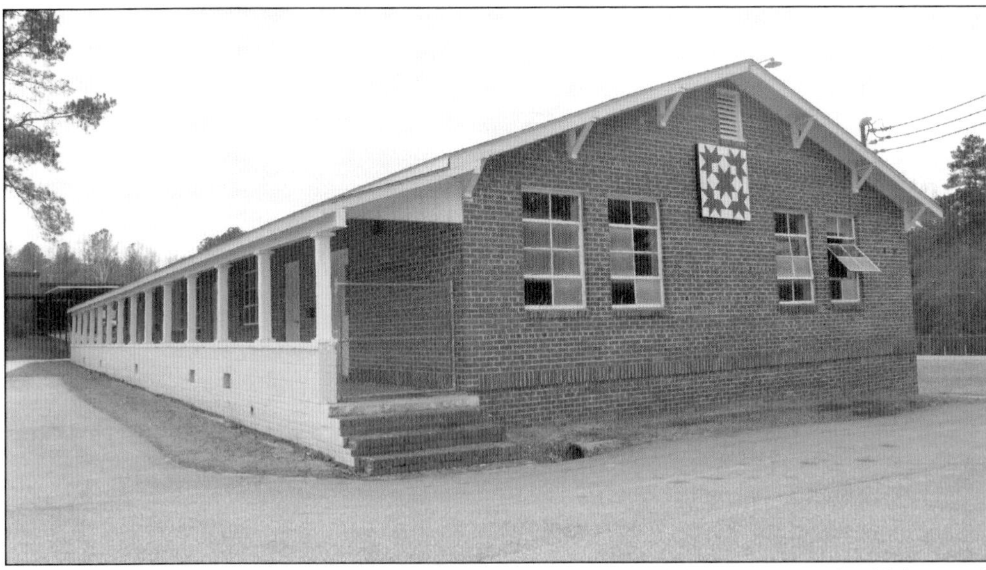

African Americans who fought during World War II volunteered their services to build the Porch Building at the Franklin County Training School in 1951. Their efforts provided the school with an additional five classrooms and gave the veterans the needed construction experience necessary to reenter the workforce. The school was renamed Riverside Union School in 1959, and efforts are currently under way to preserve the historic building. (Author's collection.)

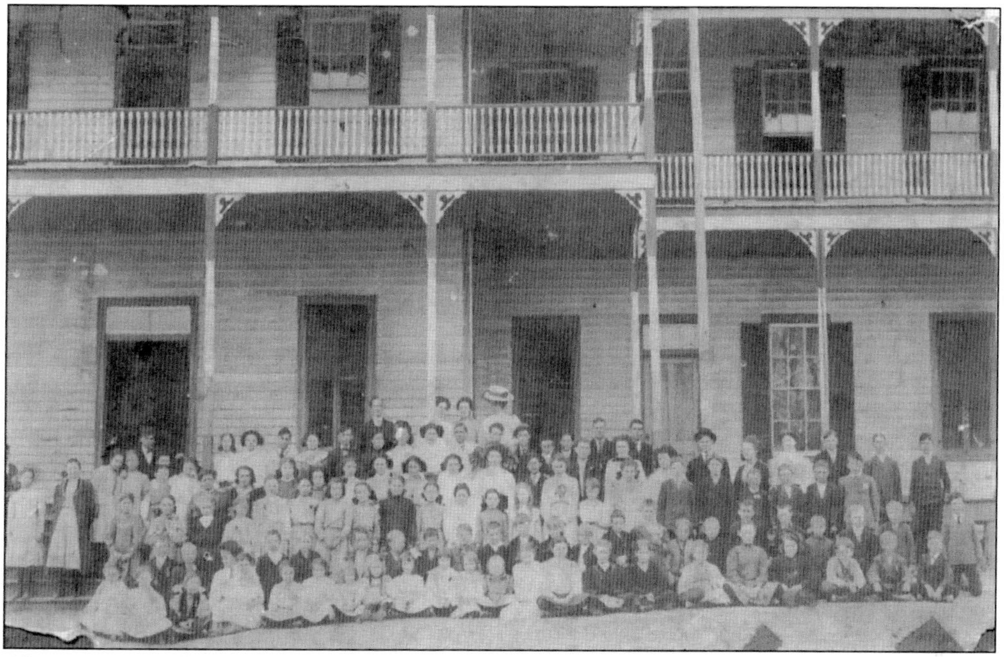

Above, Youngsville area students have gathered for a class photograph at the Youngsville Graded School in 1910. The postcard below shows the 1934 and 1935 classes of the Youngsville School, on South College Street. The school was built in 1905 and boasted an enrollment of 100 students. The classrooms each had a potbelly stove; on one morning in 1916, the entire town turned out to form a bucket brigade, saving the building from fire. The school closed in 1925 after a new school was built to ease overcrowding. The Youngsville School housed elementary and high school students for 53 years until the county consolidated its school system in 1978, and the students were then bused to Bunn. The building was eventually demolished. (Above, courtesy of Youngsville Town Hall; below, courtesy of Tommy Dement.)

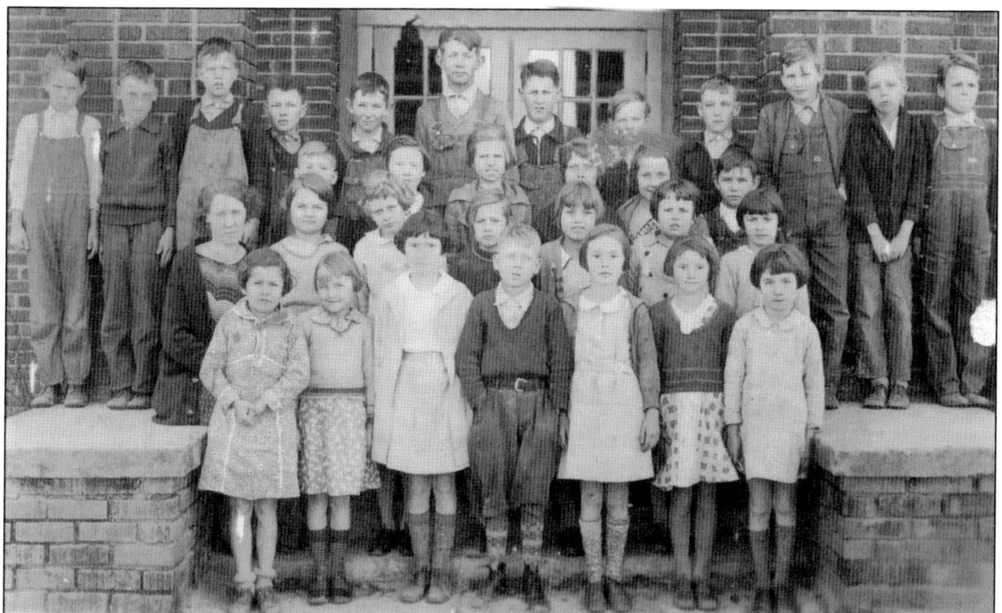

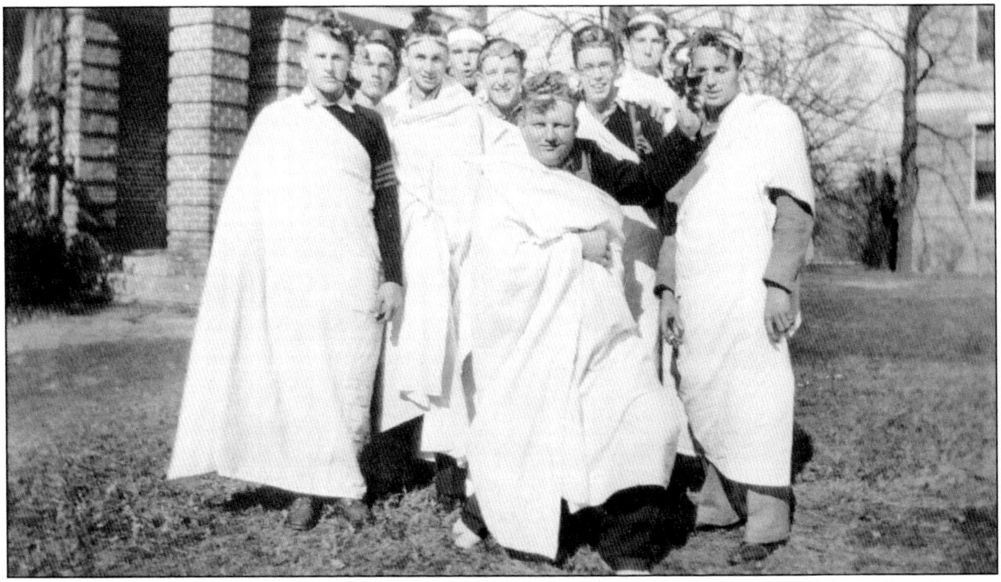

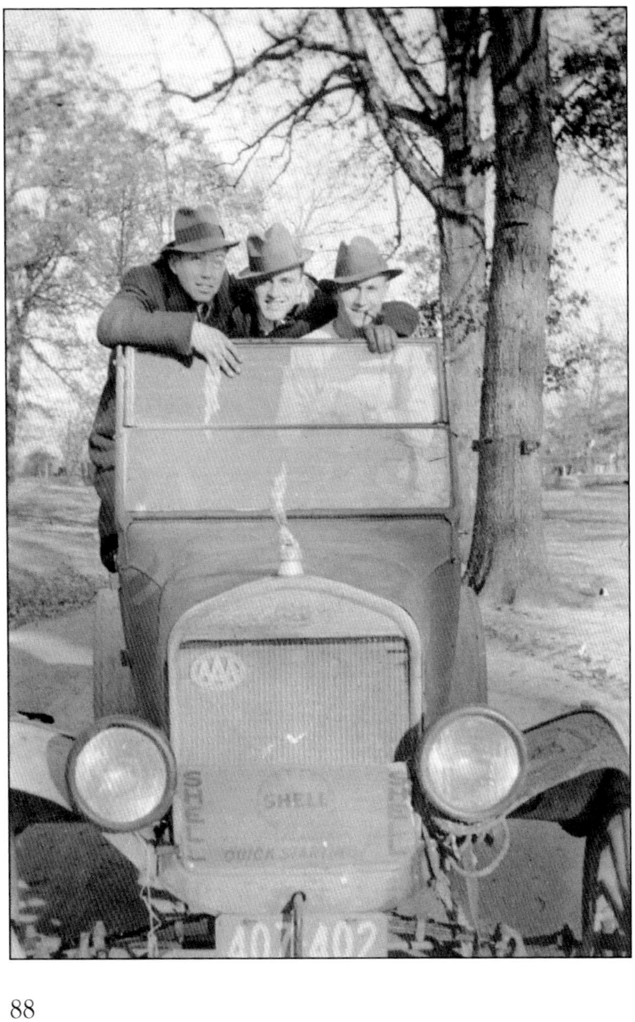

These two photographs of unidentified young men attending Louisburg College in 1934–1935 were part of the John B. Wemyss Jr. Collection at the State Archives of North Carolina. In the 1933 annual, *The Oak*, fraternities listed were Kappa Epsilon Alpha and Lambda Tau Zeta. The togas—the traditional garb of the "frat boy"—being worn by the young men in the photograph above suggest that they may have been members of one of the two organizations. The Franklin Male Academy held its first classes on January 1, 1805, and later combined with the Louisburg Female Academy to form Louisburg College. The private, Methodist, two-year institution is the heart of Louisburg today, with an enrollment of 700 students. (Both, courtesy of the State Archives of North Carolina.)

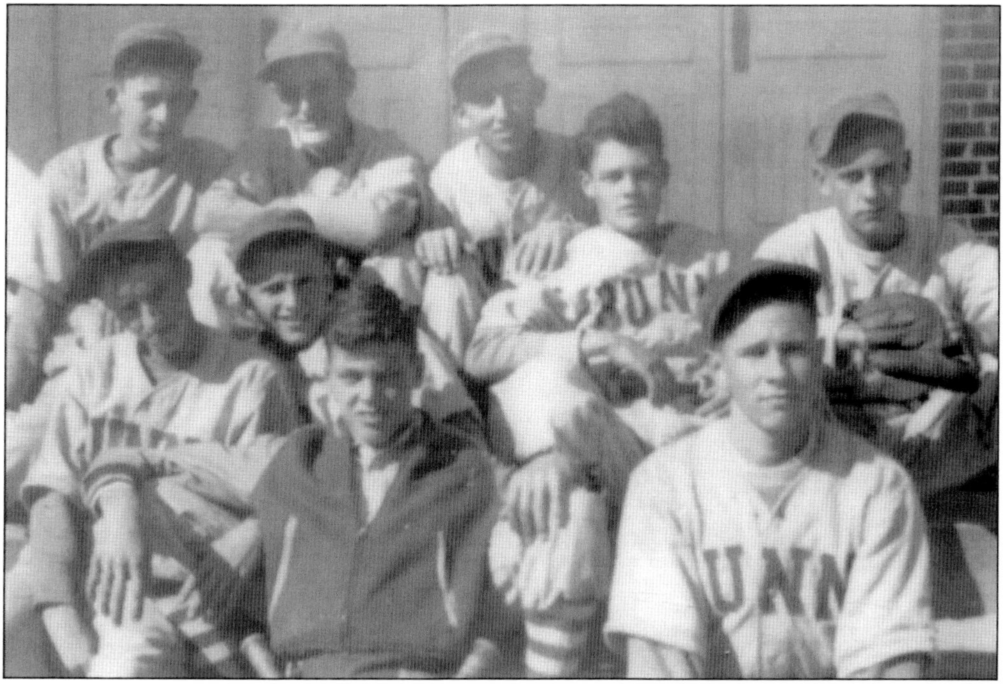

These photographs, showing the Bunn High School baseball and softball teams, were labeled "Franklin County 1941–1942 Champions." Baseball and softball have been among the extracurricular sports at all of Franklin County's schools. Other competitive sports included football, basketball, and track. Competition among the sports teams within the Franklin County school system has always motivated the young athletes to strive to win bragging rights. Bunn High School and Louisburg High School have one of the most heated rivalries; in 2013, they were voted in a *USA Today* online poll to have the "Best Rivalry in the Nation," and each school was awarded a $5,000 prize. (Both, courtesy of Sarah J. Pace.)

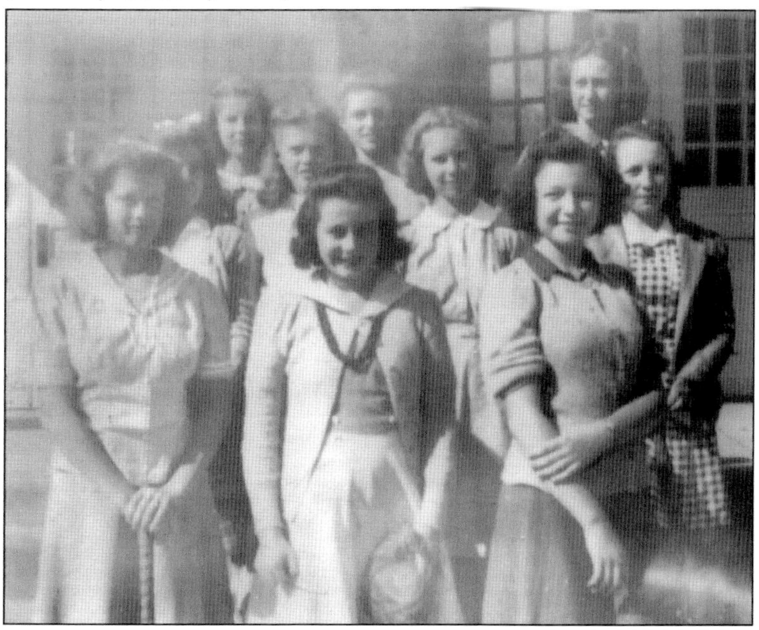

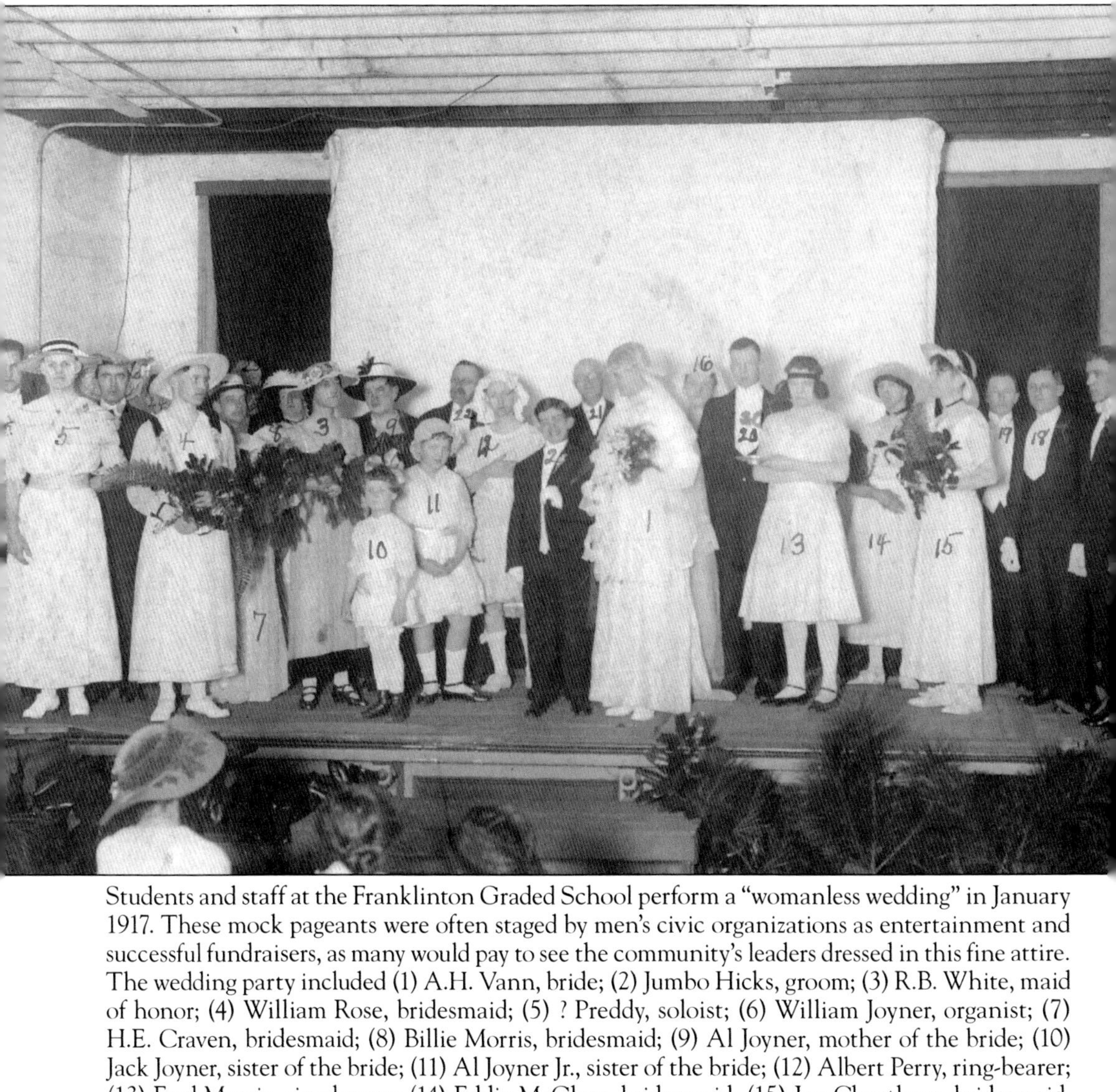

Students and staff at the Franklinton Graded School perform a "womanless wedding" in January 1917. These mock pageants were often staged by men's civic organizations as entertainment and successful fundraisers, as many would pay to see the community's leaders dressed in this fine attire. The wedding party included (1) A.H. Vann, bride; (2) Jumbo Hicks, groom; (3) R.B. White, maid of honor; (4) William Rose, bridesmaid; (5) ? Preddy, soloist; (6) William Joyner, organist; (7) H.E. Craven, bridesmaid; (8) Billie Morris, bridesmaid; (9) Al Joyner, mother of the bride; (10) Jack Joyner, sister of the bride; (11) Al Joyner Jr., sister of the bride; (12) Albert Perry, ring-bearer; (13) Fred Morris, ring-bearer; (14) Eddie McGhee, bridesmaid; (15) Joe Cheatham, bridesmaid; (16) Edwin Rose, flower girl; (17) MacDonald Dixon, groomsman; (18) Jim Purnell, groomsman; (19) Bob Rose, groomsmen; (20) John Henry Harris, groomsmen; (21) Dr. Henderson, preacher; (22) B.W. Ballard, father of the bride; (23) Walter Cooke, groomsmen; (24) unidentified; (25) Armistead Henderson, father of the groom; and (26) Daniel ?, mother of the groom. (Courtesy of Franklinton Town Hall.)

Six

Earning Time Off, Taking a Break

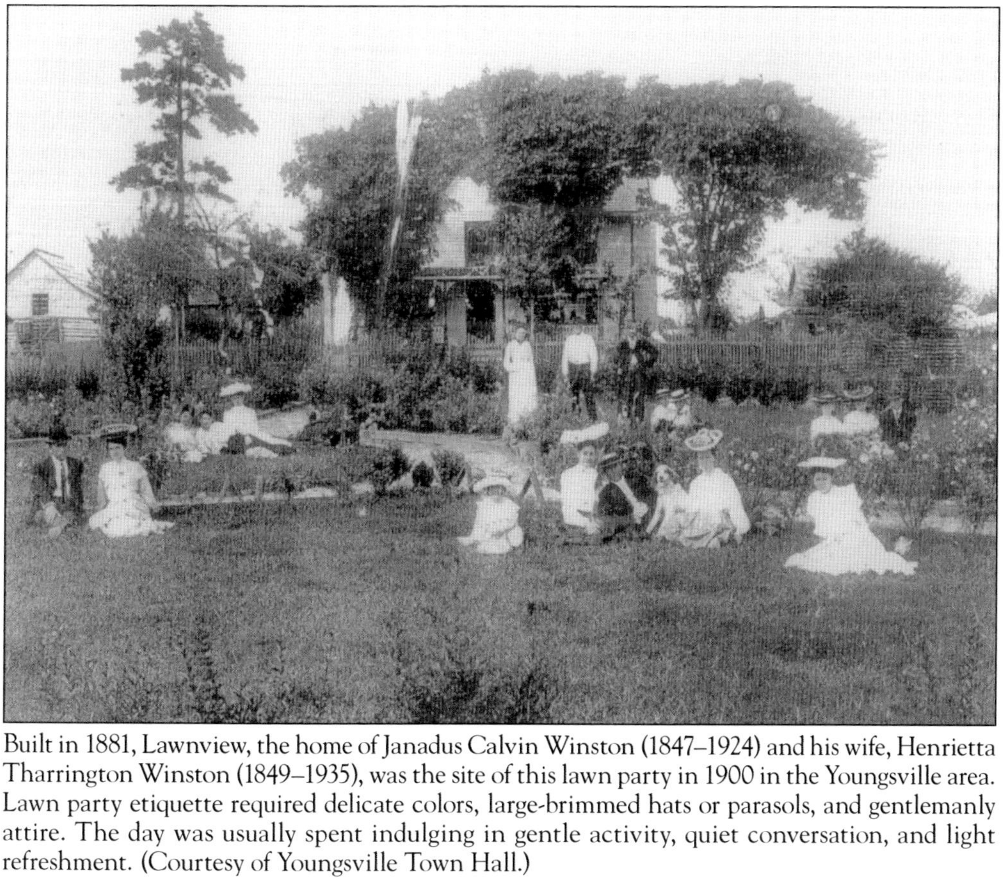

Built in 1881, Lawnview, the home of Janadus Calvin Winston (1847–1924) and his wife, Henrietta Tharrington Winston (1849–1935), was the site of this lawn party in 1900 in the Youngsville area. Lawn party etiquette required delicate colors, large-brimmed hats or parasols, and gentlemanly attire. The day was usually spent indulging in gentle activity, quiet conversation, and light refreshment. (Courtesy of Youngsville Town Hall.)

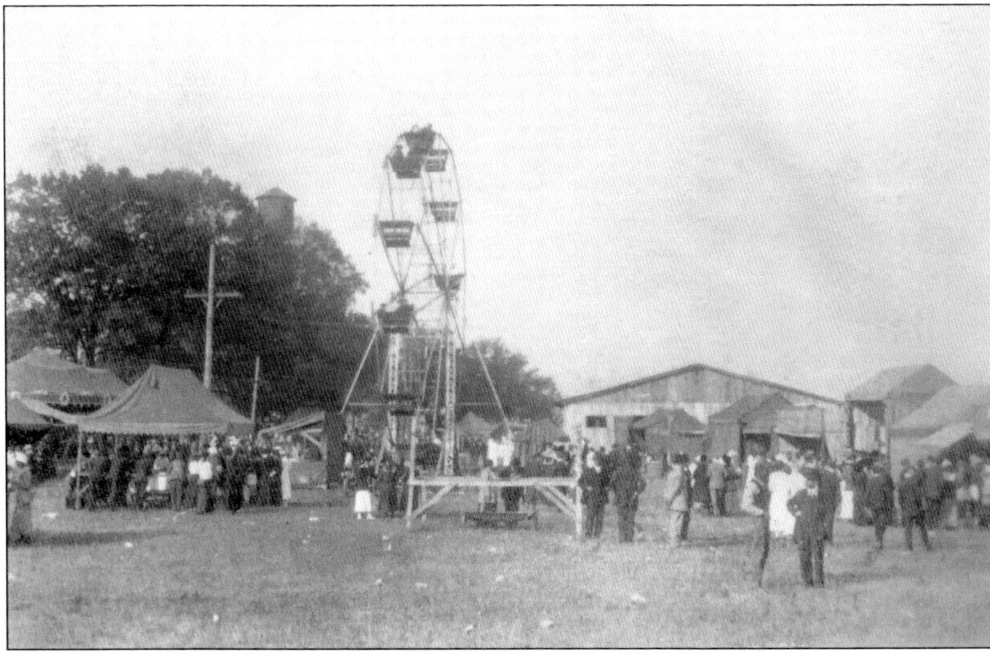

In the early 1900s, the Franklin County Fairgrounds were located on what is now Bickett Boulevard between Noble and Davis Streets. Cedar Street, which runs behind Louisburg College's auditorium, bordered the rear of the grounds. Peaking above the trees in the background of this photograph is the top point of the town's water standpipe, which was built in 1905. The fairgrounds had several buildings to house exhibits and traveling shows. From atop the Ferris wheel, there was most likely a view of the college grounds, the length of the river, the courthouse bell tower, and much of the town. (Courtesy of Sammy Beasley.)

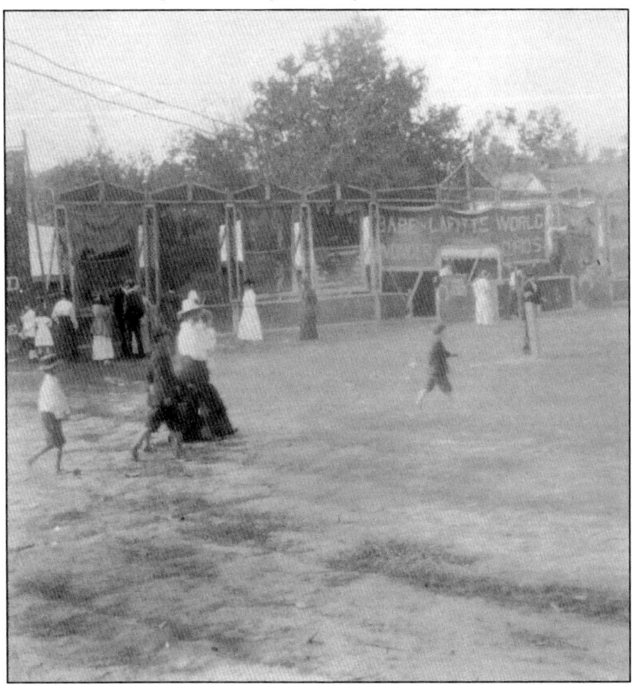

The midway marquee in this photograph promises that "wonders and curios" can be seen inside the sideshow. An advertisement in the *Franklin Times* in September 1911 announced a show featuring "Racing camels, a somersaulting elephant, the Hippobagus Equinnes, the Millers and the world's greatest equestrian artists, Every Act With The Show is a Feature Act, Nothing Old." It also offered a street parade "Grander than King's Splendor." A testament to the civility of the day, the last line of the advertisement insisted that there would be "Positively no Gambling or Profane Language" allowed on the fairgrounds. (Courtesy of Sammy Beasley.)

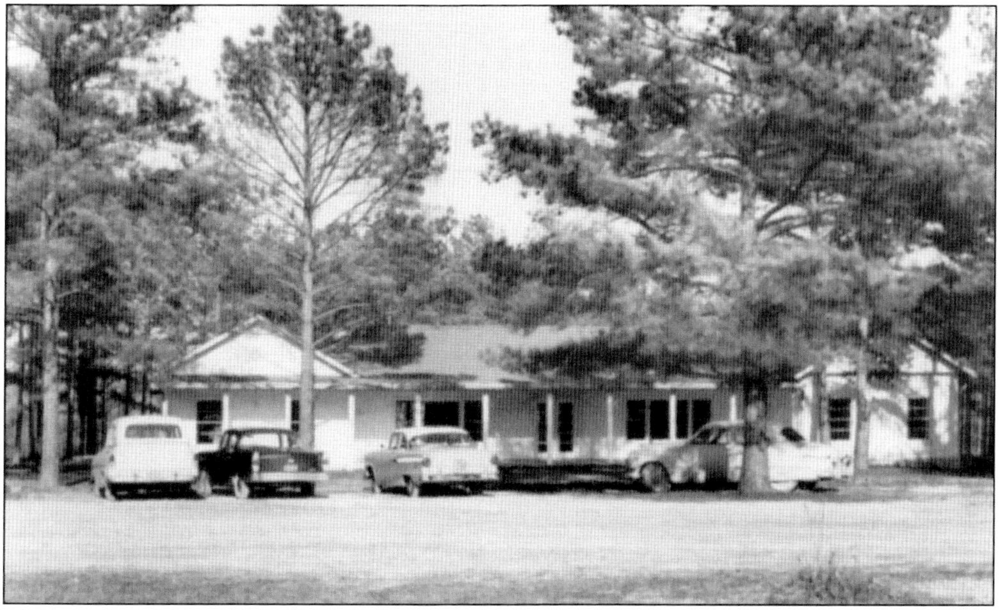

The popularity of golf in the mid-1920s prompted Dr. Harry H. Johnson to form a group of like-minded players to start Green Hill Golf Club. In 1929, the group purchased 70 acres on the outskirts of Louisburg, and one of their first events was a demonstration tournament as part of the county's 1929 sesquicentennial celebration. (Courtesy of Ted Gupton.)

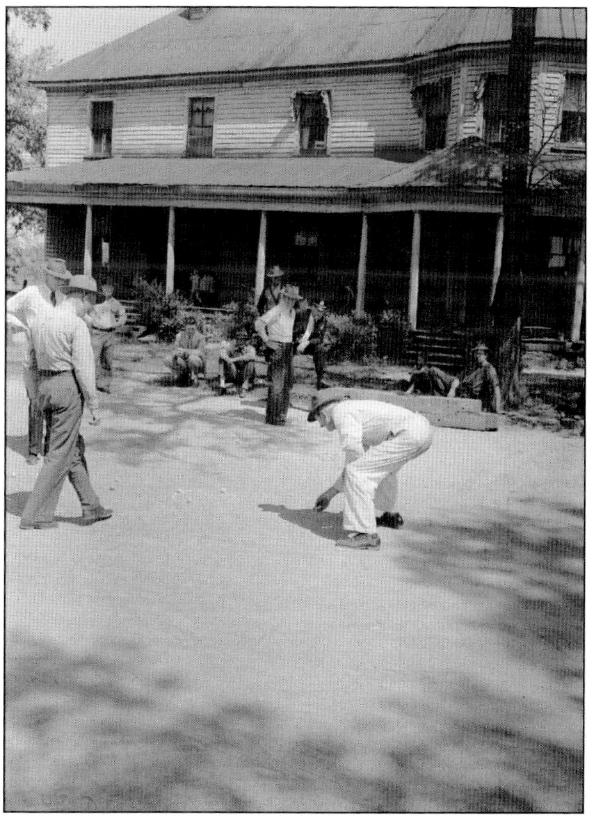

The marble game that went on in front of the Franklinton Hotel was played by grown men with billiard ball–size marbles. Most every day, teams of men could be found knocking their opponents marbles from a ring drawn in the dust. At times, the game became highly competitive, and it gained even more notoriety when the *Saturday Evening Post* ran an article about the game in 1946. In his book *Franklin County 1779–1979*, T.H. Pearce lists some of those known to have participated in the game, including early players B.W. Ballard, F.J. Whitfield, W.A. Whitfield, G.L. Whitfield, Jesse Winston, M.L. Harper, Tommy Joyner, Babe May, and the Reverend C.L. Powell and Wes Morton, Joe Pendleton, Charlie Evans, Ressie Suitt, C.F. Tillotson, and Joe Hight in the mid-1940s. None among these names was listed as having the bragging rights of being champion. (Courtesy of the State Archives of North Carolina.)

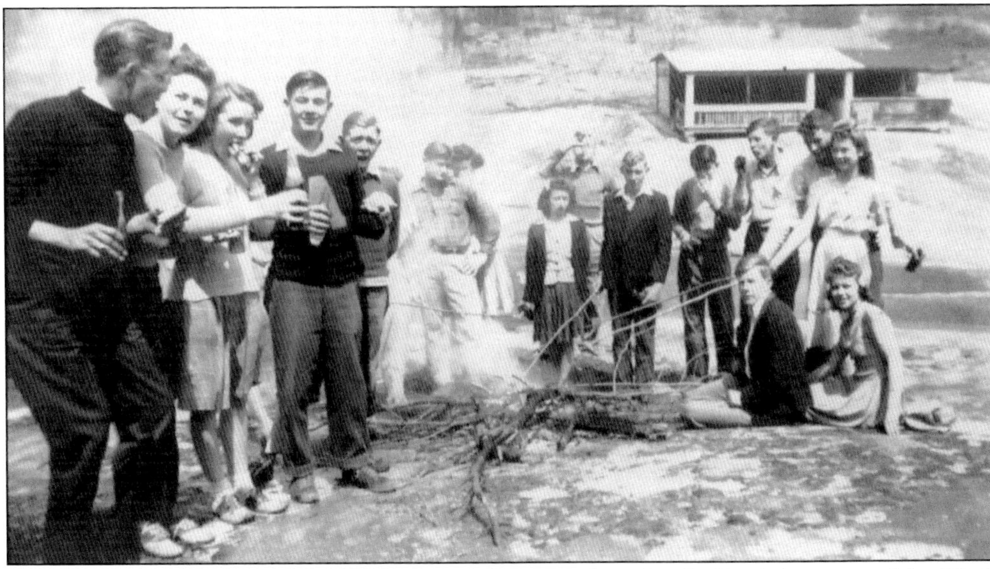

Teens gather for an outdoor cookout at a popular spot along Sandy Creek known as "the Wash Out." Note the letter sweater, saddle shoes, rolled sleeves and cuffs, and bottled sodas that represented the youth of the 1950s. Sandy Creek runs from Highway 401 to Flat Rock Creek in the northern section of the county and has been the favorite hangout for generations of youth. (Courtesy of Cindy Hunt Carroll.)

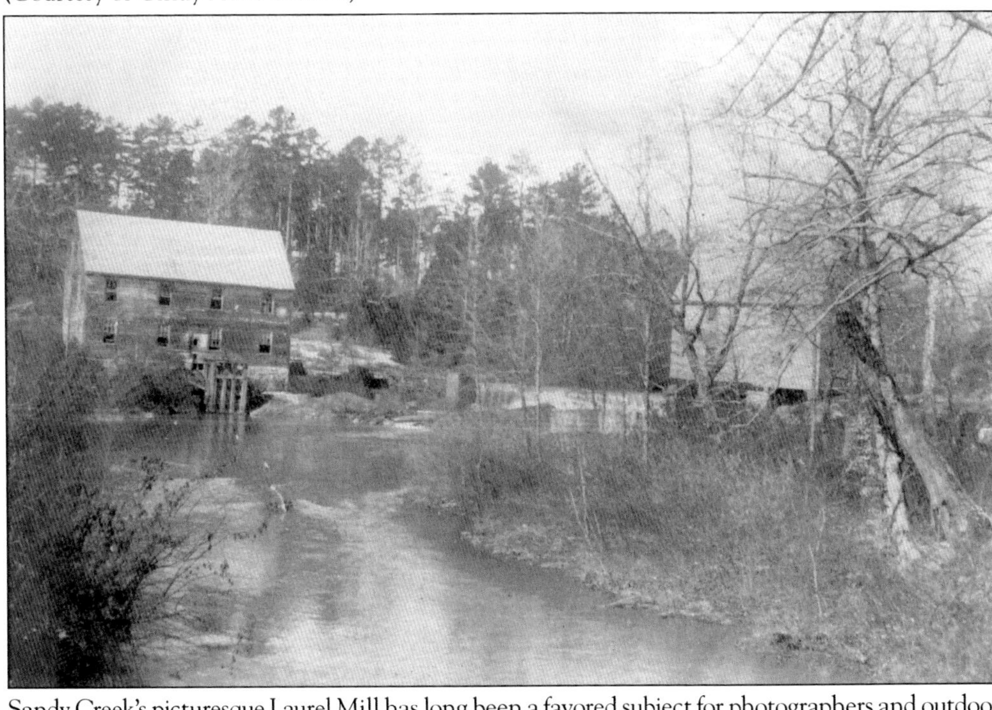

Sandy Creek's picturesque Laurel Mill has long been a favored subject for photographers and outdoor weddings. Its sloping, flat rocks and low dam offer sunbathers and fishermen a refreshing respite on a hot day. Locals may not remember the building to the left in this early-1900s photograph, but the gristmill on the right still stands and is listed in the National Register of Historic Places. (Courtesy of Sammy Beasley.)

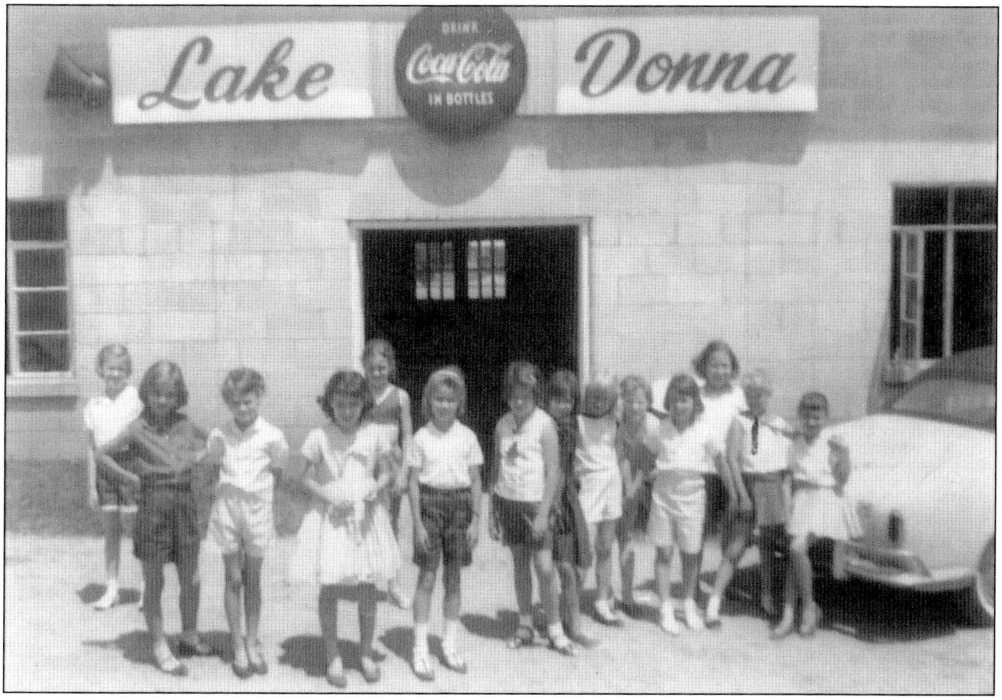

Mrs. Moss's third-grade class chose Lake Donna for their class picnic, where they are seen here. Lake Donna was built by Harry Privette and named for his daughter. The recreation area had two concrete pools with sandy bottoms and a clubhouse with a jukebox and a dance floor. The lake no longer exists, but the jukebox plays on at Woodlief's store on Main Street in Youngsville. (Courtesy of Youngsville Town Hall.)

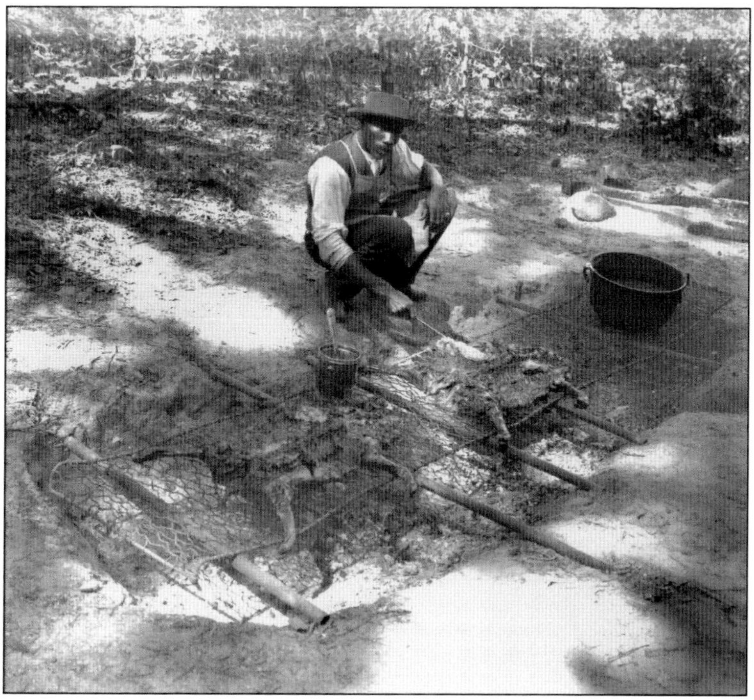

True pit-cooked barbecue is a Southern tradition, but few cooks today prepare it this literally. This unidentified man is preparing his dinner using a grate over a pit of hot coals. Today, an aboveground barrel cut in half to make a "pig cooker" is the preferred method. Either way, the result is a mouth-watering meal. (Courtesy of the State Archives of North Carolina.)

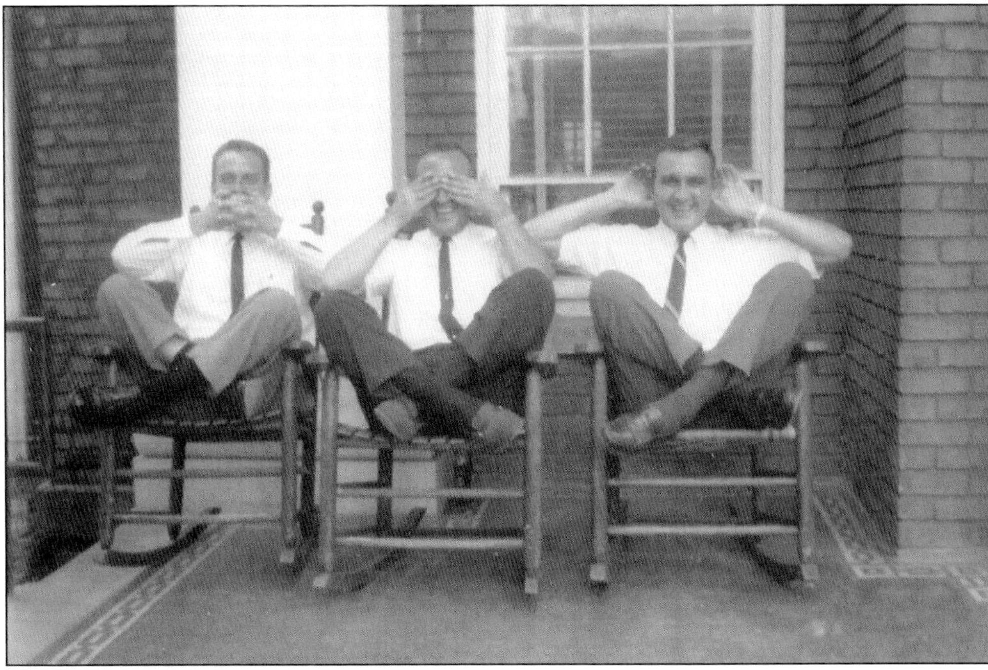

In October 1964, the Inscoe brothers of the Cedar Rock community take a day off to enjoy time on the porch and take an amusing photograph. From left to right, Grady C. Inscoe, Phillip G. Inscoe, and Jim T. Inscoe mimic the classic three wise monkeys pose of "speak no evil, see no evil, hear no evil." (Courtesy of Grady C. Inscoe.)

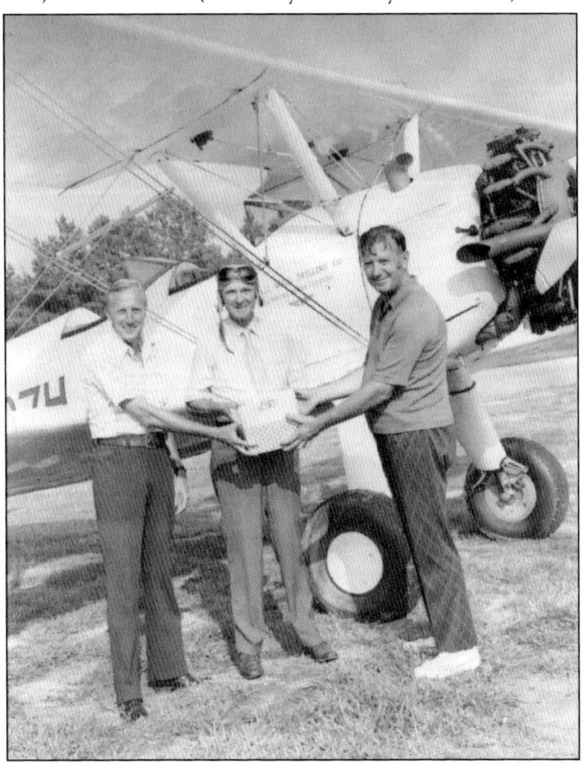

Aviation enthusiast Raymond Earl Burnette (1929–2007), Floyd Griffin (1908–2001), and Joe K. Ball Jr. (1924–1995) help Griffin celebrate his 65th birthday on July 2, 1973. Franklin County's past is rich with backyard runways and barnstorming aviators from the beginnings of aviation. Griffin and Ball worked in the 1940s as civilian instructors for Army pilots, and Burnette was responsible for bringing sport skydiving to the county. (Courtesy of Vernon Dickerson.)

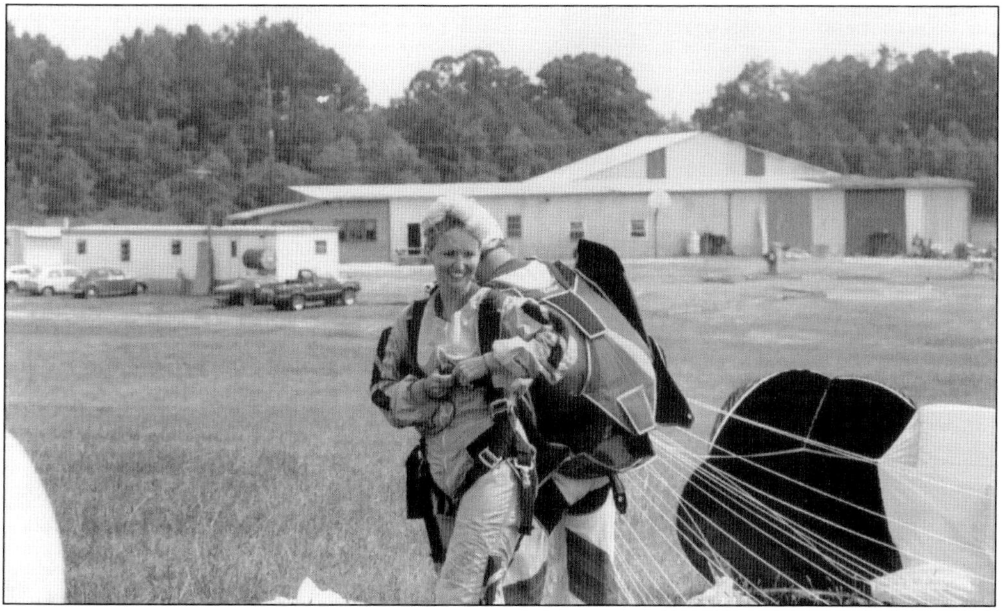

Student skydiver Diane Taylor Torrent smiles after landing her first jump in July 1987. Paul and Nancy Fayard opened Franklin County Sport Parachute Center on Highway 56 West in 1973. Training novice sport parachutists, Fayard's "dropzone" attracted weekend enthusiasts and curious spectators for 35 years. The hangar and offices in the background burned in 1998, and Fayard rebuilt them before retiring from skydiving in 2008. (Author's collection.)

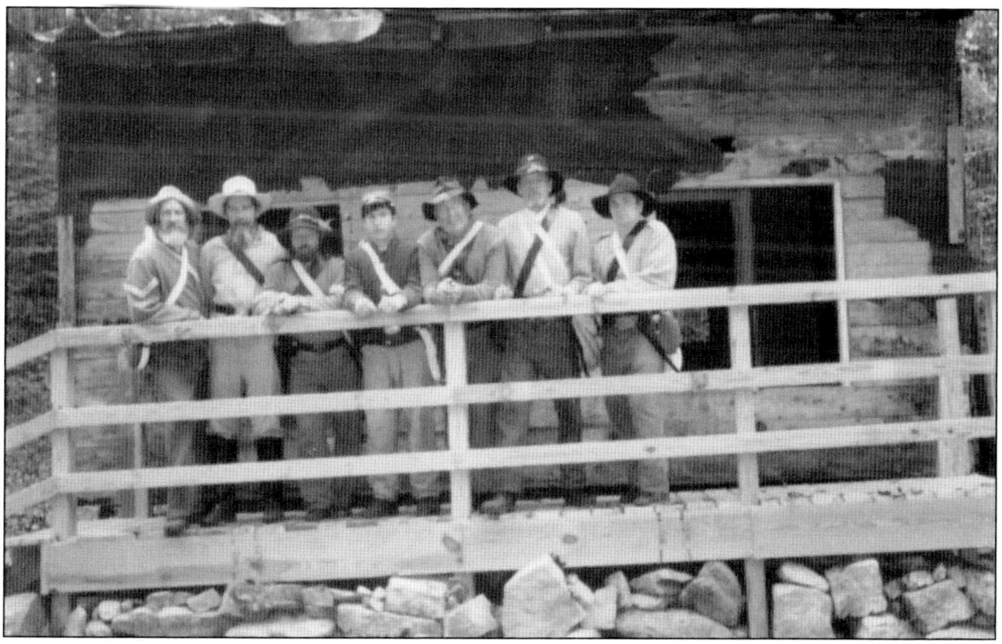

Members of the Franklin Rifles participated in the Annual Living History Reenactment at Gen. J.E.B. "Jeb" Stuart's birthplace in Ararat, Virginia, in 2005. Participants at these events dress in authentic uniform and meet on the battlefield and in encampments to relive the experiences of their ancestors while helping to educate today's youth about the struggles faced during war. (Courtesy of Tommy Dement.)

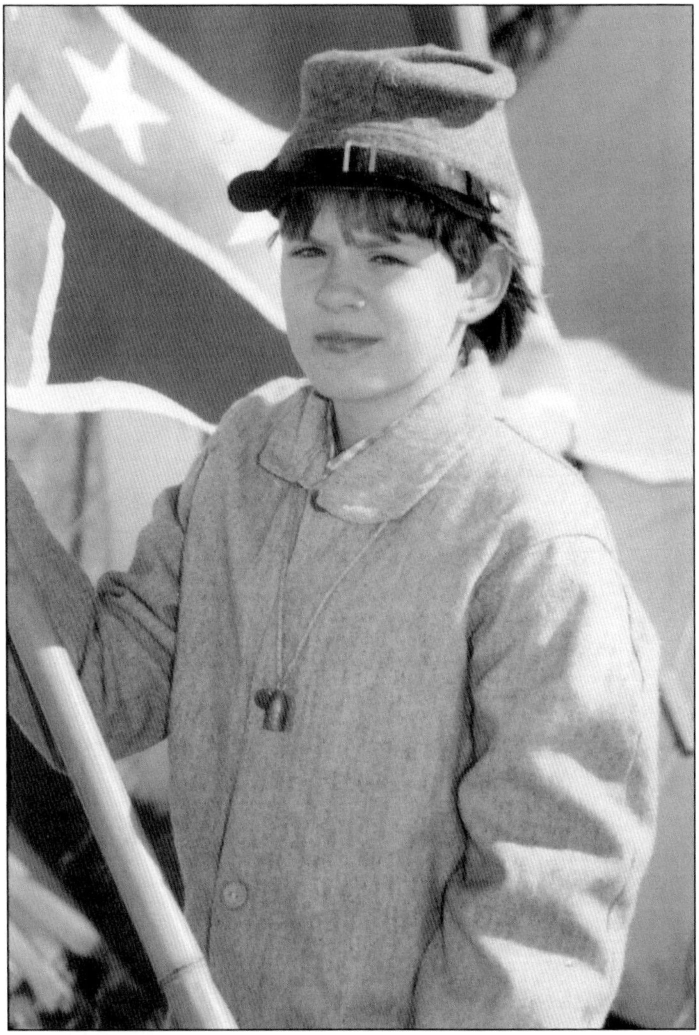

Young Brian Dement proudly carries the colors at his first reenactment for the 47th Regiment, North Carolina Volunteers at Boone Hall Plantation in Mount Pleasant, South Carolina, in 2005. Young boys on the battlefield were a common sight, often functioning as couriers, guards, water carriers, or musicians. Though they enlisted as boys, most returned to their homes as men. (Courtesy of Tommy Dement.)

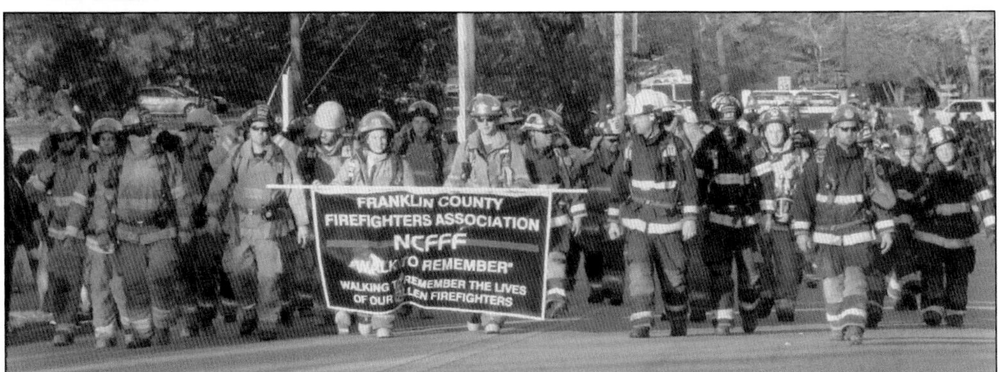

The Franklin County Firefighters Association proudly marches down Main Street Louisburg in the 2012 Christmas parade. Mostly volunteer, these brave men and women received applause and admiration along the parade route as they marched in honor of their fallen brothers. (Author's collection.)

Seven

Serving the People, Protecting the Home Front

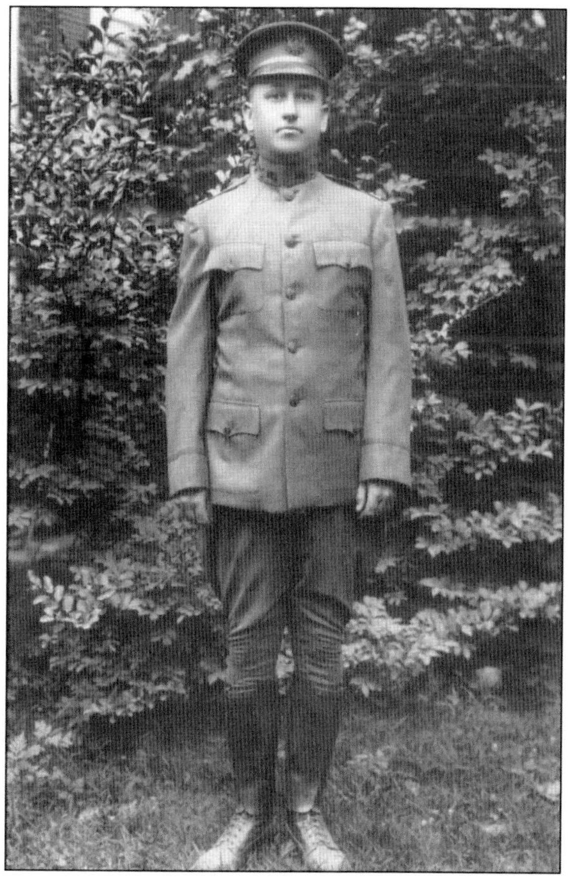

Samuel Perry Boddie (1880–1936) held the rank of major in the 30th Division, 60th Brigade, of the 120th Infantry in France during World War I. Returning home after earning a Purple Heart in battle, Boddie helped charter the Louisburg chapter of the American Legion Jambes Post No. 105. In his civilian life, he was a pharmacist, running the well-known Boddie's Drug Store in Louisburg. (Courtesy of Sammy Beasley.)

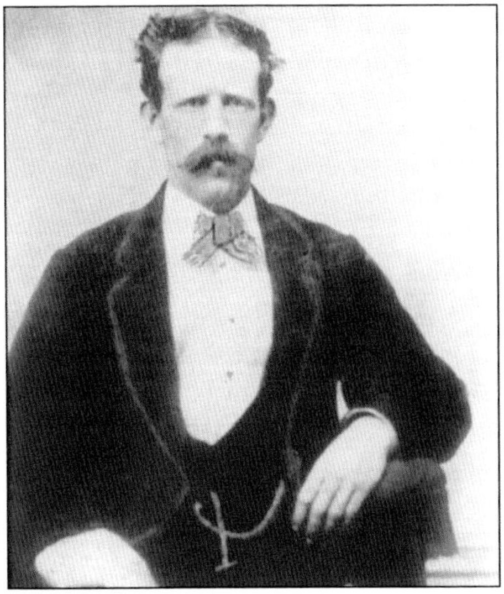

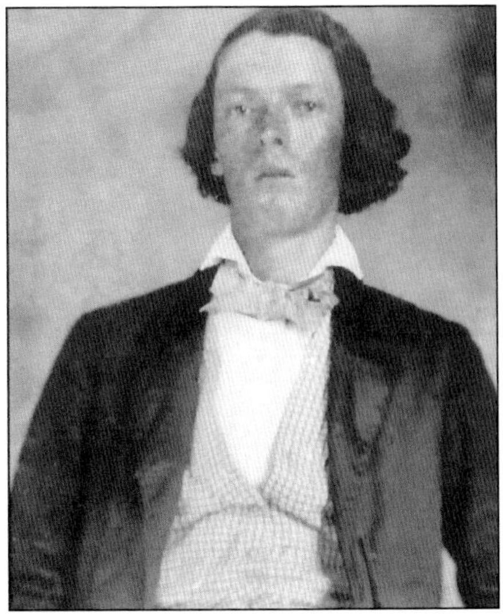

The tintype above left is believed to depict Orren Randolph Smith (1827–1913), who is credited with designing the Stars and Bars, the Confederacy's official flag. The flag first flew over the Franklin County Courthouse on March 18, 1861. Smith served in the Mexican War and earned the rank of major in the Civil War while serving with the 2nd North Carolina Battalion, Company B. The tintype above right is thought to be Henry Spencer Gupton (1844–1918), who served with Company G, 15th Regiment. Gupton enlisted at age 17 and was wounded in battle at Lee's Farm, near Yorktown. Popular during the Civil War, tintypes were often mounted in ornamental cases and remain remarkably resilient. The small photographs were carried by soldiers and treasured by loved ones awaiting their return. (Above left, courtesy of the Tar River Center for History and Culture; above right, courtesy of Ernie Mustian.)

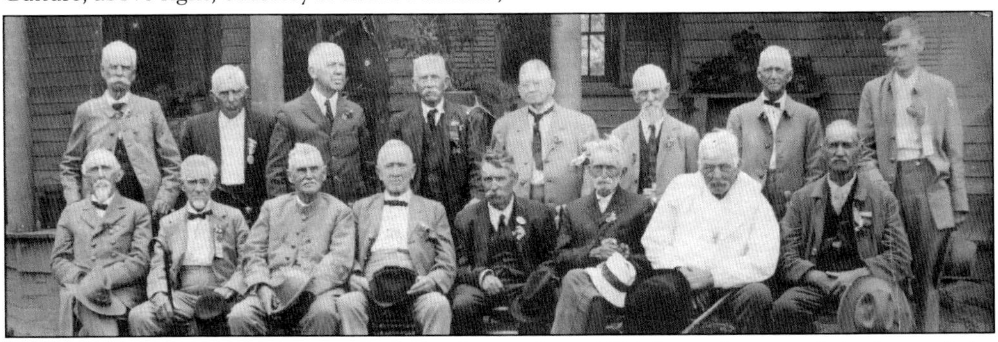

Franklin County Confederate veterans gather in June 1924 for a photograph in front of the Franklinton Hotel prior to traveling to the United Confederate Veterans Reunion in Memphis. The photograph includes, from left to right, (seated) J.W. Mustian (1847–1934), James Knox Gilliam (1840–1929), D.A. Long, N. Winston, B.E. King, R.Y. Dickerson, Joshua Lawerence Bowden (1846–1935), and Dewitt Clinton Tharrington (1845–1930); (standing) Phillip Guston Alston (1843–1928), James L. Cheaves, Joseph John Allen (1847–1929), J.H. Bobbitt, Ruffin Van Buren Collie (1844–1951), Robert B. Carr (1844–1928), P.F. Dickens, and Sidney H. Horton. Reunions were held regularly until the 61st and final reunion in June 1951. The May 30, 1949, issue of *Life* magazine featured a photograph of Franklin County veteran Ruffin Van Buren Collie, who was among the last surviving veterans of the Civil War, along with 30 Union and 38 Confederate soldiers. At the time, Collie was 105 years old; he lived another two years before passing on January 5, 1951, just short of 107 years of age. He left to survive him five generations and over 180 descendants. (Courtesy of Carrie Daniels.)

Thomas Soloman Collie (1842–1921) served in the Civil War as a private in Company L, 15th Regiment and was among many who were wounded and captured at Gettysburg. After being imprisoned at Bedloe's and David's Islands, Collie returned to Franklin County and served as a county commissioner for the Cedar Rock district from 1883 to 1902 and as their chairman from 1902 to 1916. (Courtesy of Sarah J. Pace.)

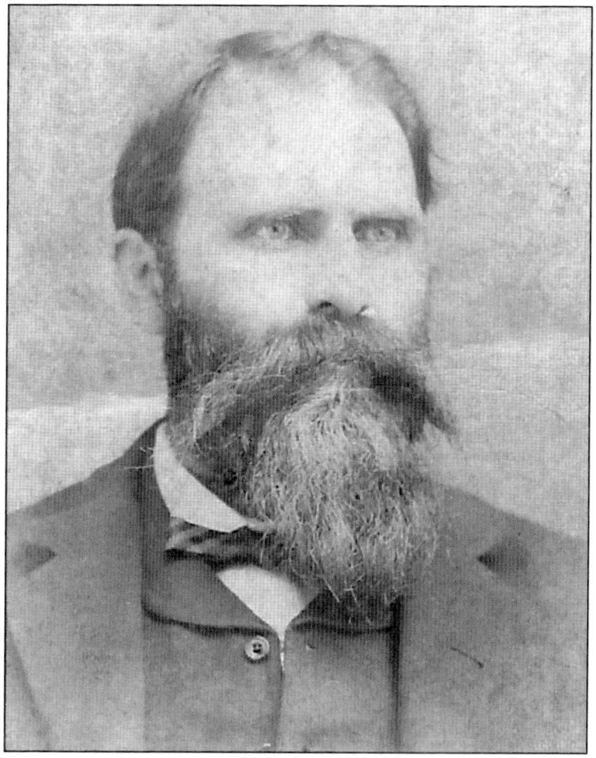

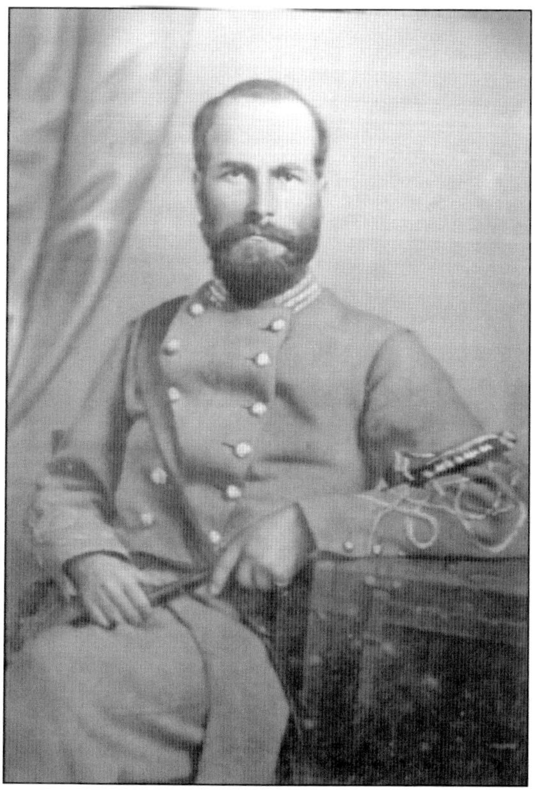

Joseph Jonathan Davis (1828–1892), the commander of Company G, 47th Regiment, North Carolina Infantry, was imprisoned at Johnson's Island for two years. Upon his release, he served in the North Carolina House of Representatives from 1868 to 1870, as a US congressman from 1875 to 1881, and as a state supreme court justice from 1887 to 1888. In 1902, the United Daughters of the Confederacy honored his memory, naming their Louisburg branch the Joseph J. Davis Chapter No. 537, which is still active today. (Courtesy of the Raymond and Barbara Burnette collection.)

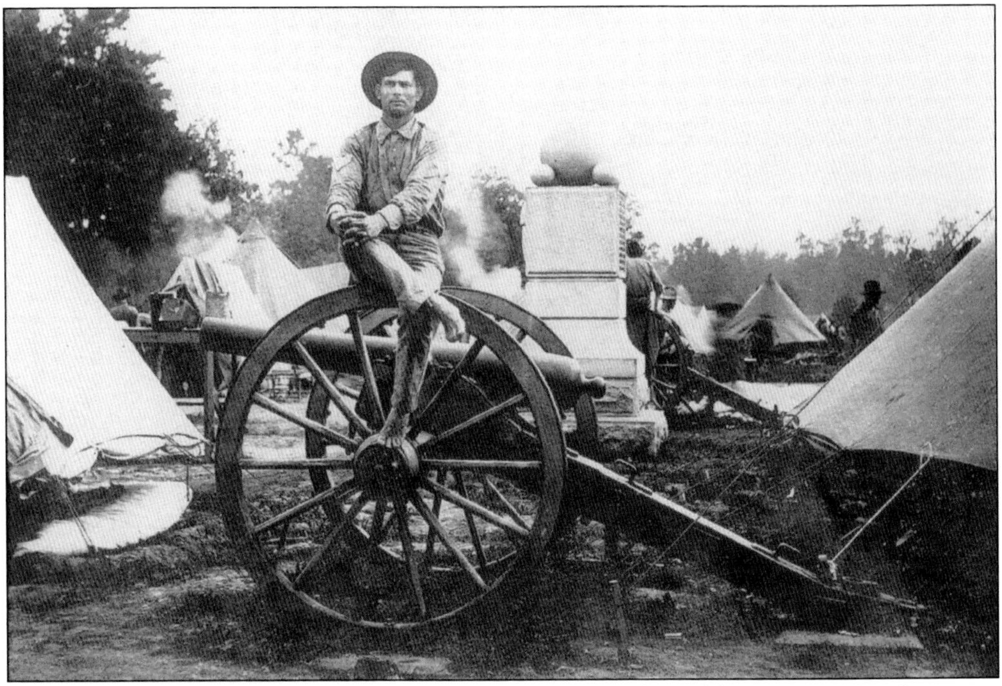

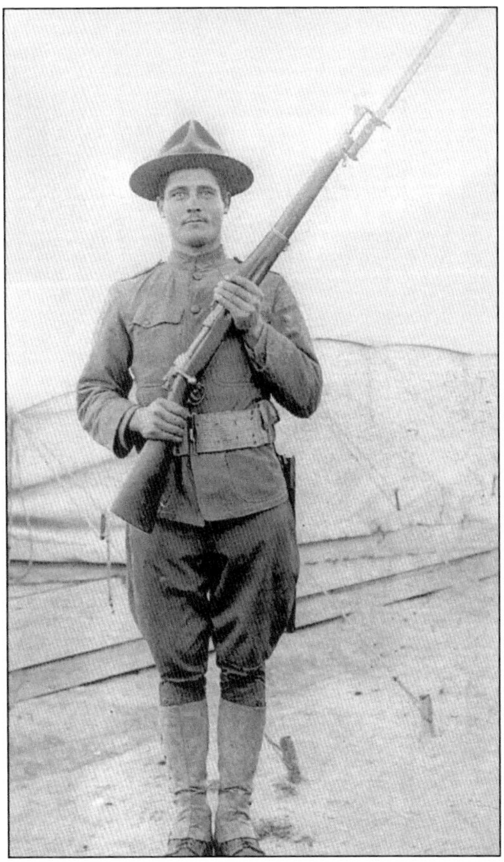

Barefooted Franklinton native Hugh Elmore Strickland (1876–1932) sits atop a cannon at Chickamauga, Georgia, on August 25, 1906. From July 28 through August 25, 1906, the 3rd North Carolina Infantry of the North Carolina State Militia, along with units from six other states, participated in encampment and maneuver drills at Chickamauga State Park. Strickland was a sergeant, and he autographed this photograph to his colonel. (Courtesy of Carrie Daniels.)

Alert resident Tollie Foster Faulkner (1891–1975) served in World War I from September 27, 1917, until his release on July 23, 1919. He is seen here dressed in his uniform holding a bolt-action Springfield rifle with a 16-inch bayonet. The Springfield was officially adopted by the US military on June 19, 1903, and it remained in service until the early days of the Vietnam War. (Courtesy of Cindy Hunt Carroll.)

Rev. Edward Hill Davis (1860–1953, left) and Dr. Daniel T. Smithwick (1867–1956, right), both noted Franklin County historians, stand before the Fenton Foster home on May 25, 1948. Davis is best remembered for his comprehensive book *Historical Sketches of Franklin County*, published in 1948, while Smithwick's contributions as the first official county historian cannot be numbered. (Courtesy of the State Archives of North Carolina.)

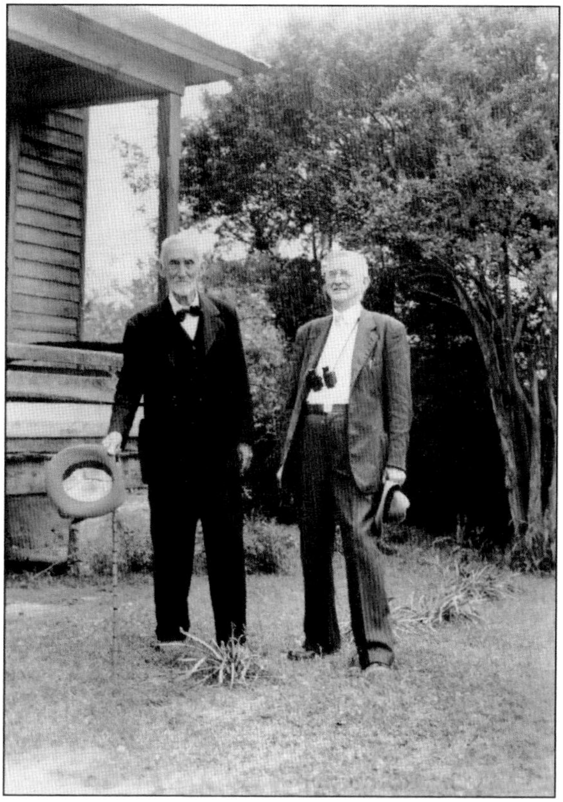

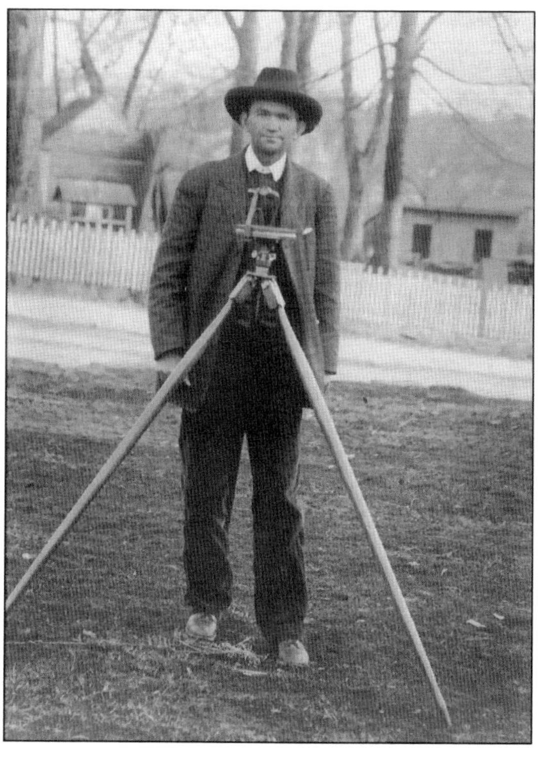

Joseph Turner Inscoe (1870–1961) of the Cedar Rock district is seen here on the grounds of Louisburg College in 1910. Inscoe worked as the county's land surveyor from 1892 to 1912 and was known to use the long-standing structures of the campus to aid in calibrating his instruments. In 1915, he represented Franklin County in the general assembly and worked as a poll taker with the elections board. Inscoe was actively involved in his community and, in 1947, served with the committee to build Franklin Memorial Hospital. As an active Baptist and Mason, he was among the leaders of Cedar Rock Baptist Church. The Inscoe family continued the tradition of surveyors for three generations, surveying much of Franklin County. Joseph Inscoe's descendants insured his legacy would survive by having the bulk of their surveys digitized and preserved for future research. (Courtesy of Jim Inscoe.)

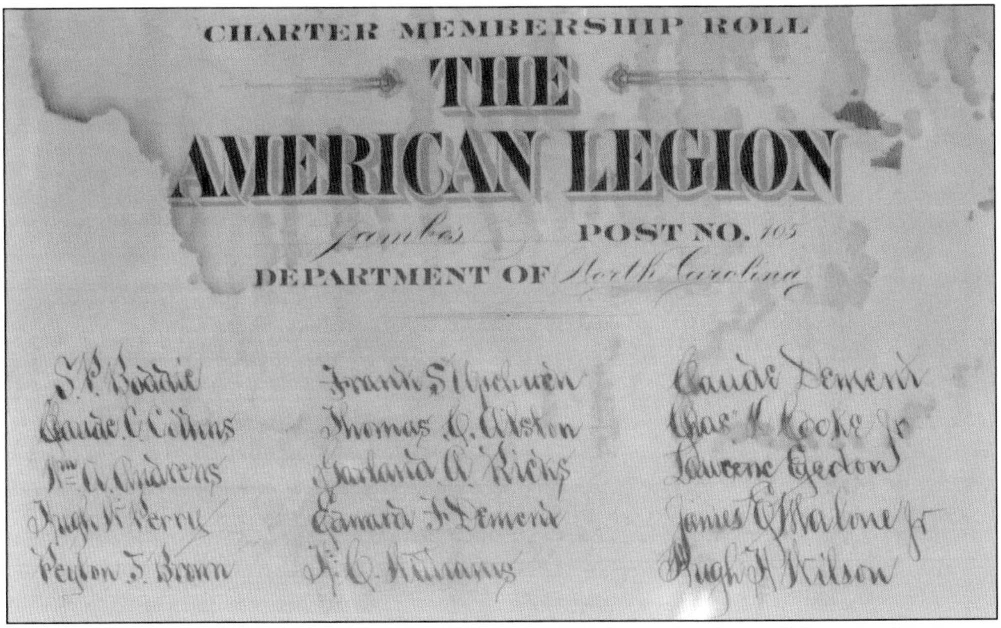

The American Legion Jambes Post No. 105's original 1920 membership roll lists the 15 charter members who served together in the 120th Infantry during World War I. These Franklin County men honored six of the fallen brothers who served with them by forming the name of their post using the first letter of each man's last name: Joyner, Ayscue, Macon, Burnett, Ellington, and Strickland. (Author's collection.)

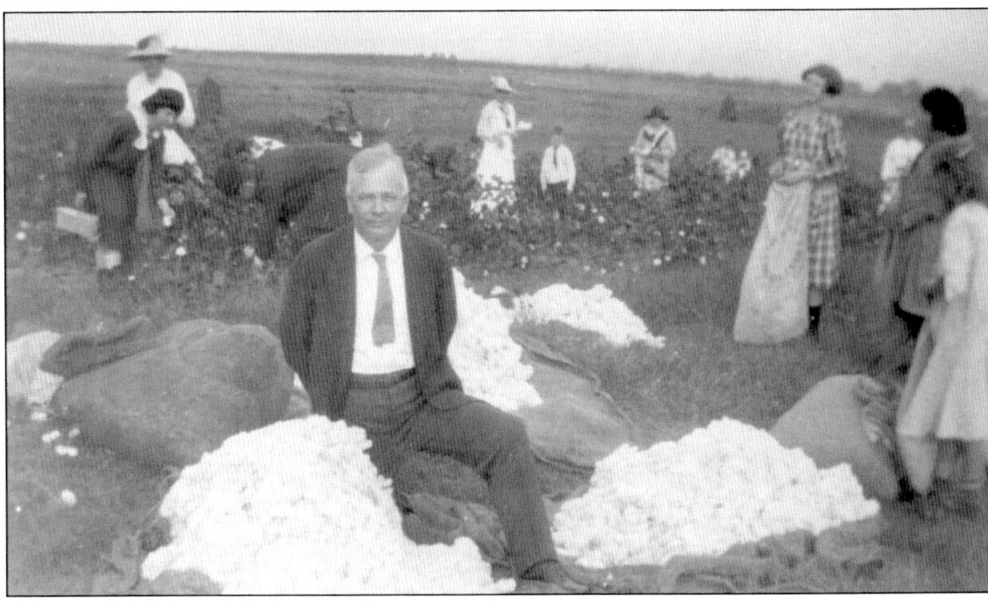

Thomas Walter Bickett (1869–1921), seen here in a cotton field in October 1918, was practicing law in Louisburg when elected governor in 1917. Known as North Carolina's "War Governor," he took office just before the country entered World War I. Upon his retirement in 1921, he suffered a fatal stroke and was buried at Louisburg's Oakwood Cemetery. Louisburg dedicated Bickett Boulevard in 1947 to honor his strong roads agenda. (Courtesy of the State Archives of North Carolina.)

Franklin County ABC officer Joseph Cecil Joyner (1899–1939) smiles from behind his desk in the county courthouse. The First Citizens Bank calendar on the wall dates this photograph just eight months before his sudden death in November 1939. (Courtesy of Stan Joyner.)

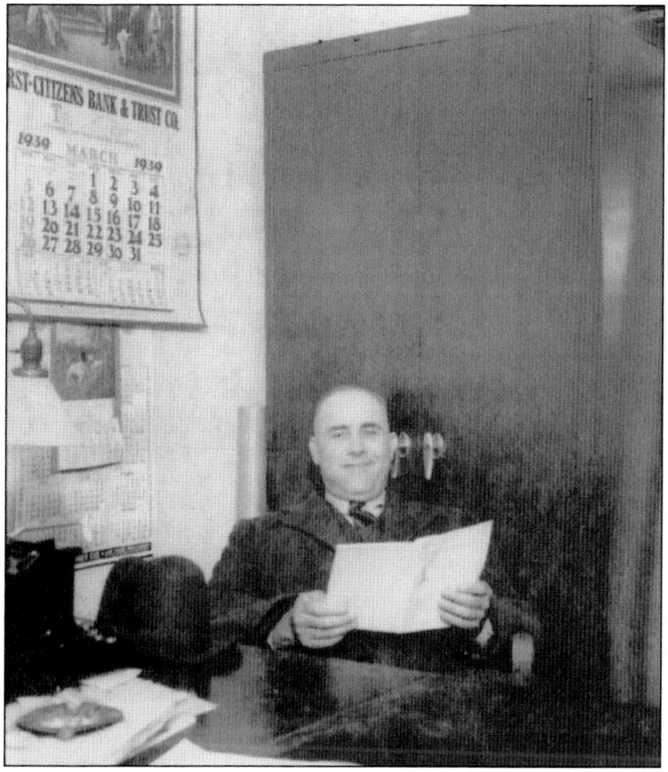

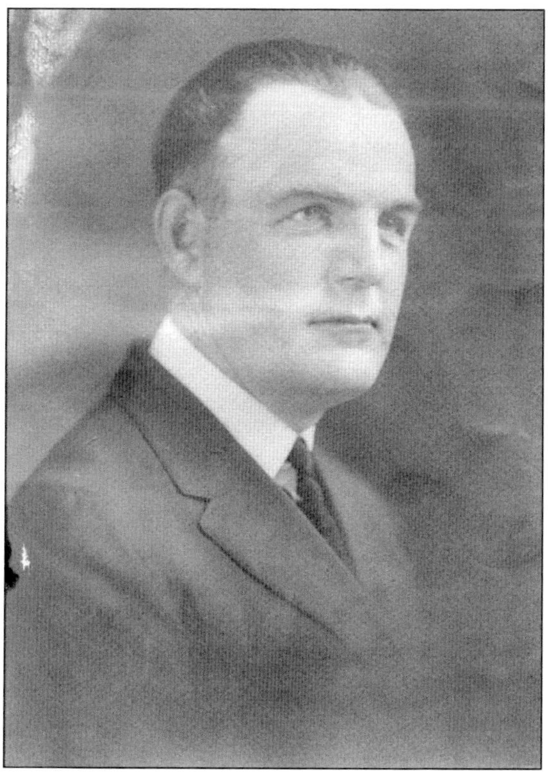

This photograph of William Norwood Fuller (1890–1941) was found among the forgotten records in the courthouse basement. Fuller served as the Franklin County accountant from 1932 to 1939, and it was under his supervision that the courthouse underwent major renovations and modernization between 1936 and 1937. Fuller is credited with keeping the major project on time and within budget. (Courtesy of the Franklin County Courthouse.)

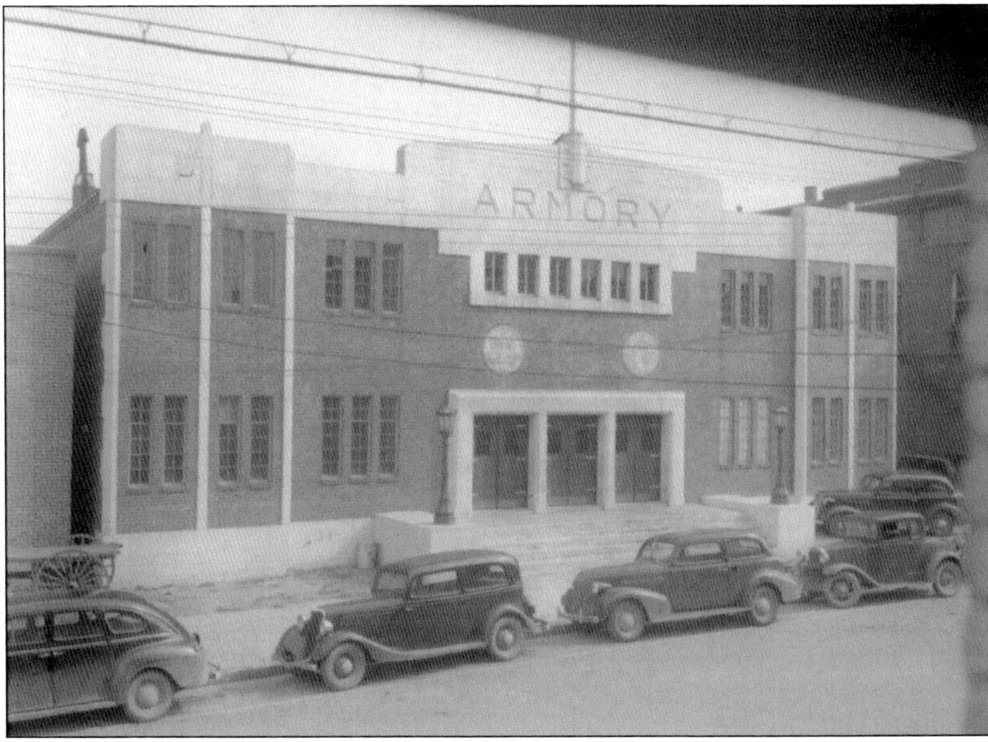

The Louisburg Armory, on Nash Street, was dedicated on September 24, 1940. Located where town hall sits today, it was used by the 113th Field Artillery and for town offices, recreation, parties, and dances. When fire destroyed the building on April 17, 1971, it was rebuilt on Bickett Boulevard in 1974. A medallion salvaged from the fire is displayed at the new facility today. (Courtesy of the State Archives of North Carolina.)

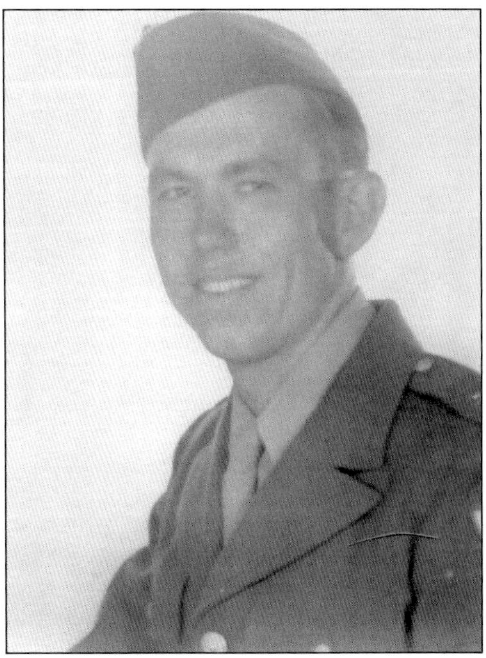

George Everet Phelps (1924–2013) served in the US Army in Company C, 1258th Engineers Combat Battalion during World War II. The 1258th served under Gen. George S. Patton's command and participated in the Battle of the Bulge, from December 16, 1944, to January 25, 1945, the largest battle of the war to the United States, costing 19,000 American lives. Phelps returned to Louisburg to marry and raise a family. (Courtesy of Karen Phelps Fuller.)

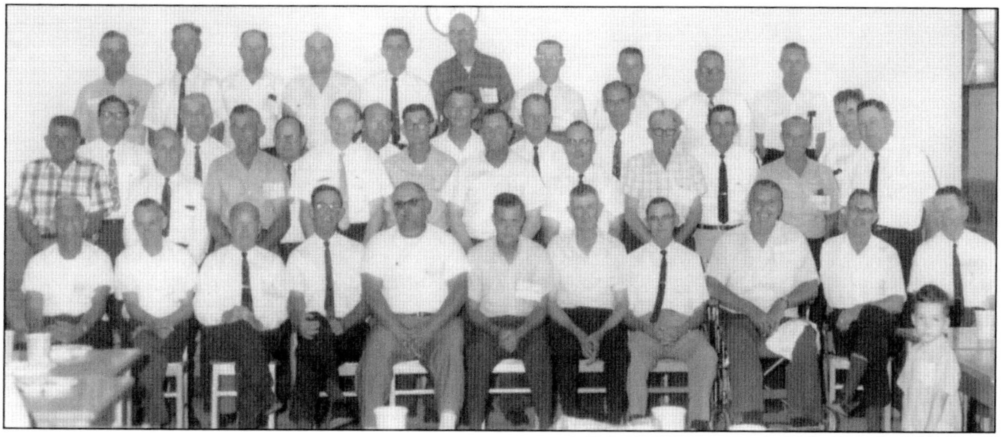

Franklin County World War II veterans, many of them Youngsville National Guardsmen, gather for a reunion photograph in the Youngsville School cafeteria around 1970. The young boy at the bottom right is unidentified. From left to right are (first row) James R. Abrams, unidentified, Kaiser Hendricks, Jesse Ed Preddy (1918–1977), C.C. Dupree, Willie Boone, Clyde E. Hudson (1910–1971), unidentified, Rayford Rogers (1922–1972), Vernon Stone, and Charles Cyrus (1921–1998); (second row) Frank Hedrick (1917–1998), Melvin J. Young (1909–1998), Grover Burgess, Gen. Edward F. Griffin, unidentified, Bland Hill (1918–1977), Herbert Frazier (1923–2008), E.L. Perry, B.T. Harris, Foster Pace, and A.C. Price; (third row) Ebbie Jones Pearce, Davis F. Hill, Romp Hendricks, Bob Cooper, J.W. Pearce, Hubert Waters, Herman Lidsey, and (far right) Bob Cheatham (1918–2005); (fourth row) Elton Beamon, M.O. Lester, Frederick Preddy (1917–1986), Claude T. Satterwhite (1922–2003), Jones H. Winston (1920–1986), Samuel Hobgood (1908–2002), Hilery Medlin (1913–1989), Charles A. Moore, Bill Hendricks, and Howard Moore. (Courtesy of Youngsville Town Hall.)

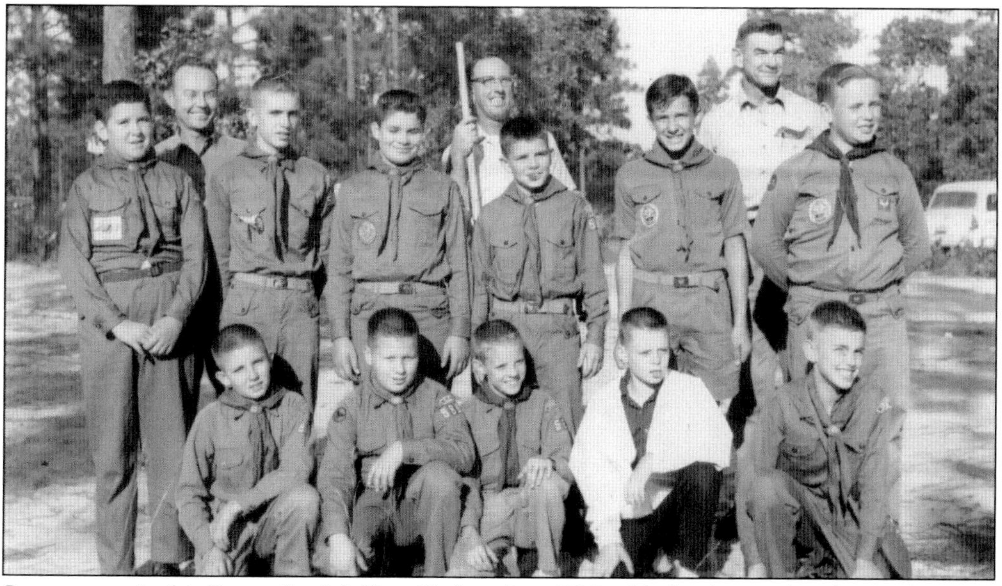

Scoutmaster Archie Brown (back left) and helpers Jesse Ed Preddy (back center) and Bob Cheatham (back right) lead this Youngsville Boy Scout Troop during a fall 1962 Camporee at Fort Bragg. These future leaders are, from left to right, (first row) Jesse Preddy, E.J. Wilder, and three unidentified boys; (second row) Ronnie Catlett, unidentified, C.L Wrenn, Johnnie Mitchell, Ralph Brown, and Wade Holden. (Courtesy of Franklin County Library, Lib Cheatham Collection.)

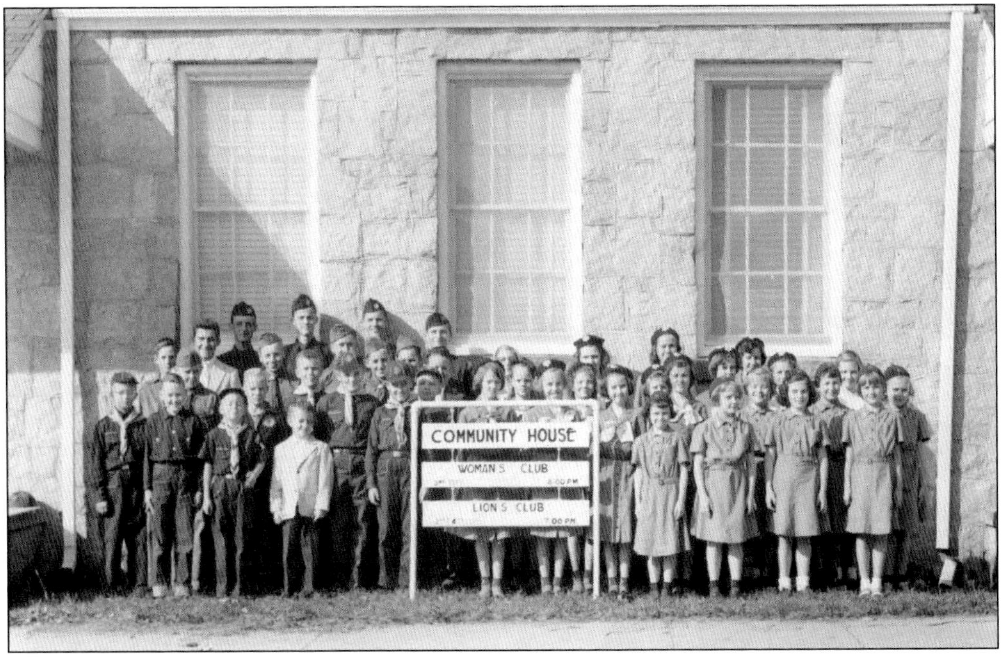

The Youngsville community has long been active in Scouting, as evidenced by this large group of Boy and Girl Scouts at the Youngsville Community House in 1955. In 1972, Franklin County opened the 110-acre Homestead Girl Scout Campground on Highway 39, which offered opportunities for all youth from the North Carolina Coastal Pines Council to gather locally, until budget cuts forced its closing in 2010. (Courtesy of Youngsville Town Hall.)

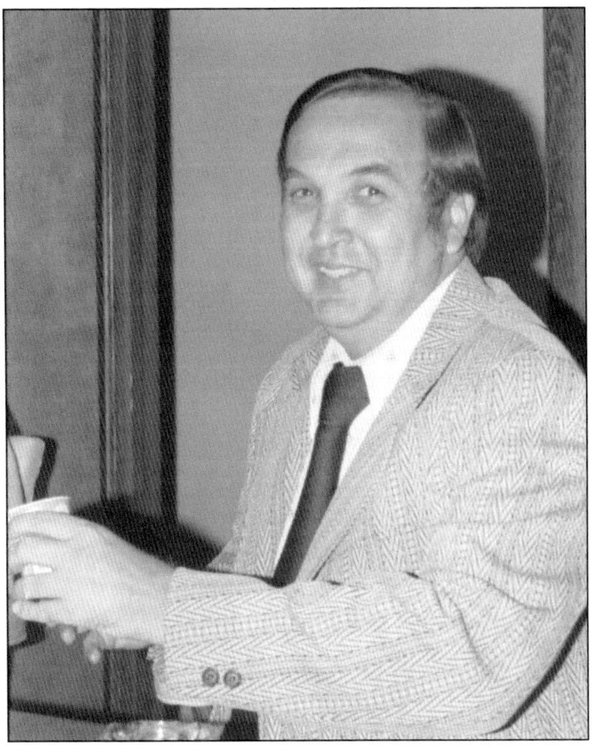

Ralph S. Knott (1933–2011) served as clerk of the Superior Court of Franklin County for 39 years, from 1962 to 2001. The longest-serving clerk in Franklin County history, Knott was also chairman of the State Clerk of Superior Court Legislative Committee for 23 years and served for two years on the North Carolina Court Commission. Knott was active in the Franklin County Democratic party and was chosen as "Citizen of the Year" by the Franklin County Chamber of Commerce. Instrumental in establishing the Vance-Granville Community College satellite campus in Franklin County, Knott was also known to be the driving force behind the Parks and Recreation Department and was the chairman of the Franklin County Leadership Committee. (Courtesy of the Raymond and Barbara Burnette collection.)

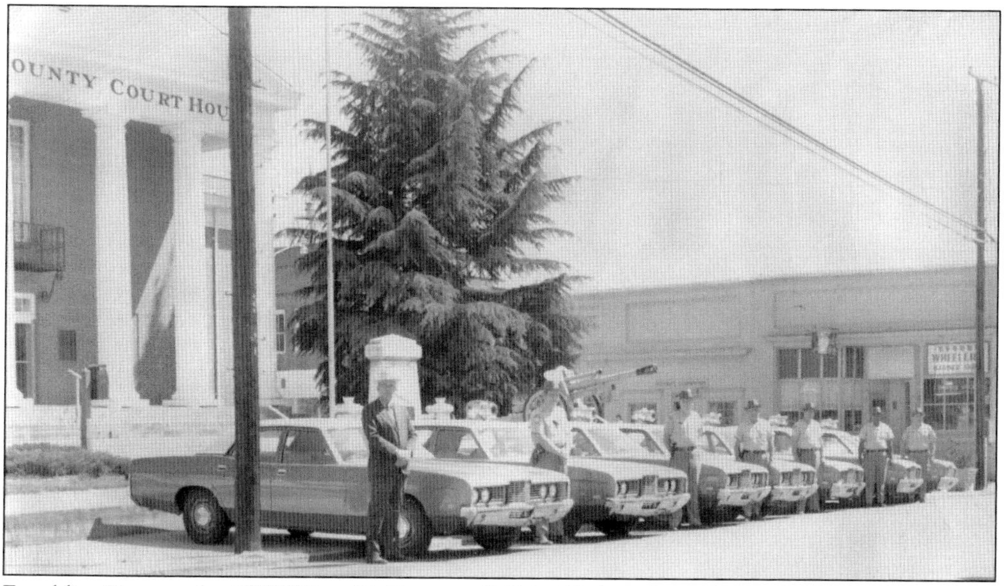

Franklin County sheriff William T. Dement (1924–1990) and six deputies proudly display the force's patrol cars in front of the courthouse around 1968. Dement served as county sheriff from December 1, 1966, until November 30, 1986, and continued to be known as "Sheriff" until his death in 1990. In the background along Court Street are Cicero's Sandwiches and Wheeler's Barber Shop. (Courtesy of Peggy Jones.)

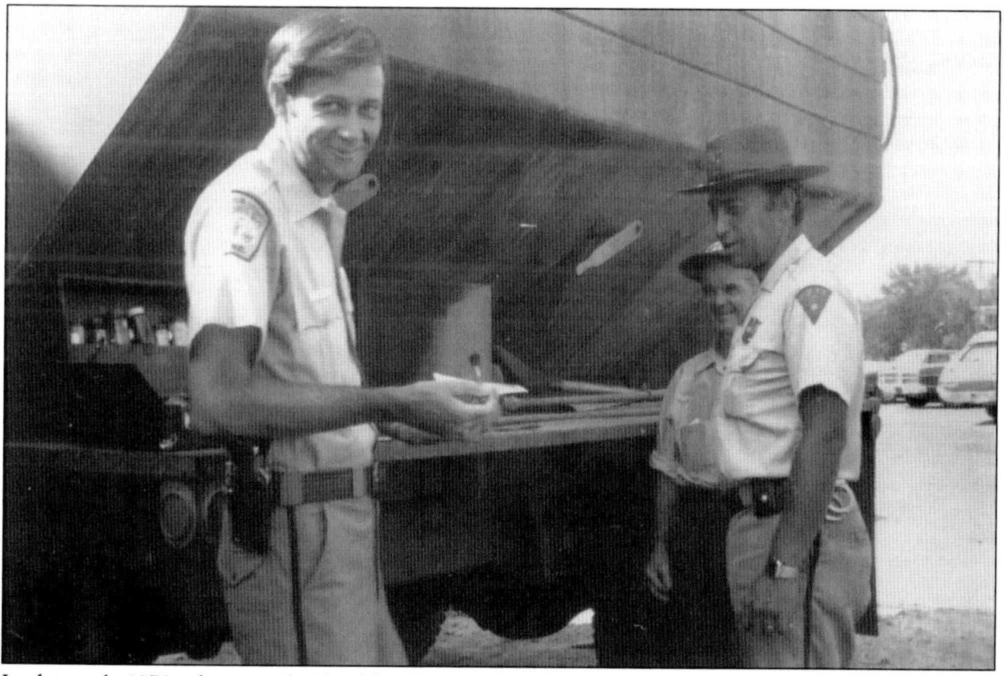

In this early-1970s photograph, Franklin County sheriff's deputy William Astor Bowden (1935–2010, left) and Youngsville chief of police Jack Stroud (center) investigate a theft at the Youngsville Milling Company as M.D. Hoyle looks on. Bowden served as a deputy and later worked with the *Franklin Times* before retiring as a lieutenant with the Capital Police. (Courtesy of Franklin County Library, Lib Cheatham Collection.)

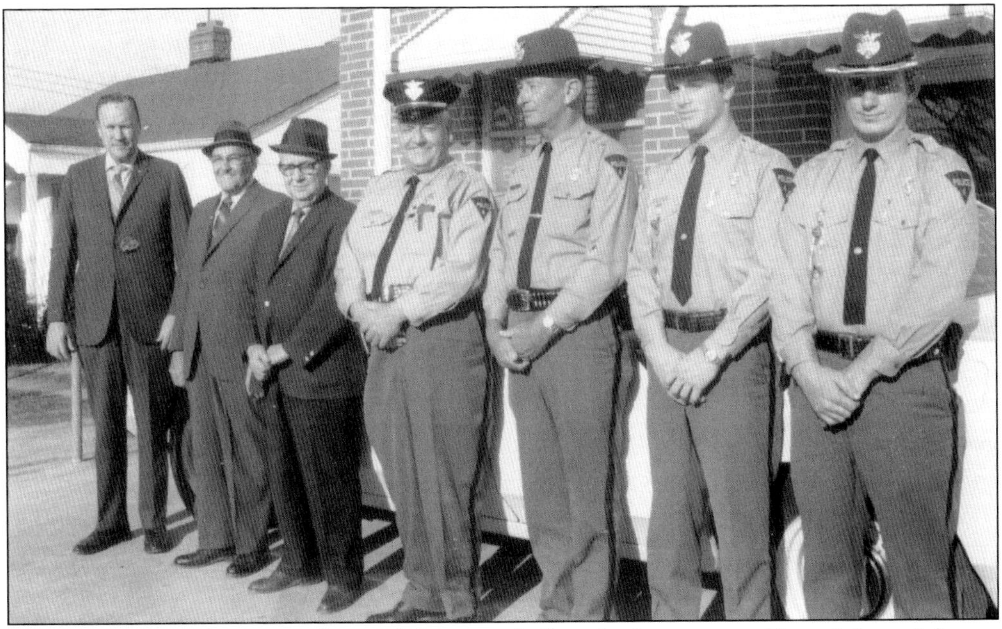

Youngsville officials pose in front of the town hall with the new car. From left to right are Youngsville mayor Wiley Marvin Roberts, commissioners David H. Cyrus and James T. Allen, and policemen Earl Minor, J.W. Pearce (chief), Raymond Lee Bragg, and Walter Woodlief. (Courtesy of Franklin County Library, Lib Cheatham Collection.)

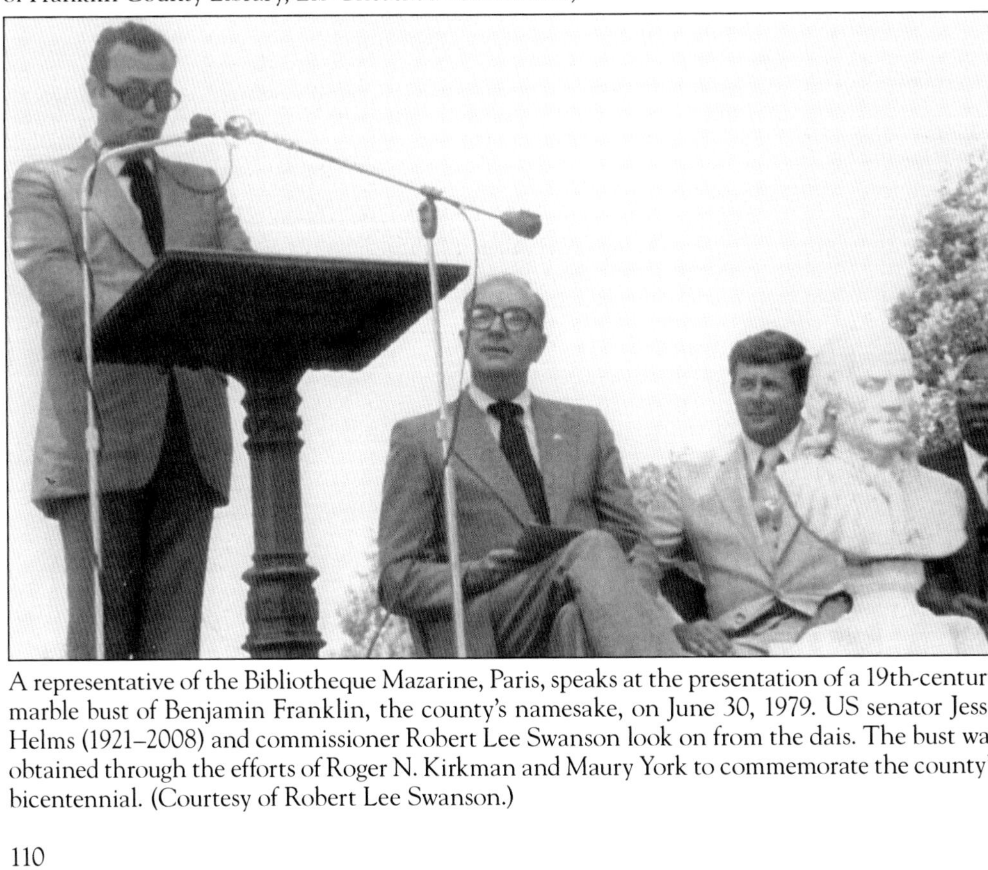

A representative of the Bibliotheque Mazarine, Paris, speaks at the presentation of a 19th-century marble bust of Benjamin Franklin, the county's namesake, on June 30, 1979. US senator Jesse Helms (1921–2008) and commissioner Robert Lee Swanson look on from the dais. The bust was obtained through the efforts of Roger N. Kirkman and Maury York to commemorate the county's bicentennial. (Courtesy of Robert Lee Swanson.)

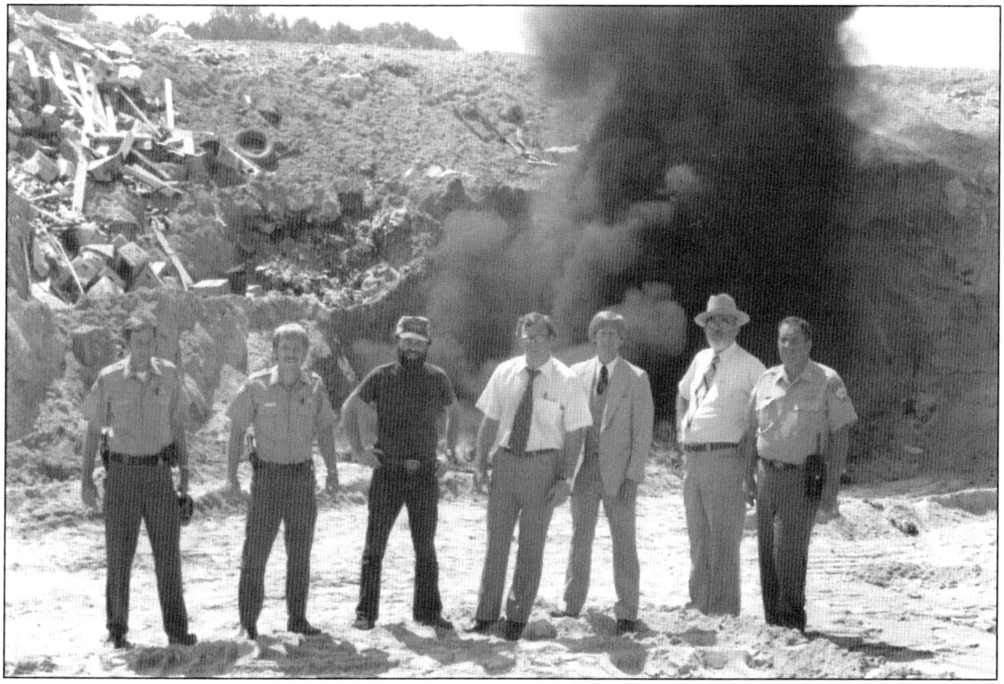

With the landfill as a backdrop, law enforcement line up for a group photograph in the 1970s as pounds of marijuana go up in smoke. An unsuccessful landing at Ball's Airport resulted in the confiscation of an airplane's illegal cargo and the pilot's arrest. From left to right are Astor Bowden, Wesley Denton, Luther King, unidentified, Pete Tomlinson, Sheriff William T. Dement, and Vernon Scarborough. (Courtesy of Franklin County Sheriff's Department.)

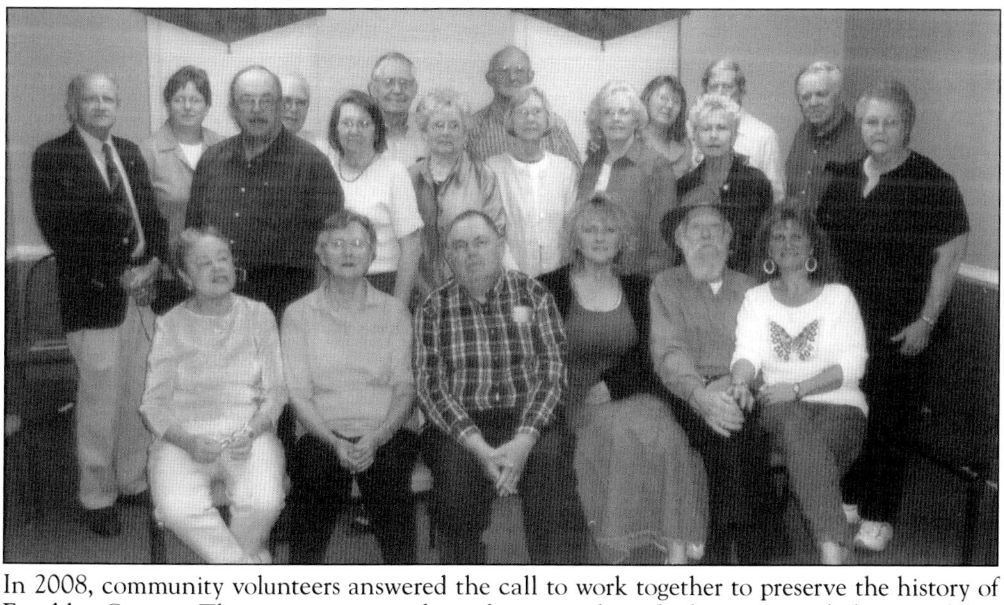

In 2008, community volunteers answered the call to work together to preserve the history of Franklin County. The committee was formed to compile and edit stories and photographs of Franklin County's past and present citizens. Working for long, unpaid hours, they produced two volumes of *Franklin County Heritage* books. In 2009, the group evolved into the Heritage Society of Franklin County. (Courtesy of Annette Goyette.)

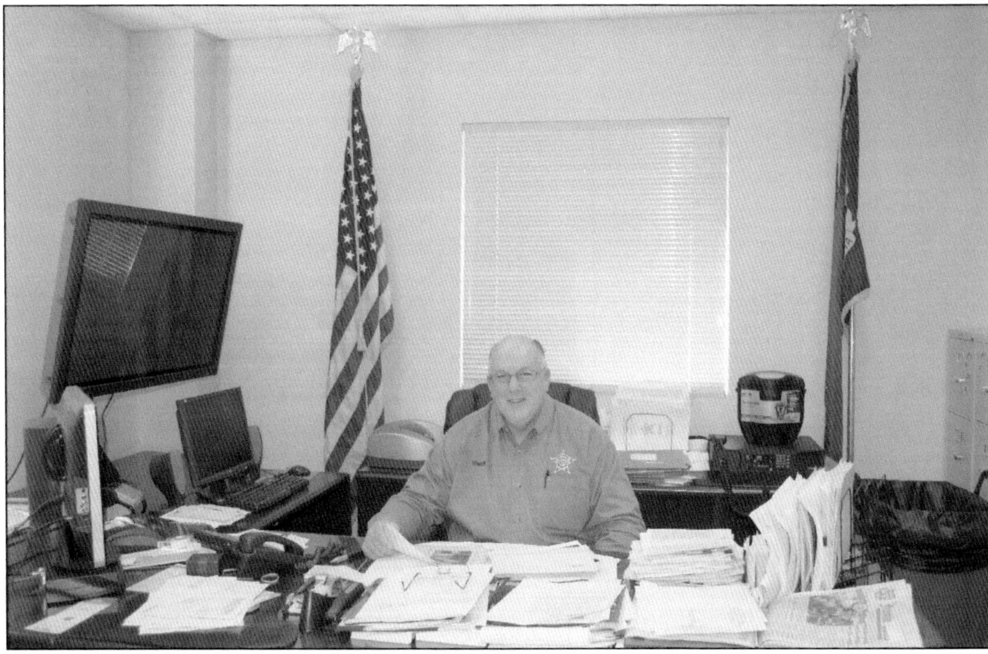

Sheriff Jerry W. Jones smiles as he works from his office at the Franklin County Sheriff's Department, on T. Kemp Road in Louisburg. First elected in 2002, Sheriff Jones is currently serving his second term. A lifelong Franklin County resident, he once served as mayor of Bunn, volunteered with both the fire department and the rescue squad, and was president of the Franklin County Fire Fighters Association. (Author's collection.)

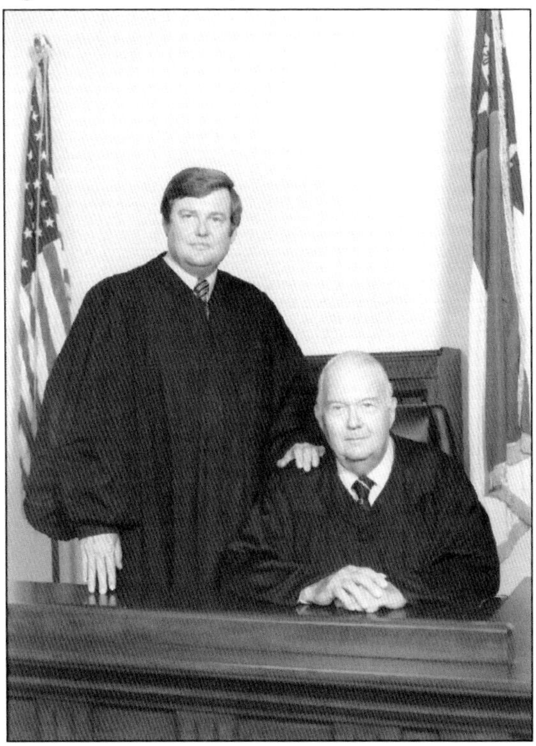

Superior Court judge Robert H. Hobgood stands by his father's side in the Franklin County Courthouse in 1987. The Honorable Judge Hamilton H. Hobgood (1911–1995) served for 24 years as a North Carolina Superior Court judge, from 1955 to 1979. He then continued as a senior resident superior court judge and then a retired/recalled judge traveling throughout the state until 1989. A Louisburg native, Judge Hobgood was a lawyer, state senator, and judge who presided over more than 60,000 cases. Franklin County's courthouse annex was named in his honor to commemorate his years of service to the judicial system. His son Hon. Judge Robert H. Hobgood is currently the senior resident superior court judge for the ninth judicial district of the third division of the superior court, serving Franklin, Granville, Vance, and Warren Counties. He began serving as senior resident superior court judge on January 1, 1980. (Courtesy of Judge Robert H. Hobgood.)

Eight

Leaving a Landmark, Erecting Monuments

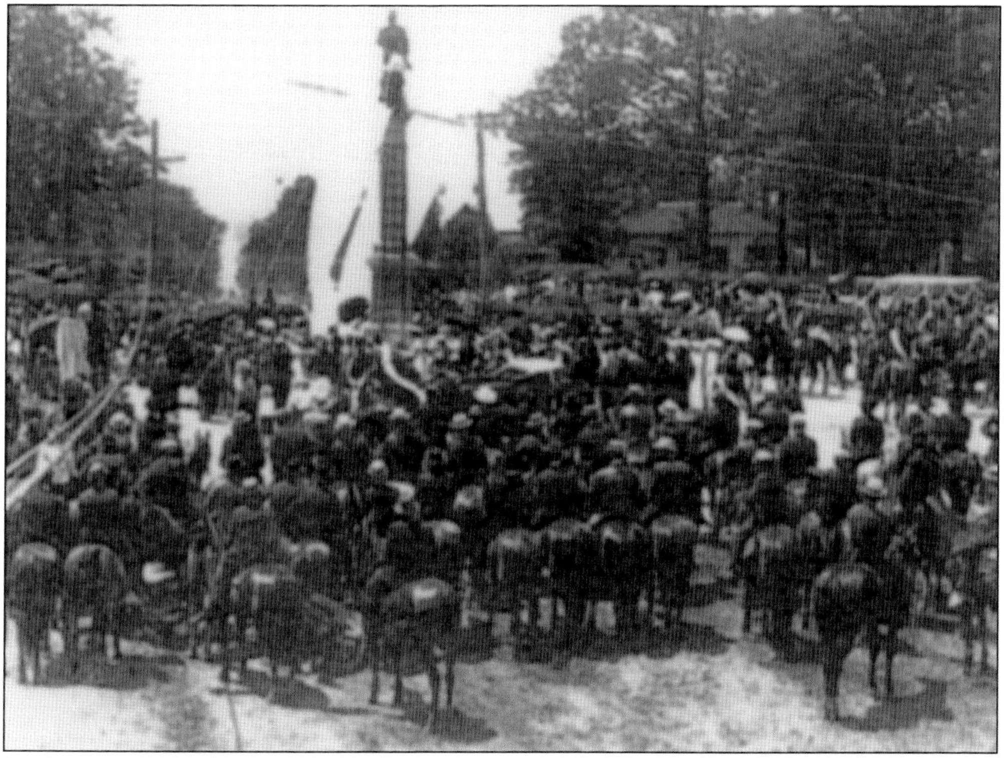

On May 13, 1914, the United Daughters of the Confederacy unveiled a 30-foot monument on North Main Street in Louisburg honoring Civil War soldiers. Among the 5,000 attending were North Carolina governor Locke Craig, North Carolina attorney general Thomas W. Bickett, and the county's Confederate veterans in dress uniform. A military band played "Dixie" while parading past the Louisburg College location where Sherman's troops camped 50 years earlier during their march through the South. (Courtesy of Sammie Beasley.)

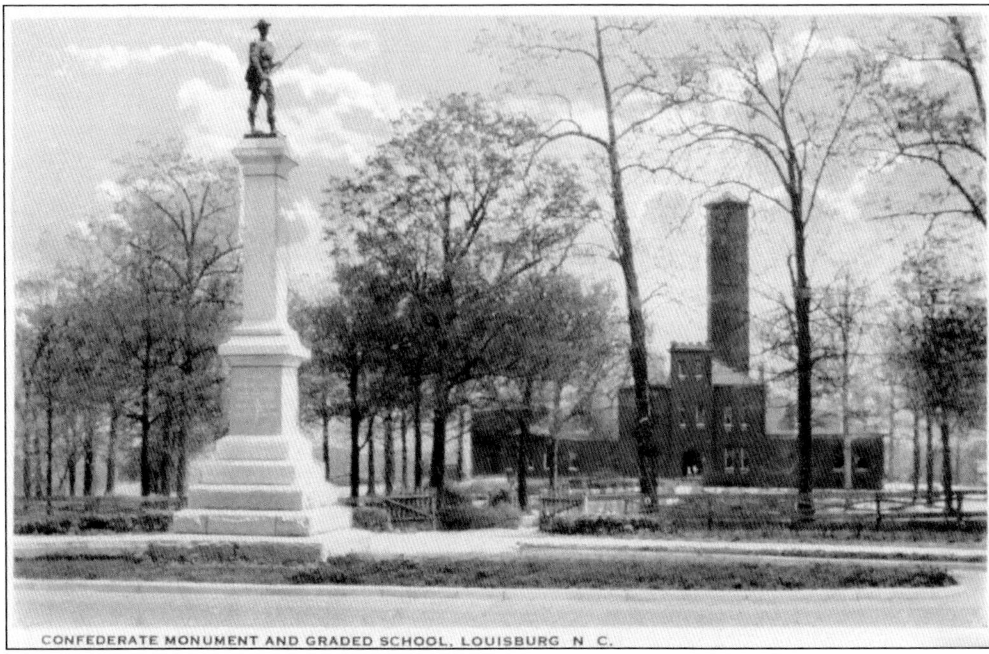

An early postcard of Louisburg's Confederate monument shows the Mills Graded School and the steel standpipe in the background, where Louisburg College's Seby B. Jones Performing Arts Center stands today. The curbing dates this photograph to after 1922, when the town's streets were paved. Louisburg College students and parade watchers will also note the absence of the brick sitting wall along the perimeter grounds. (Courtesy of Freddie Edwards.)

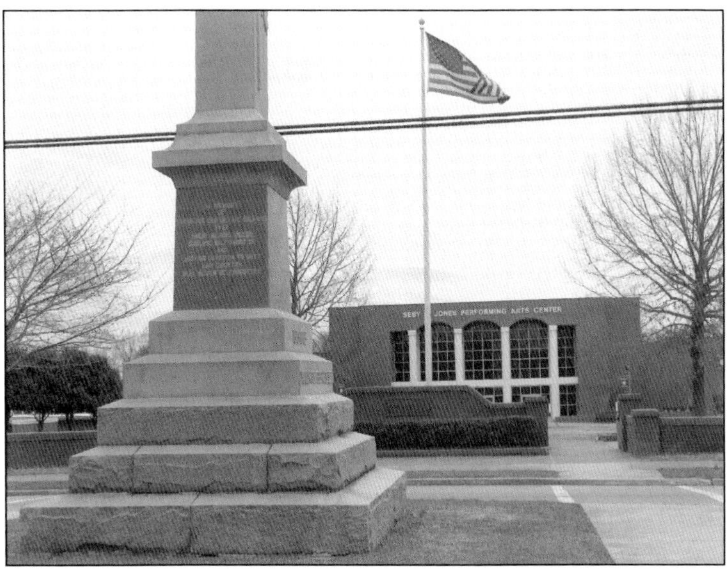

One of the four inscriptions on the Confederate monument's base reads, "In Memory of Franklin's Confederate Soldiers That Their Heroic Deeds, Sublime Self-Sacrifice and Undying Devotion To Duty and Country May Never Be Forgotten." A rededication ceremony was held for the monument's centennial anniversary in May 2014. (Author's collection.)

Freemasonry existed in what is now Franklin County long before the county was formed. This marker located on Route 1407 in the northern section of the county marks the spot where the Blanford Bute Masonic Lodge first met. Originally chartered from the Blandford Lodge of Petersburg, Virginia, the site of the Blanford Bute Lodge is in the Alert section of the Sandy Creek Community. (Author's collection.)

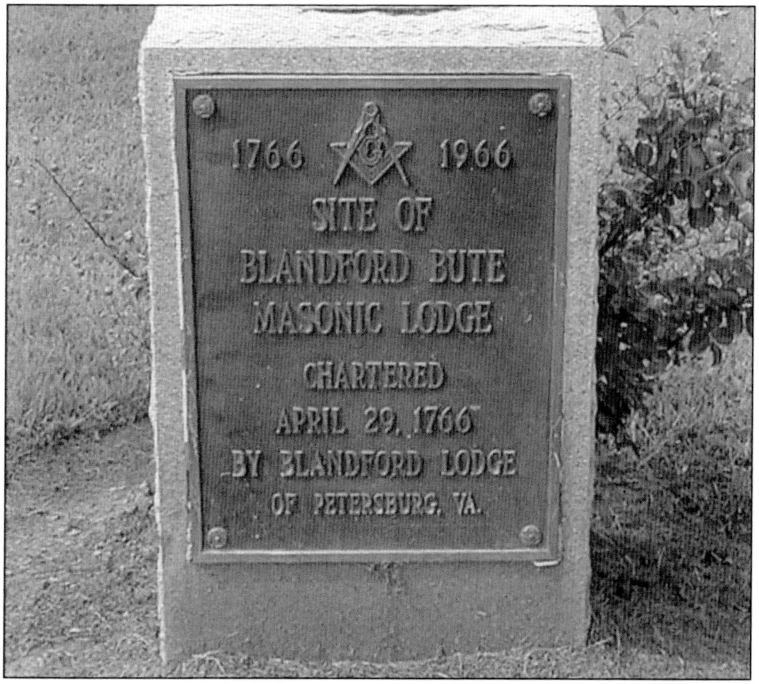

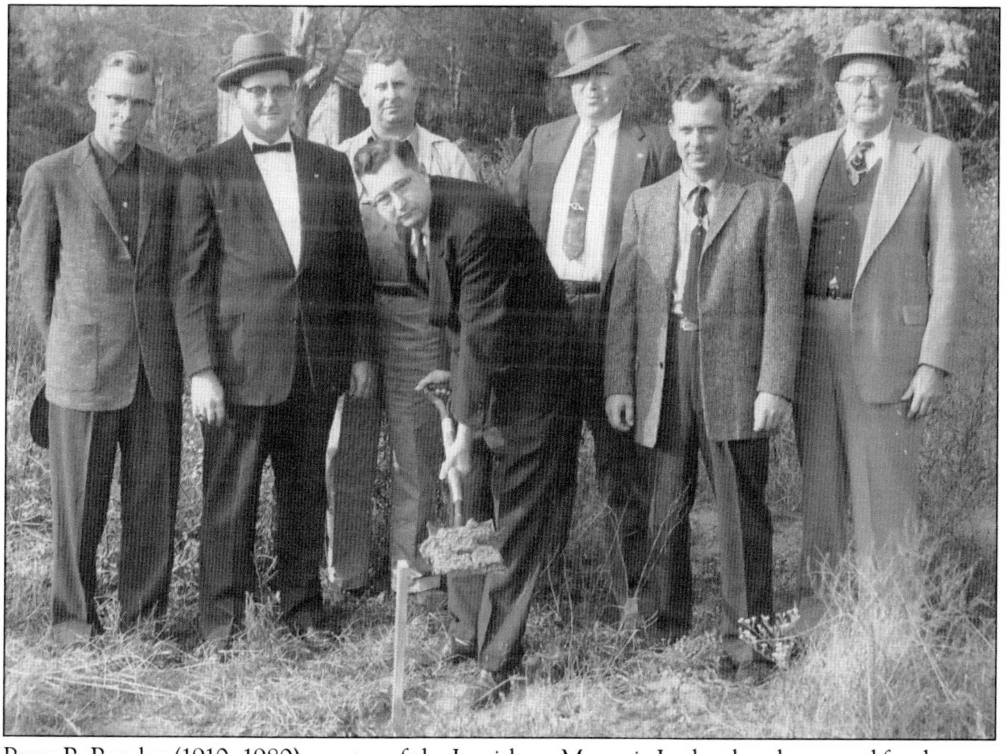

Perry B. Beasley (1910–1980), master of the Louisburg Masonic Lodge, breaks ground for the new building on the corner of Bickett Boulevard and Jolly Street in November 1957. From left to right behind him are R.W. Knott, Herman Spencer, Stewart Merritt, S.C. Foster Jr., Milton Fleming, and I.P. Wheeler. (Courtesy of Sammy Beasley.)

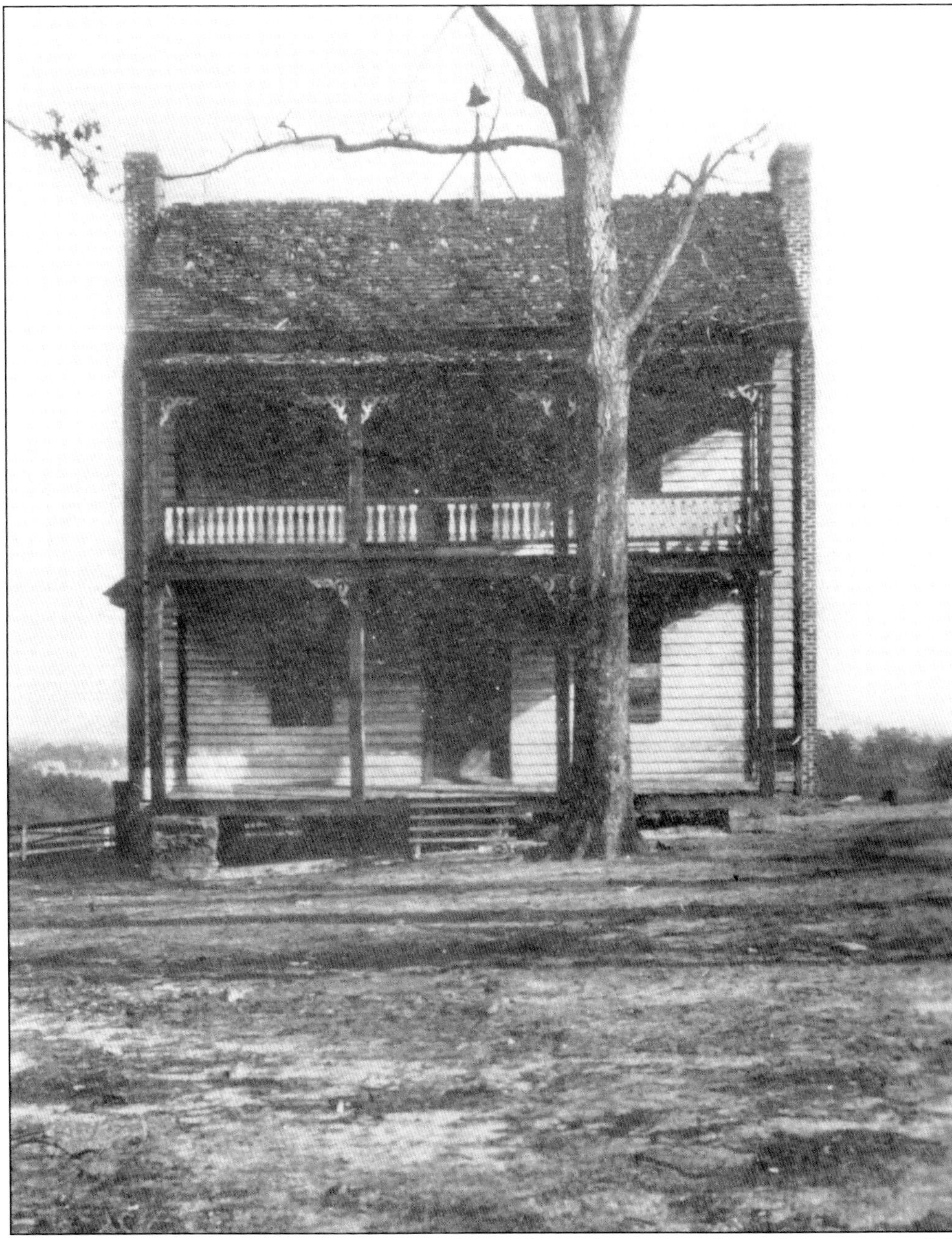

The lower level of Louisburg College's original Franklin Male Academy housed classrooms, while the upper level served as the school preceptor's residence. Matthew Dickinson lived and worked there from 1804 to 1808 while serving as both college president and professor to the male students of the academy. Note the class bell atop the roof. (Courtesy of Sammy Beasley.)

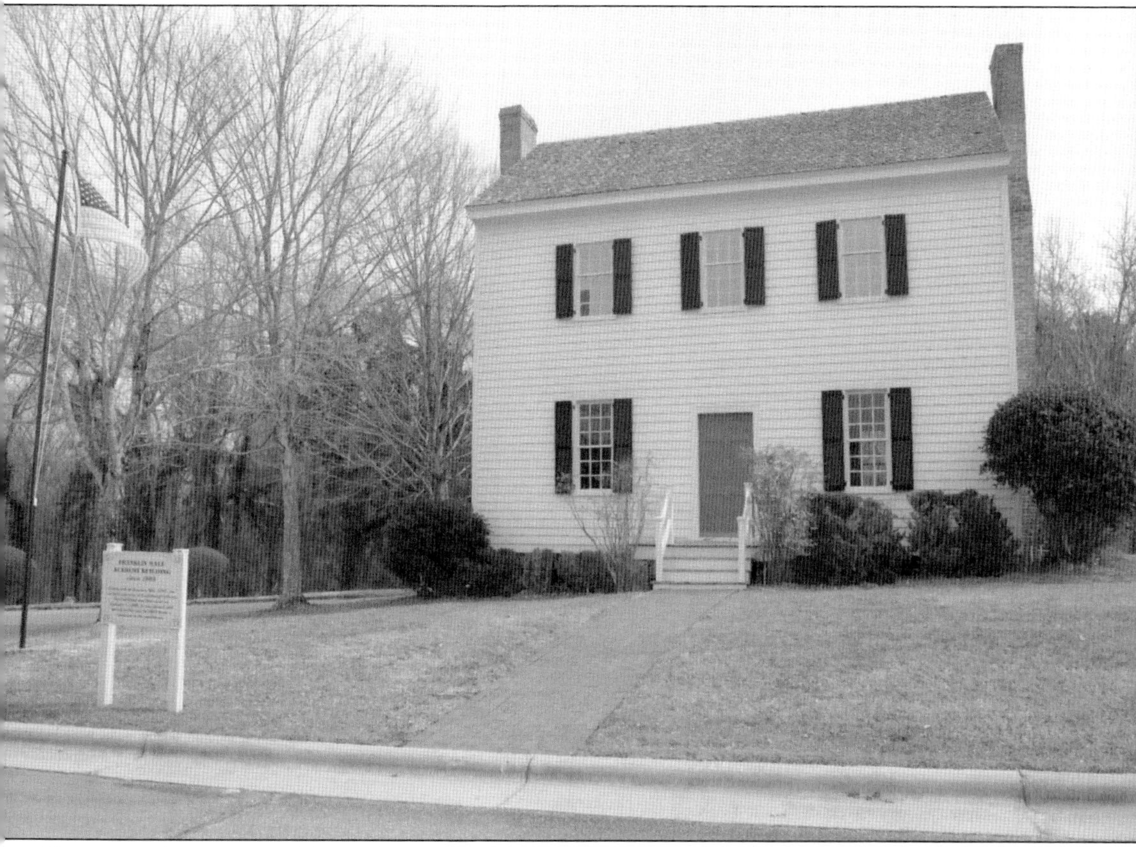

The original academy building still stands as a testament to the college's longevity and commitment to the county. The sign in front of the restored Franklin Male Academy building reads, "Chartered on January 6th, 1787, the earliest ancestor of Louisburg College. This building was first used on January 1, 1805. It was closed and moved to this site in 1905 from a location to the southwest." (Author's collection.)

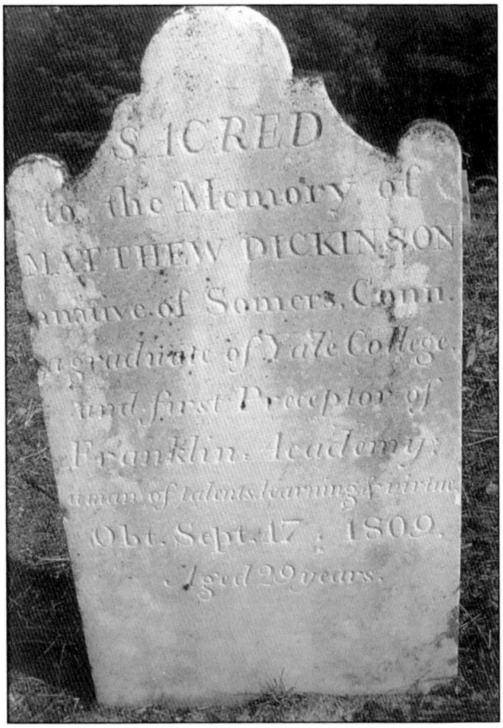

Yale graduate Matthew Dickinson (1780–1809) was Franklin Male Academy's first preceptor, from 1804 to 1808. Dying at 29 of a "bilious fever," he was laid to rest at Glebe, the home of his mentor, Alexander Falconer. Dickinson's family sent the carved headstone at left by wagon from Connecticut to be placed where it stands today on the Edwards and Foster farm off Highway 401 North. When Louisburg College requested to move the grave to their campus to commemorate its 225th anniversary, historians and descendants of the Dickinson and Edwards families expressed concern against disturbing the 203-year-old grave, and a compromise was reached to maintain the cemetery. Below, in September 2012, Dickinson family descendants Pamela Genovesi (left) and Jackie Clark (right) traveled to Louisburg to attend the unveiling of artist Will Hinton's rubbing of the headstone, on display in Dickinson's original academy building. (Both, author's collection.)

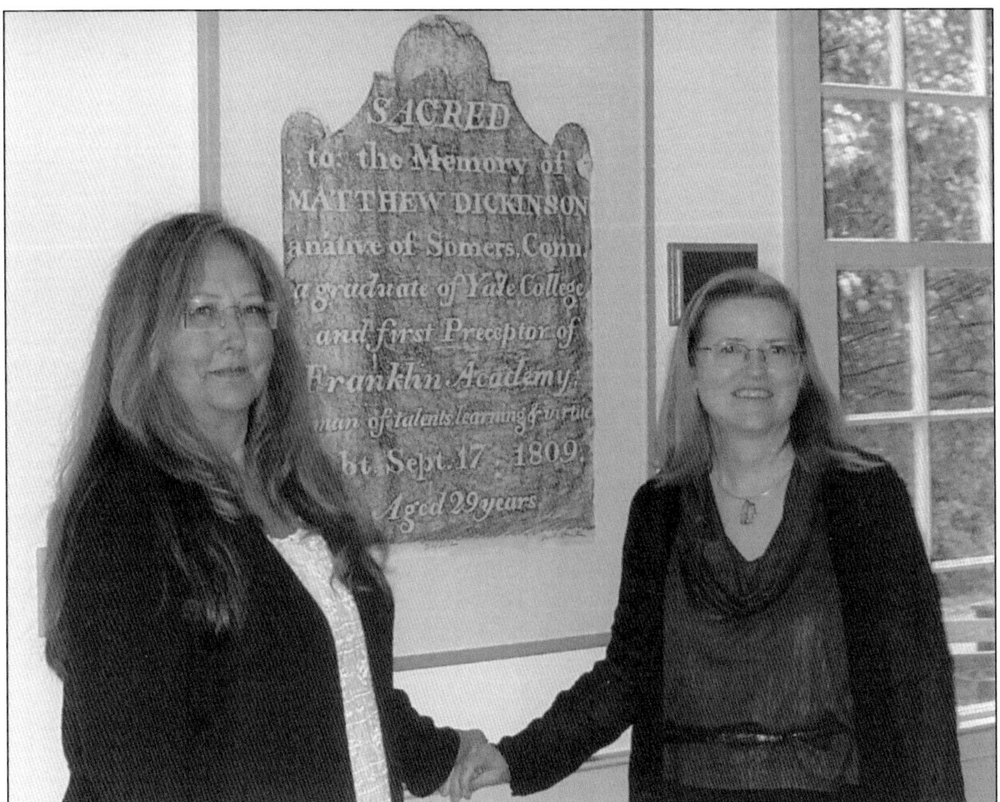

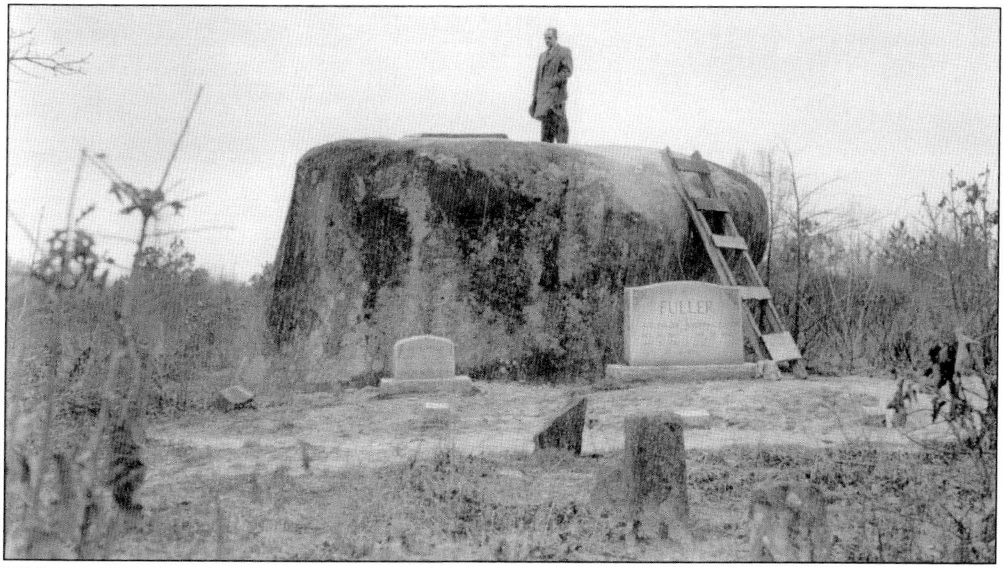

William A. Jeffreys (1817–1845) died of typhoid fever and had a great fear of a ground burial. His father contracted a stonemason to carve a tomb into a granite boulder on their Harris Crossroads property. Sealed with a marble slab, the inscription read, "Sacred to the Memory of William Andrew Jeffreys of Franklin County, Attorney at Law and Senator, Born Jan. 13, 1817, died Oct. 3, 1845. He was a kind husband and parent, a loyal and honest man and a faithful and public servant." A marker placed in 1942 was removed by 2008 at the request of the landowners. Vandals had broken the marble slab above the boulder, forever depriving the opportunity of future visitors to appreciate the efforts of Jeffreys's family to honor his dying wish. (Above, courtesy of the State Archives of North Carolina; below, courtesy of the North Carolina Office of Archive and History.)

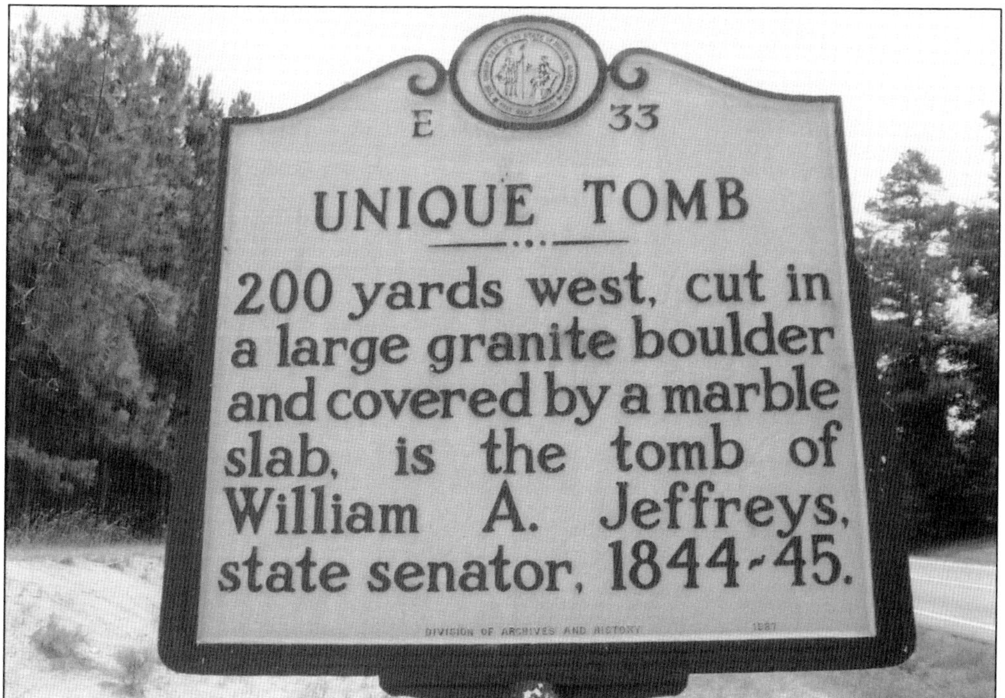

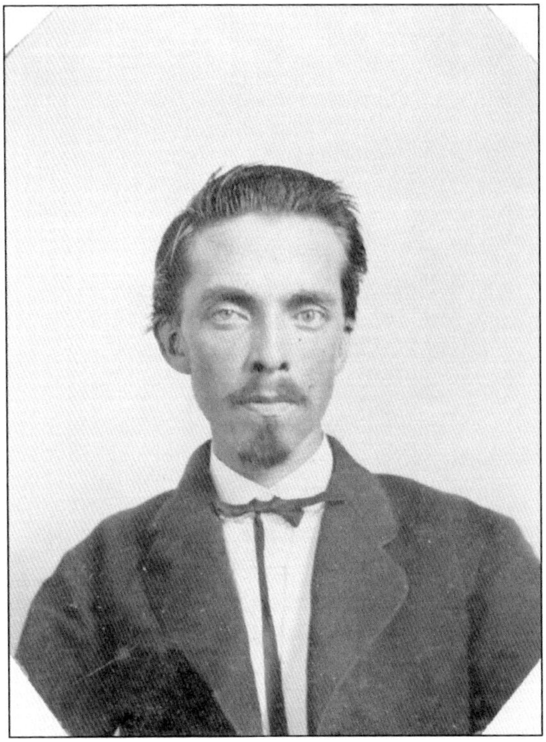

Franklin County poet and published author Edwin Wiley Fuller (1847–1876) attended Louisburg Male Academy during the Civil War and wrote *Angel in the Cloud* as a student in 1871. His second work, *Sea Gift*, published in 1873, gained widespread acclaim after his death and became known as "the Freshman's Bible" to students at the University of North Carolina at Chapel Hill. Slightly autobiographical, it depicted a student at the University of North Carolina during the Civil War. An 1871 first edition of *Angel in the Cloud* was recently discovered on the shelves of the Franklin County Library and was placed behind the circulation desk. It can be viewed by request and is a treasured addition to the library's collection. The marker below, placed in 1968, points to Fuller's house, which still stands today on Main Street in Louisburg. (Left, courtesy the State Archives of North Carolina; below, author's collection.)

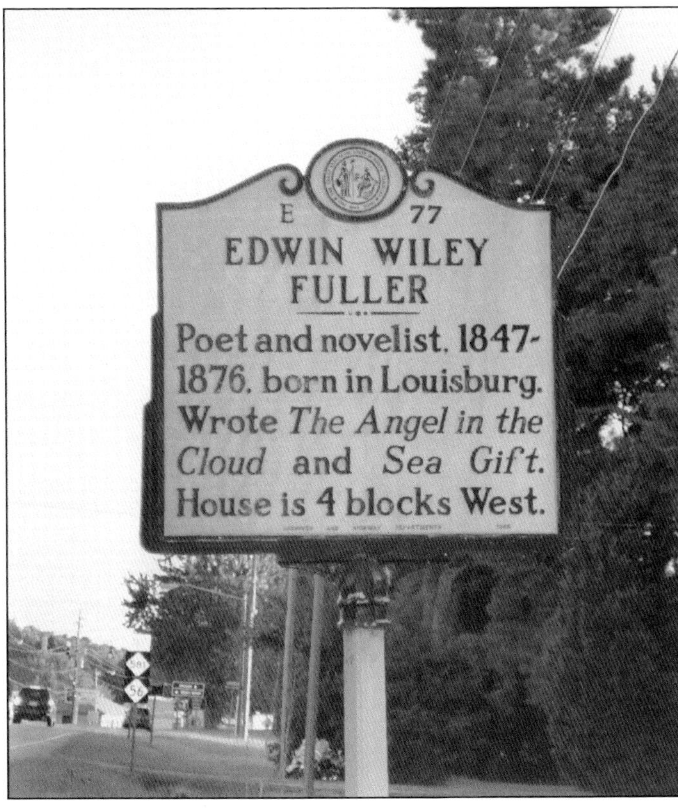

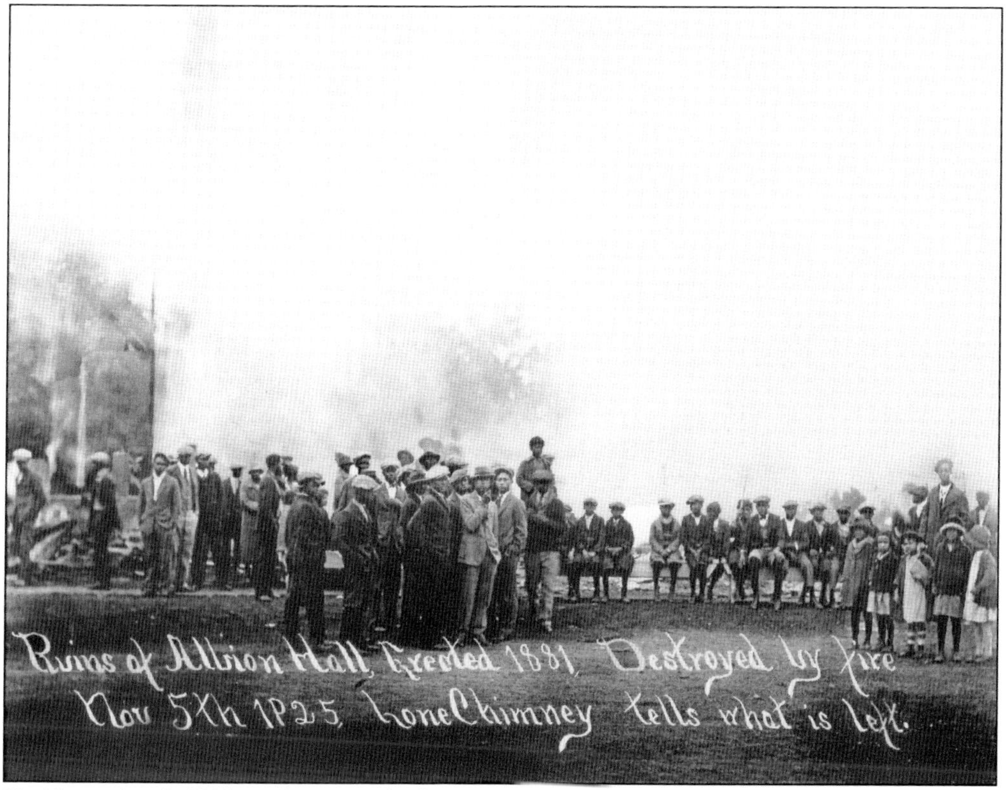

On November 5, 1925, students watched as Albion Hall, erected in 1881, was destroyed by fire. The classroom building was one of the 10 structures at Albion Academy, which offered an education to over 500 African American students and was known to be one of the finest and best-equipped schools in the state. In 1924, tuition was $5, with room and board an additional $12 per month. (Courtesy of Franklinton Town Hall.)

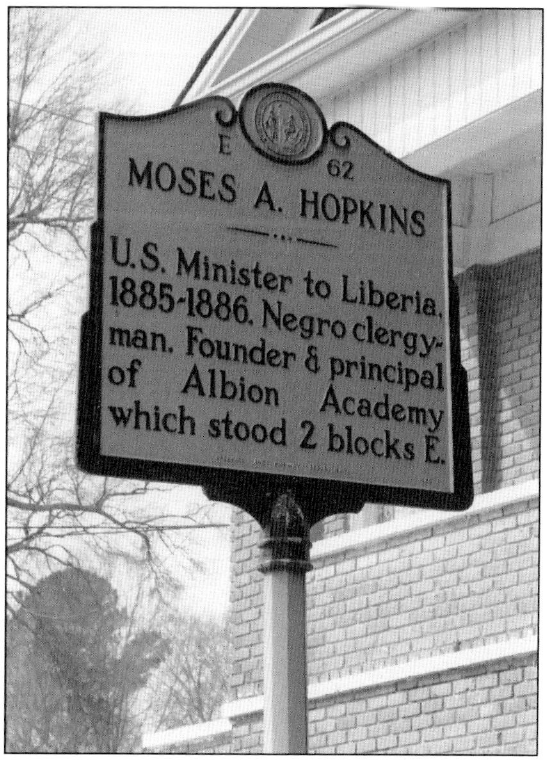

This marker on South Main Street in Franklinton honors the founder of Albion Academy, Moses A. Hopkins (1846–1886). The son of slaves, Hopkins was not educated until adulthood, but he went on to graduate at the top of his class at Lincoln University. The first African American to graduate from Auburn Seminary, Hopkins was ordained and moved to Franklinton to minister and educate the county's youth. (Author's collection.)

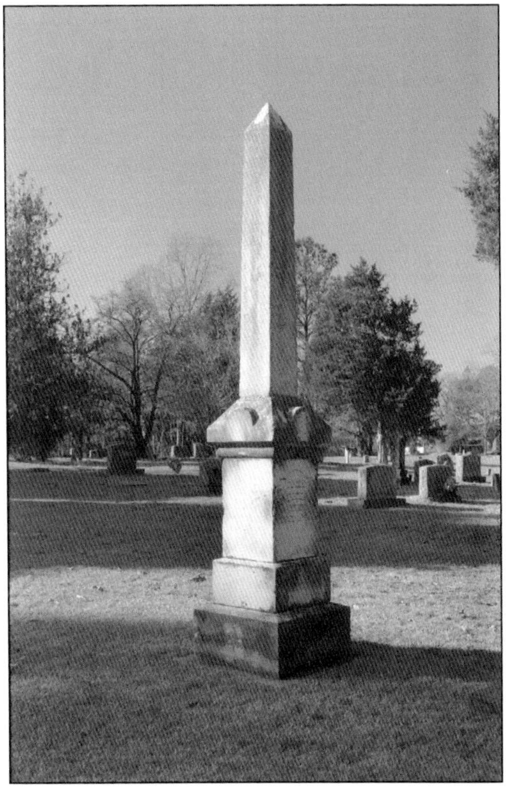

Confederate veteran Joshua L. Bowden's (1846–1935) daughter Ethel (1888–1928) organized the Justice community to raise the $475 needed for this monument to honor the Confederate dead. Dedicated on May 10, 1912, the marble obelisk reads, "To Our Confederate Dead 1861–1865, To live in hearts we leave behind, is not to die." Originally at Justice Academy, it was moved to Duke Memorial Baptist Church in 1977. (Author's collection.)

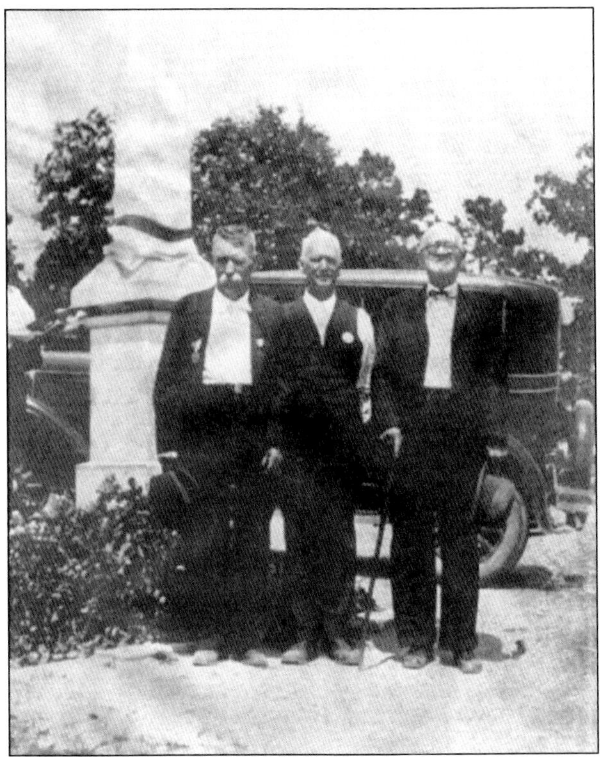

From left to right, Ruffin Van Buren Collie (1844–1951), Joshua Lawrence Bowden (1846–1935), and A.A. Strother stand before the Justice Confederate monument erected in 1912. Bowden is credited with founding the Justice community around Bowden's store and post office, which he operated with his wife, Patience Yelverton Bowden (1848–1917). The once thriving community consisted of a cotton gin, a gristmill, and the Justice Academy, where the monument originally stood. (Courtesy of Sammy Beasley.)

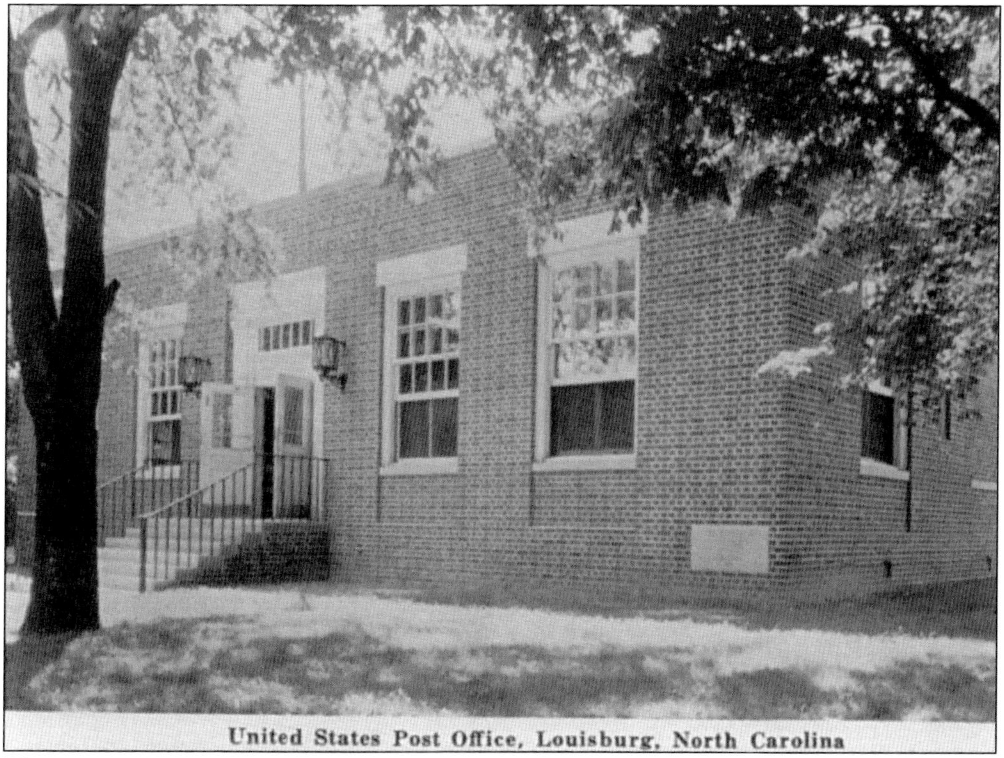

This postcard depicts the Louisburg post office, on the corner of Main and Franklin Streets, which was built in 1937 as part of the Works Progress Administration (WPA). Enacted by Pres. Franklin D. Roosevelt to provide jobs for those out of work due to the Depression, the WPA also completed other projects in Franklin County, including the Porch Building on West River Road, cemetery surveys, and the post office mural. (Author's collection.)

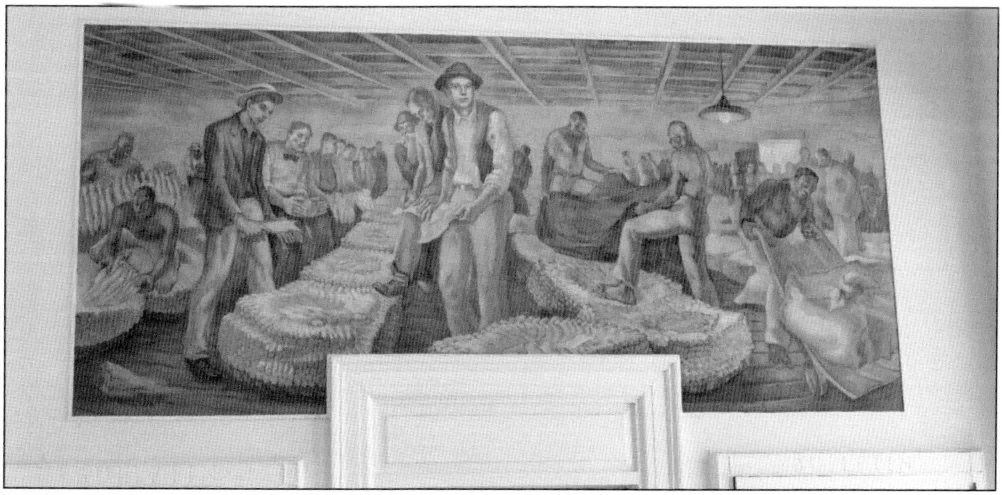

The WPA oil-on-canvas mural *Tobacco Auction* gracing the Louisburg Post Office was completed in 11 months by Richard Hay Kenah (1907–1982) in June 1939. His Brighton, Pennsylvania, studio also produced murals for post offices in Bridgeport, Ohio, and Bluefield, West Virginia. After considering the designing of the Stars and Bars as his subject, Kenah chose to represent the area's planters and their main objective: the sale. (Author's collection.)

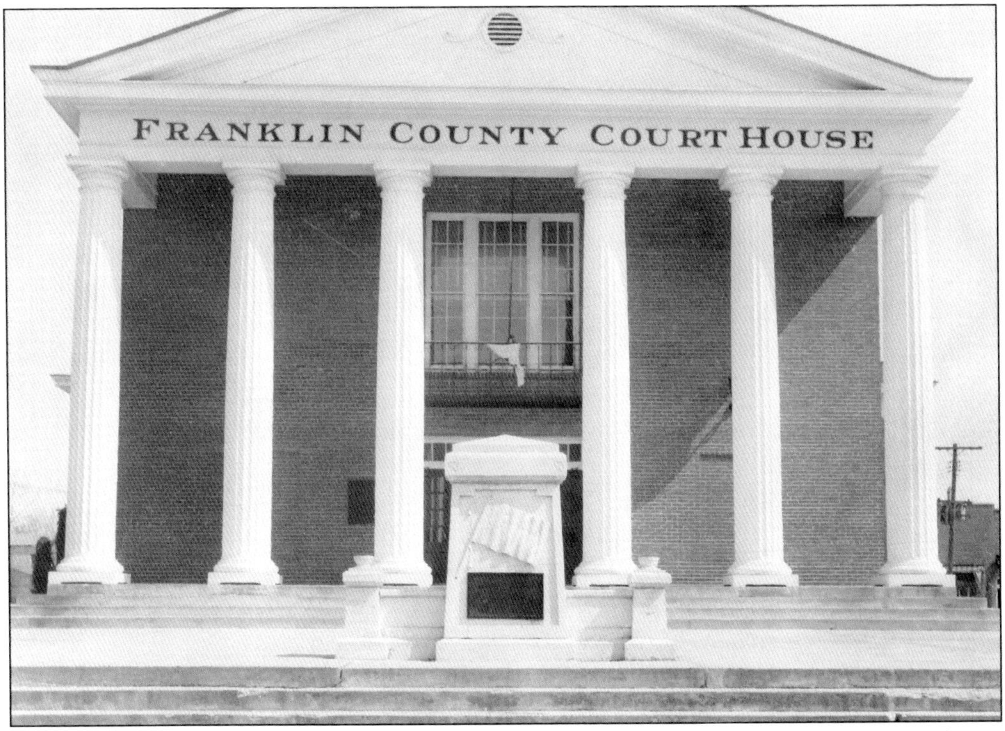

Dedicated in 1923 and seen here in 1938, the monument in front of the Franklin County Courthouse commemorates the raising of Orren Randolph Smith's design of the Stars and Bars, the first Confederate flag flown over Louisburg on March 18, 1861. Sewn by Catherine Rebecca Murphy, Smith's rendition of the flag is carved into the monument's face and depicts red and white stripes to represent state, church and press. The seven-star circle symbolized unity and equality of the seven states that had seceded. A nautically inspired long blue streamer and white star were flown over the flag in 1861 to represent North Carolina's homeward-bound journey, as the state did not secede until May of that year. (Both, courtesy of the Franklin County Courthouse.)

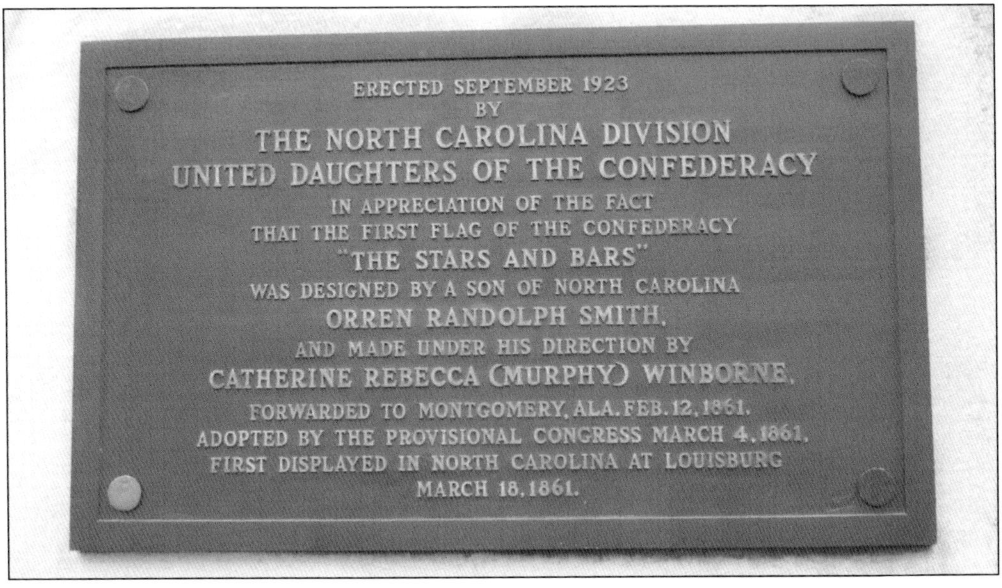

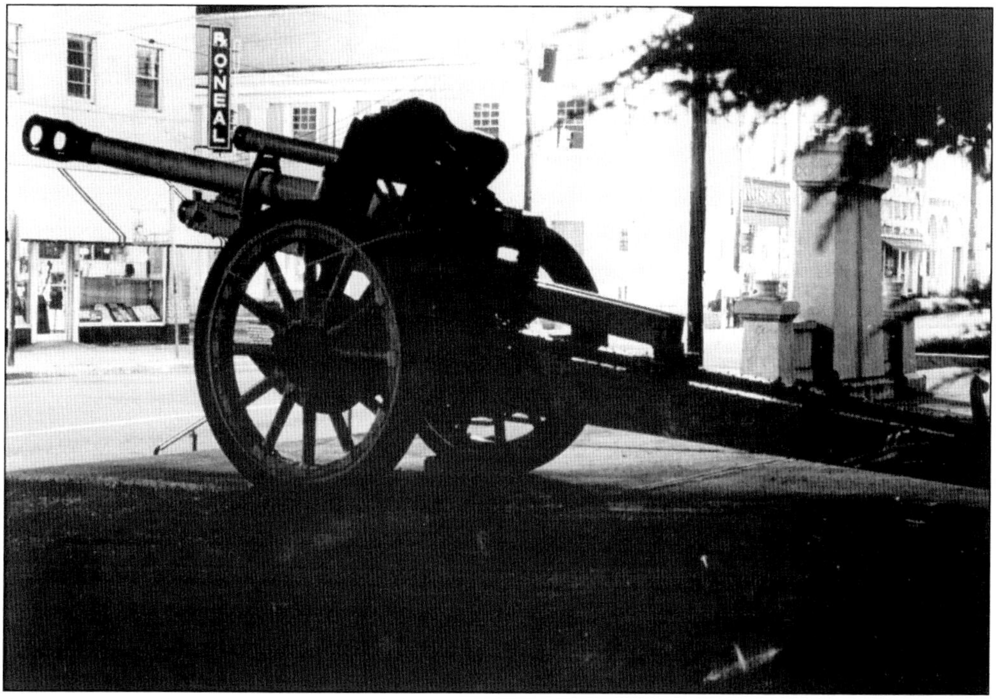

On Armistice Day, November 11, 1948, the captured German cannon at the courthouse was dedicated by American Legion Jambes Post commander Edward F. Yarborough (1910–1996). It replaced the original World War I cannon, which was scrapped for ammunition during World War II. Following courthouse remodeling in the 1970s, the cannon was moved, and it now guards the American Legion Post No. 105 on M.C. Wilder Road. (Courtesy of Cecil W. Robbins Library.)

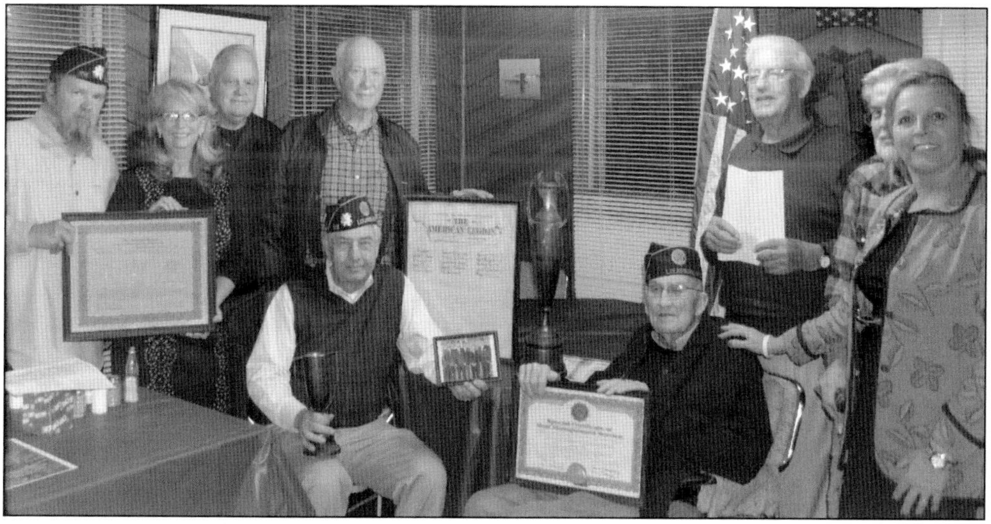

The Heritage Society of Franklin County returned a recently discovered collection of lost artifacts to the American Legion Jambes Post 105 on February 18, 2014. Trophies, photographs, and certificates dating to 1920 were uncovered while cleaning a long-unused office in Louisburg's downtown district. Pictured from left to right are Roger Kornegay, Diane Taylor Torrent, Neal Blake, Clyde Perdue, Charlie Smith, Willie Robertson, Garland Mustian, Cecil Wilkes, and Patricia Burnette Chastain. (Author's collection.)

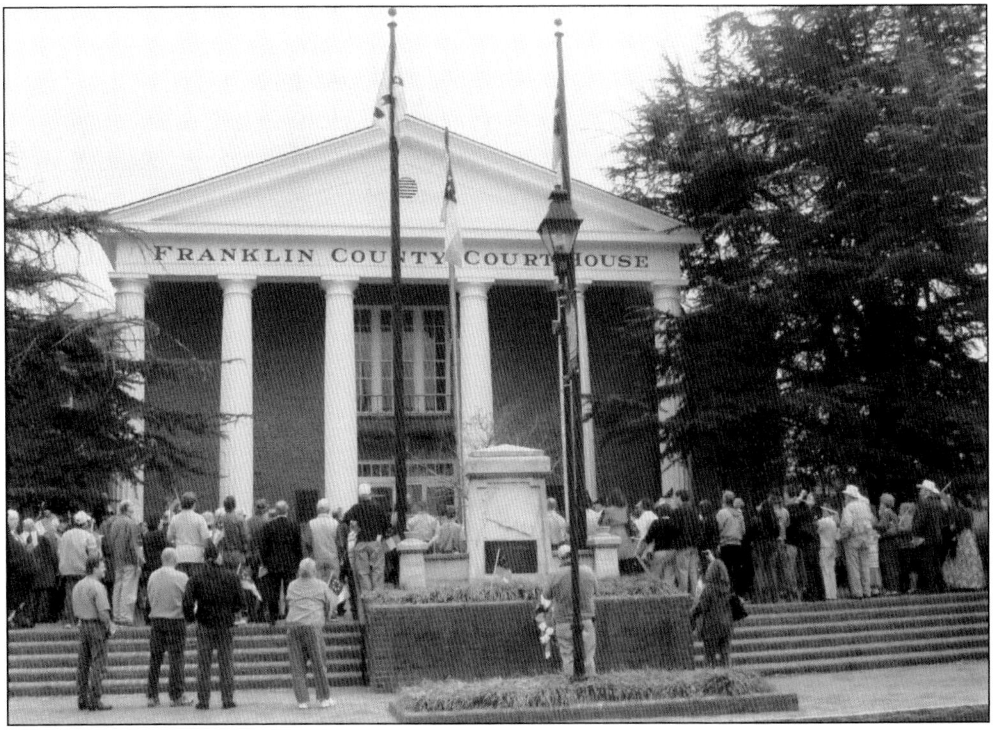

March 20, 2011, saw the Stars and Bars again fly over the courthouse when the Franklin Rifles Sons of Confederate Veterans Camp 310 and the Joseph J. Davis United Daughters of the Confederacy 535 held a flag day ceremony in remembrance of the Civil War's sesquicentennial. The replica flag flew from the original, charred, 100-foot pine pole from 1861 that General Sherman's troops attempted to burn while camping in Louisburg in May 1865. (Courtesy of Sammy Beasley.)

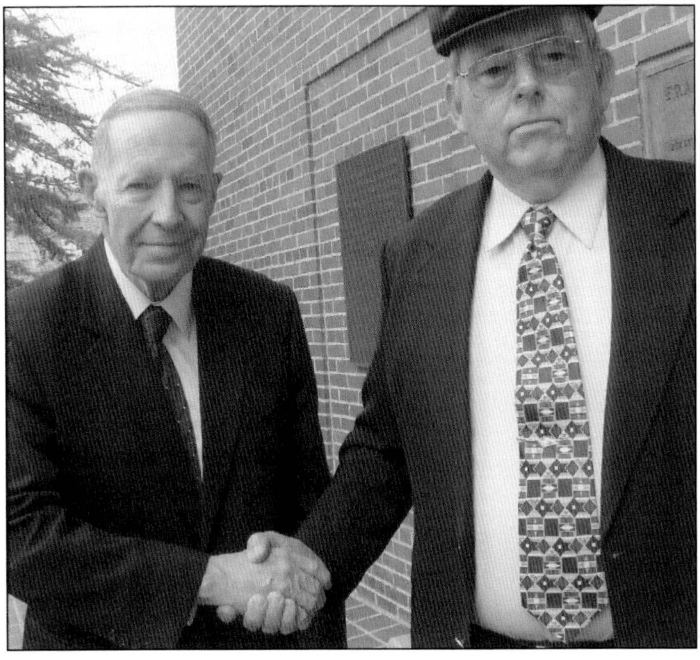

The Honorable I. Beverly Lake, North Carolina Supreme Court justice and Sons of Confederate Veterans (SCV) member, was the keynote speaker before the gathering of citizens, which included Boy Scout Troop 619, American Heritage Girls Troop 619, the Regimental Band, and the Sons and Daughters of the Confederacy at the March 2011 flag day. Seen here greeting Justice Lake is the event organizer, Sammy Beasley, an SCV member and local historian. (Courtesy of Sammy Beasley.)

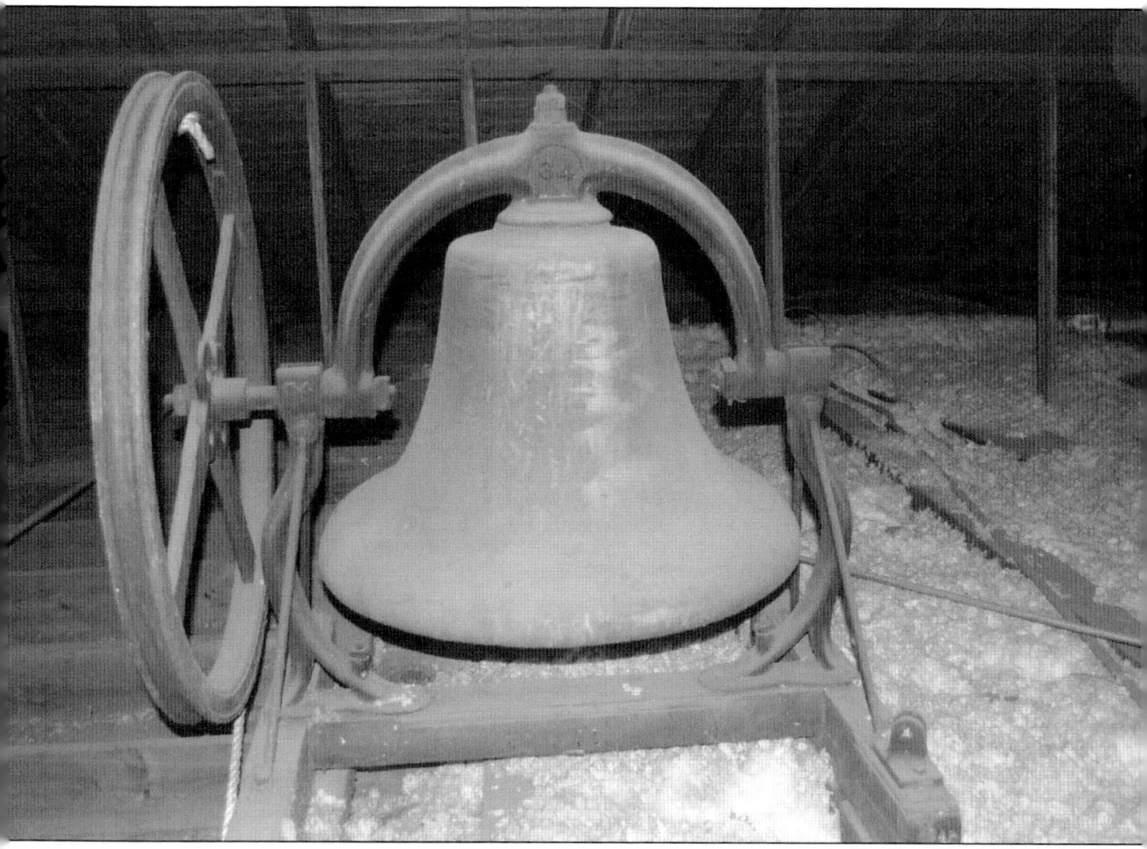

Unseen for years and protected from the elements, the bell in the courthouse attic was cast just following the Civil War by the Cincinnati Bell Foundry, Blymyer Norton and Company of Cincinnati, Ohio. It sits on a wooden brace between the sturdy rafters of the original courthouse. The facade of the courthouse was changed in 1936 when extensive renovations eliminated the old bell tower and forever hid the bell from view. In days past, the tradition was to toll the bell at the beginning and end of a work day, at midday break, or to memorialize a solemn occasion. The county's courthouse bell had sat silent since last being rung to mark the passing of longtime county clerk of court Ralph Knott in 2011. On the day this photograph was taken, the current clerk, Patricia Burnette Chastain, again rang the 34-inch bell to accompany the joyous notes of the 2013 Christmas parade as it passed the courthouse square. (Author's collection.)

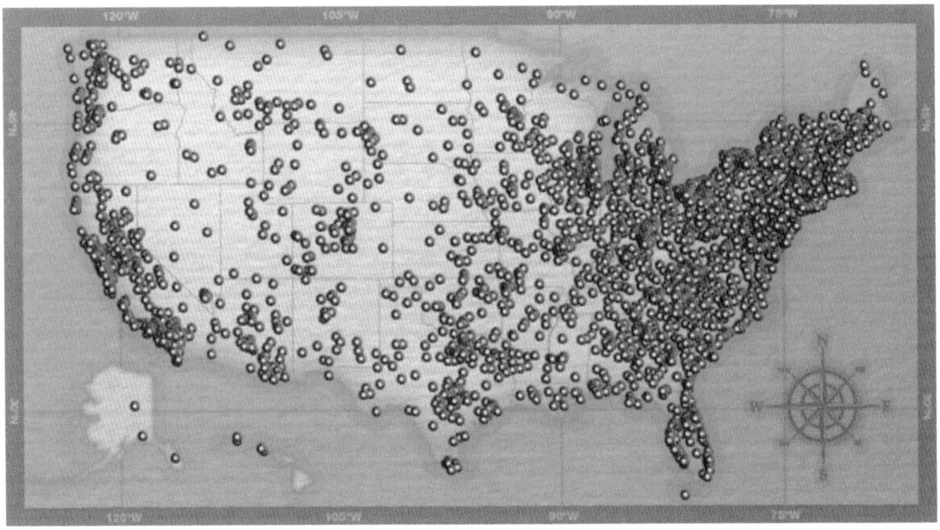